LEGAL MALPRACTICE LAW
IN A NUTSHELL

By

VINCENT R. JOHNSON

Professor of Law
St. Mary's University

WEST®

A Thomson Reuters business

Mat #40757234

© 2011 Thomson Reuters

> 610 Opperman Drive
> St. Paul, MN 55123
> 1–800–313–9378

Printed in the United States of America

ISBN: 978–0–314–19523–4

DEDICATION

To Phyllis M. Humphreys,
the high school teacher who introduced me
to the world of books

PREFACE

This book, *Legal Malpractice Law in a Nutshell*, offers a comprehensive survey of the theories under which lawyers are sometimes held liable to clients or nonclients. The initial chapters of the book focus on key features of the dynamic field of lawyer professional liability. The topics include prominent causes of action (such as professional negligence, breach of fiduciary duty, and fraud), the role of experts in malpractice litigation, important defenses, and the rules governing damages and fee forfeiture.

The later chapters of the book explore issues of considerable practical significance. Those subjects include the vicarious liability of lawyers and law firms, conflicts of interest, strategies for reducing errors and claims, and the role and limits of malpractice insurance.

This book started in Professor Thomas L. Shaffer's Professional Responsibility class at Notre Dame Law School decades ago. As a student, I left that class worried that malpractice liability lurked around every corner in law practice. History has proven that concern to be correct.

The actual writing of this book began soon after Susan Saab Fortney and I published our textbook,

Legal Malpractice Law: Problems and Prevention (Thomson/West 2008), and compiled for the American Law Institute another volume, *A Concise Restatement of the Law Governing Lawyers* (ALI 2007). If Susan had not been tapped to lead Texas Tech University School of Law as Interim Dean, she would have been my co-author on this volume. Susan contributed to the early stages of the work and has provided advice and encouragement to me at numerous junctures.

This book was written in many places: in a basement in Belgrade, Serbia; on a bus to Suzhou, China; on the train from Vienna to Passau; in a high-rise hotel in Beijing; at stops along the Danube bike trail; in the Old China Hand Reading Room in Shanghai; at airports in Detroit, Pittsburgh, and Seattle; frequently on airplanes; and mainly in San Antonio.

This volume is dedicated to one of my best teachers, Phyllis M. Humphreys. In Pennsylvania, at Derry Area Senior High School, she opened my eyes to reading and the world of books. As a teacher, she set a fine example by her professionalism, good humor, and resourcefulness. Mrs. Humphreys took a cheerful, optimistic, far-sighted approach to the challenges and opportunities of teaching mostly working class kids in a rural school district. Now retired, she continues to embody the finest traditions of American education.

Vincent R. Johnson
San Antonio, Texas
September 25, 2010

ACKNOWLEDGMENTS

Preparation of the manuscript for this book was assisted by several students at St. Mary's University School of Law in San Antonio, Texas. Those talented assistants included: Joshua P. Garza, Trevor Andrew Hall, Vanessa N. Hernandez, Nicholas Kemmy, Melissa A. Lesniak, Stephen C. Loomis, Allen K. Lowe, Elizabeth McKim, Haley O'Neill, Erik Steenken, Somer R. Stone, Miguel Vela, and David L. Wheelus. With attention to detail and plain hard work, these students greatly improved this book. Trevor Hall and Haley O'Neill did particularly outstanding editing. I am indebted to each of these nascent lawyers, and to several other unnamed students who volunteered to perform various small tasks as the work progressed. I appreciate the support for this project provided by St. Mary's University.

When I taught Professional Responsibility at George Washington University, my research assistants were Christopher Meeks and Zachary Martz. They located many of the cases discussed in this book.

My wife Jill Torbert is a constant reminder of what it means to be a good lawyer. She deserves my thanks every day.

VII

Over the past two decades, I have had the pleasure of occasionally working with lawyers on legal malpractice cases, generally as an expert witness. I hope that this book reflects the wisdom those fine men and women have shared with me about this field of law.

Certain examples and ideas mentioned in this volume are drawn from my torts books: *Advanced Tort Law: A Problem Approach* (LexisNexis, 2010) and *Studies in American Tort Law* (Carolina Academic Press, 4th ed. 2009) (with Alan Gunn). Some of the language in Chapter 7 comes from my article "The Unlawful Conduct Defense in Legal Malpractice," 77 *UMKC L. Rev.* 43 (2008).

OUTLINE

_____

Chapter 1: Introduction to Legal Malpractice Law

Chapter 2: Overview of Theories of Liability

Chapter 4: Breach of Fiduciary Duty

Chapter 6: Remedies for Legal Malpractice

Chapter 8: Vicarious Liability

Chapter 9: Important Malpractice Issues

Chapter 10: Preventing Legal Malpractice

Chapter 11: Legal Malpractice Insurance

TABLE OF CASES

A

B

C

D

E

H

I

J

K

L

M

R

S

T

U

V

W

Y

TABLE OF STATUTES

TABLE OF STATUTES

TABLE OF BOOKS, ARTICLES, & OTHER SOURCES

ABA Formal Op. 97-407 (1997), 77, 404

American Bar Association Special Committee on Evaluation of Disciplinary Enforcement, *Problems and Recommendations in Disciplinary Enforcement* (1970), 3

American Bar Association Standing Committee on Lawyers' Professional Liability, *Profile of Legal Malpractice Claims: 2004-2007* (2008), 6

Baxter, Brian, *Former Bingham Associate Files Date Rape Suit Against Firm*, www.law.com, July 1, 2009, 336

Buhai, Sande L., "Act like a Lawyer, Be Judged like a Lawyer: The Standard of Care for the Unlicensed Practice of Law," 2007 *Utah L. Rev.* 87, 88-89, 363

Burger, Ethan S., "The Use of Limited Liability Entities for the Practice of Law: Have Lawyers Been Lulled into a False Sense of Security," 40 *Tex. J. Bus. L.* 175 (2004), 346

Carter, Terry, "How Lawyers Enabled the Meltdown: And How They Might Have Prevented It," *A.B.A. J.*, Jan. 2009, at 34,152

Colo. Bar Ass'n, Ethics Comm. Formal Op. 113 (2005), 458

Cooper, Benjamin P., "The Lawyer's Duty to Inform His Client of His Own Malpractice," 61 *Baylor L. Rev.* 174 (2009), 134, 457

Cowan, Alison Leigh, *et al.*, "A Lawyer Seen as Bold Enough to Cheat the Best of Investors," *N.Y. Times*, Dec. 14, 2008, at A1, 345

Crystal, Nathan, "Enforceability of General Advance Waivers of Conflicts of Interest," 38 *St. Mary's L.J.* 859 (2007), 382

D.C. Rules of Prof'l Conduct R. 1.8 (2010), 397

LEGAL
MALPRACTICE
LAW
IN A NUTSHELL

CHAPTER ONE

INTRODUCTION TO LEGAL MALPRACTICE LAW

A. DUTIES TO CLIENTS AND NONCLIENTS

Legal malpractice law is the emerging body of principles that governs the civil liability of lawyers for losses incidental to the practice of law. In some cases, these rules work to hold lawyers accountable for harm to persons resulting from errant practices. In other cases, the relevant principles insulate lawyers from damage awards when it would be unfair to impose legal responsibility. Thus, legal malpractice law attempts to strike a fair balance between the public's interest in consumer protection and the legal profession's need for freedom of action.

Claims against lawyers may be asserted by either clients or nonclients. Broadly conceived, legal malpractice law encompasses both of these categories of potential liability. While most of this book is concerned with lawyers' obligations to current or former clients, Chapter 5 focuses specifically on duties to nonclients.

The law of legal malpractice is rapidly developing. This is a dynamic and challenging field of law.

B. THE RISE OF LEGAL MALPRACTICE LAW

Prior to the 1970s, there were relatively few reported cases holding lawyers accountable for legal malpractice. For a variety of reasons, injured persons faced obstacles in mounting a successful legal malpractice action. On one hand, an aggrieved client (let alone a nonclient) faced difficulties in securing counsel to handle a malpractice claim. In a day when the legal profession was much smaller and more homogeneous than it is today, lawyers were reluctant to represent persons suing other lawyers. On the other hand, the judiciary was not yet receptive to legal malpractice actions. Because professional liability was something of a novelty, the malpractice principles applicable to lawyers were simply underdeveloped.

Today, everything is different. The legal profession has grown immensely and so have concerns about consumer protection. For these and other reasons, legal malpractice claims have significantly increased. The contours and nuances of the law governing lawyer liability are matters of great and ever-increasing importance. This is true both for those engaged in the practice of law, as well as for consumers of legal services and others affected by lawyers' work.

The issues raised in legal malpractice actions are matters of real consequence. Whether and to what extent liability is imposed directly affects how lawyers practice law. The rulings of courts on liability claims influence how much care lawyers exercise with respect to such matters as communicating information to clients, following clients' instructions, avoiding conflicts of interest, and safeguarding client information and property.

Imposing liability deters misconduct, not only by lawyers who are held liable, but by other members of the profession who become aware of malpractice lawsuits, settlements, and court rulings. The range of persons affected by information about malpractice filings and court rulings is substantial. Lawyers learn about the commencement or disposition of legal malpractice actions from public records, printed reports, and online databases. Popular professional media, such as *The National Law Journal* and *American Lawyer*, as well as electronic publications such as abovethelaw.com and law.com, regularly report stories involving suits against lawyers, adverse judgments, and settlements.

The dramatic shift of legal malpractice law from an obscure supporting role in civil litigation to center stage undoubtedly has many causes. However, two contributions are indisputable. The first is the increased attention now accorded to issues of lawyer professional responsibility generally. The second involves developments relating to the fields of medical malpractice and accounting malpractice.

1. The Clark Report and Watergate

In the early 1970s, two events catalyzed a reexamination of the standards to which lawyers are held and the mechanisms for enforcing those standards. The first was a report issued by an American Bar Association (ABA) committee chaired by former U.S. Supreme Court Justice Tom C. Clark. *See* American Bar Association Special Committee on Evaluation of Disciplinary Enforcement, *Problems and Recommendations in Disciplinary Enforcement* (1970) (better known as the "Clark Report"). Justice Clark's committee determined that the system for disciplining lawyers for unethical conduct was scandalously deficient. The Clark Report recommended immediate action to protect both the public and the integrity of the legal profession. The second development was the discovery during the Watergate crisis (1972–1974) that lawyers had been involved in all types of pernicious practices in presidential politics during the Nixon Administration.

As a result of these two events—the Clark Report and Watergate—the organized bar conducted a "top to bottom" review of issues relating to lawyer conduct. In this examination, state and national bar associations, law schools and their accrediting agencies, scholars, concerned lawyers, and critics of the legal profession all played an important role.

The increased attention to legal ethics concerns resulted in numerous changes. Starting with legal education, the American Bar Association now requires that all ABA- accredited law schools offer professional responsibility training. The bar admission process also requires that lawyers successfully complete an examination on rules of professional conduct. States have also improved the procedures for investigating grievances and disciplining lawyers. Not surprisingly, an extensive body of literature has emerged addressing issues related to lawyer conduct. For example, the American Law Institute has greatly advanced understanding in this area by promulgating the *Restatement*

(Third) of the Law Governing Lawyers (2000). More-over, as a result of the increased number of legal malpractice decisions, important theories of lawyer liability that were once unclear have become better understood. *See* Vincent R. Johnson, "Justice Tom C. Clark's Legacy in the Field of Legal Ethics," 29 *J. Legal Prof.* 33 (2005).

2. Developments in Medical and Accounting Malpractice

At the same time that the issues of lawyer conduct were being accorded greater attention in the legal profession generally, changes were taking place in related fields of law. Suits against doctors and accountants became commonplace. As a result, it no longer seemed strange to think about whether another class of professionals—lawyers—could be held liable for losses caused by deficient practices. Indeed, it was only logical that, if doctors and accountants could be held liable for negligence or under other legal theories, lawyers could also be held accountable for their misdeeds. The expansion of professional malpractice liability in the 1970s and 1980s paralleled the passage of consumer protection laws in every state and the adoption of strict products liability principles through-out the country. Each of these legal developments greatly increased the chances that persons innocently harmed by business enterprises could recover compen-sation for their losses.

In the twenty-first century, lawsuits against lawyers and findings of lawyer liability are no longer novel. Though it is difficult to measure growth in this area of the law, analysts attentively track the patterns of litigation, reporting on increases or fluctuations in the number and size of court judgments and in the amounts paid by lawyers or their insurers to settle liability claims. *See* American Bar Association Standing Committee on Lawyers' Professional Liability, *Profile of Legal Malpractice Claims: 2004-2007* (2008). These studies indicate that the legal malpractice field has grown tremendously over the last forty years. Undoubtedly, legal malpractice has evolved as a very important area of civil law.

C. NO END IN SIGHT

In recent years, state legislatures have enacted numerous statutes to limit the liability of doctors. However, widespread "tort reform" for the benefit of lawyers is not on the horizon. Only a few states have attempted to pass comprehensive legislation. One notable example is the Alabama Legal Services Liability Act. *See* Ala. Code § 6-5-570 *et seq.* (Westlaw 2010). Lawyers, it seems, are not viewed with the same sympathy as those who practice medicine—or at least they have not effectively lobbied for legislative protection from legal liability. Therefore, the risk of being sued for legal malpractice is likely to remain a serious threat for many years to come.

The practice of law is a complex enterprise in which many clients may inevitably be disappointed with the results obtained in litigation, business transactions, or other legal representation. As a result, virtually every lawyer potentially faces a legal malpractice claim by an unhappy client. Indeed, a lawyer's mere assertion of rights under a client contract can thrust the lawyer into the crosshairs of litigation. For example, a suit to collect unpaid legal fees can easily trigger allegations of legal malpractice, which, under applicable rules of civil procedure, may be a mandatory counterclaim. *See, e.g., Levy and Craig v. D.S. Sifers Corp.*, 147 P.3d 163 (Kan. Ct. App. 2006).

D. PRACTICING LAW DEFENSIVELY

Good lawyers practice law defensively in order to minimize the risks of being sued or found responsible for harm caused by improper conduct. Some law firms have developed detailed procedures to reduce the risk of errors that might give rise to legal malpractice claims and to document compliance with ethical obligations. Those procedures, sometimes embodied in a law firm handbook or policy manual, define what is acceptable firm practice with respect to such important matters as acceptance or rejection of new clients, termination of representation, identification and resolution of conflicts of interest, fee arrangements, and service on corporate clients' boards of directors.

Today, avoidance of malpractice liability is also a pervasive theme in the continuing legal education programs that lawyers in most states are required to attend as a condition for annual renewal of a license to practice law. This is a desirable development. As the standards of conduct for lawyers continue to evolve and theories of liability proliferate, information about limiting exposure and protecting clients from harm must keep pace with developing ideas about what good practice requires. Chapter 10 explores various strategies for preventing legal malpractice.

E. THE COSTS OF LEGAL MALPRACTICE

Avoiding a malpractice claim does more than save a lawyer or law firm from liability for an adverse judgment or settlement, as well as the expenses of presenting a defense. It also preserves the mental well being and productivity of the lawyers who are involved in fending off allegations of liability.

Legal malpractice litigation is often complex and frequently takes years to run its course. While a suit is pending, a lawyer who is a named defendant is likely to suffer considerable distress when confronting the possibility that ruinous results may follow if the claim is successful. If the claim is a matter of public record, or a topic of discussion in the legal community, the lawyer may suffer harm to reputation and loss of business. Professional colleagues in other law firms might understandably be less inclined to refer a case to a lawyer who is the defendant in pending malpractice litigation, for negligent referral is itself a basis on which lawyers are sued for malpractice (*see* Chapter 8). Even if business does not decline, there is the inevitable stigma of having to defend a malpractice claim. Harm to reputation may be hard to quantify, but it nevertheless can be a very considerable loss.

If the lawyer does not have malpractice insurance, the costs of mounting a defense can be a heavy burden on a law practice. Moreover, even if the lawyer has insurance, the lawyer must pay the deductible under the policy. There are limits to what insurance will cover in the way of defense costs and liability. The mere fact that a lawyer's malpractice insurer had to pay out money to defend a claim or satisfy a judgment or settlement is likely to make the lawyer's future insurance premiums rise. Malpractice insurance is discussed in Chapter 11.

Aside from "out of pocket" costs, a pending malpractice suit is certain to impair the defendant lawyer's productivity. It takes a great deal of time to respond to demands under the discovery rules to produce documents, answer interrogatories, or give depositions. This is particularly so where, as is often the case, a malpractice claim arises out of a complex series of transactions spanning many years and involving numerous actors. Typically, defending a claim entails constructing a detailed history of the relevant facts, many of which may have faded or disappeared from memory. This often must be done under circumstances where documentary evidence is either sorely lacking or, alternatively, so abundant that it is necessary to sift through hundreds or thousands of documents to identify relevant material.

Even when the defendant lawyer is not directly involved in responding to discovery requests, it is essential for the lawyer to monitor the developments on both sides of the litigation. Of course, other members of the targeted lawyer's firm may be forced to spend time on tasks related to the litigation, such as explaining what role they played in the underlying facts or evaluating the terms on which a claim should be settled. A malpractice claim presents a serious threat to a lawyer and law firm's productivity, even if the claim is ultimately found to lack merit.

F.   LEGAL MALPRACTICE LAW AS A SPECIALTY FIELD

Legal malpractice law is now its own specialized area of the law. Some lawyers devote all or part of their law practices to suing other lawyers or to defending lawyers charged with wrongdoing. Many law professors serve as expert witnesses in legal malpractice litigation. This is particularly true of professors who teach both professional responsibility and torts because, substantively, legal malpractice law lies at the intersection of those two major fields of study.

Not surprisingly, there has been an explosion of legal literature bearing upon issues of lawyer liability. Treatises, textbooks, and numerous law journal articles and symposia now focus on the standards that animate the law of legal malpractice. The leading treatise is Ronald E. Mallen & Jeffrey M. Smith, *Legal Malpractice* (2009 ed.).

CHAPTER TWO

OVERVIEW OF THEORIES OF LIABILITY

A. CULPABILITY

Generally speaking, the law does not hold lawyers strictly liable for harm suffered by clients or nonclients, except for rules related to vicarious liability (*see* Chapter 8) and breach of contract (*see* Part A-3 of this Chapter). In every malpractice suit based on tort principles (including claims for breach of fiduciary duty, discussed in Chapter 4), the plaintiff must show that the defendant lawyer acted culpably. Specifically, the plaintiff must prove that the defendant intended to cause harm or failed to exercise reasonable care to prevent foreseeable losses from occurring.

1. Intent

Intent means that the defendant desired to cause a result that the law forbids or acted with substantial certainty (*i.e.*, certainty for all practical purposes) that the result would follow. Respectively, these two kinds of intent are called "purpose" and "knowledge." *See Restatement (Third) of Torts: Liability for Physical and Emotional Harm* § 1 (2010). For example, if a lawyer deliberately embezzles money belonging to a

11

client, the lawyer commits the intentional tort of conversion because the lawyer acted with "purpose." The lawyer sought to exercise dominion and control over the money in a manner inconsistent with the client's rights. Similarly, if a lawyer knowingly assists a client in breaching the client's fiduciary duties to a third person, the lawyer may be liable to the third person for the tort of intentionally aiding and abetting a breach of fiduciary duty because the lawyer acted with "knowledge." (*See* Chapter 4 Part E.) On the assumed facts, the lawyer was substantially certain that the breach being assisted would occur.

2. Negligence and Recklessness

Lack of care takes two different forms: negligence and recklessness. Negligence is the failure to exercise ordinary care. For example, a lawyer acts negligently if the lawyer carelessly fails to calendar the filing date for a lawsuit and therefore neglects to commence the action before it is barred by the applicable statute of limitations. On the other hand, recklessness reflects an extreme lack of care, which is sometimes defined as conscious indifference to a known risk of serious harm. Thus, a lawyer who asserts a false statement of fact as though it were true, even though the lawyer does not know whether the statement is correct, may be found to have acted recklessly and subject to liability for the tort of deceit. (*See* Chapter 5 Part B, discussing "scienter" as an element of deceit.)

3. Strict Liability for Breach of Contract

Clients may assert breach of contract claims based on nonperformance of express or implied promises. For example, a lawyer who bills a client for amounts in excess of what the retainer agreement allows, or for tasks not performed, is subject to liability for breach of contract (and probably on other grounds as well). *See Charnay v. Cobert*, 145 Cal. App. 4th 170, 51 Cal. Rptr. 3d 471, 484 (2006).

Culpability is generally not an issue with respect to such claims because the law of contracts cares little about why a material breach occurs. In *Evra Corp. v. Swiss Bank Corp.*, 673 F.2d 951 (7th Cir. 1982), a case not involving lawyer liability, Judge Richard Posner explained:

> [C]ontract liability is strict. A breach of contract does not connote wrongdoing; it may have been caused by circumstances beyond the promisor's control—a strike, a fire, the failure of a supplier to deliver an essential input ***. And while such contract doctrines as impossibility, impracticability, and frustration relieve promisors from liability for some failures to perform that are beyond their control, many other such failures are actionable although they could not have been prevented by the exercise of due care.

673 F.2d at 956-57. Of course, a lawyer's breach of contract that is intentional, reckless, or negligent, rather than innocent, will cast the lawyer in an especially unfavorable light in the eyes of the judge or jury. Thus, even in contract actions, a lawyer's culpa-

bility may adversely influence, sometimes in subtle ways, the resolution of issues in the case.

In some lawsuits, the jury is given considerable leeway to determine what was impliedly promised by the lawyer. In *Pierce v. Cook*, 992 So. 2d 612 (Miss. 2008), an attorney jointly represented a husband, wife, and child on a medical malpractice claim. During the course of the representation, the attorney had an adulterous affair with the wife. In affirming a $1.5 million award to the husband, the Supreme Court of Mississippi said that it was for the jury to determine whether the contract to provide services in the medical malpractice litigation was breached.

In certain situations, a breach of contract claim is more viable than other theories of legal malpractice. In one recent case, a former client who had settled a claim against an insurance company was told several years later that its law firm had discovered that the "lawyer" who had represented it was not licensed to practice law. In a subsequent suit against the law firm, the New York Appellate Division affirmed dismissal of the client's legal malpractice claim because there was no evidence that the nonlawyer's lack of a license caused damage. However, the court allowed the client's breach of contract claim to go forward because the firm had continuously held out the nonlawyer as a licensed attorney and had billed for his services. *See Natural Organics Inc. v. Anderson Kill & Olick, P.C.*, 67 A.D.3d 541, 891 N.Y.S.2d 321 (2009).

B. MULTIPLE CLAIMS IN A SINGLE LAWSUIT

Applicable rules of civil procedure allow a plaintiff to assert multiple theories of liability in a single lawsuit. These theories may reflect different levels of culpability. If a lawyer fails to convey to a client information material to the representation, the aggrieved client might alternatively allege that the lawyer committed intentional fraud, negligence, or breach of a contractual promise to relay the information. In determining whether the plaintiff established one or more of the causes of action, the factfinder will decide whether the defendant intended to cause harm, failed to exercise care, or made an innocent mistake. If the claim is for breach of contract, the factfinder will also have to determine whether the lawyer made an express or implied promise relating to the matter in question.

1. Concerns About Fracturing

Some decisions reflect concern about the improper fracturing of a single legal malpractice suit into multiple causes of action. Thus, a judge may dismiss a breach of contract claim in a case that also alleges negligence, if the breach of contract claim amounts to nothing more than an argument that the representation was incompetent and negligent. *See Oberg v. Burke*, 2007 WL 1418546, *4 (Mass. Super. Ct.).

In *Sitar v. Sitar*, 50 A.D.3d 667, 854 N.Y.S.2d 536 (2008), a lawyer engaged in an impermissible conflict of interest by representing both the buyers and the sellers in the sale of a closely held corporation. An appellate court in New York found that the aggrieved sellers stated a legal malpractice claim because the lawyer, as a result of the conflict, had allegedly failed to disclose to the plaintiff information critical to determining the purchase price of the business. However, the court dismissed the plaintiff's claims for fraud and negligent misrepresentation because those causes of action arose from the same facts as the legal malpractice claim and the plaintiff did not allege distinct damages.

It is important for a plaintiff pleading alternative claims to emphasize how the facts support distinct, rather than redundant, theories of liability. If there is a claim for breach of contract, this may mean proving that promises were expressly made by the defendant and not just implied by the defendant's conduct.

In some states, alleging alternative causes of action against an attorney is not permitted. For example, in Alabama, there is "only one *** cause of action against legal service providers *** known as the legal service liability action," which "embraces all claims for injuries or damages or wrongful death whether in contract or in tort and whether based on an intentional or unintentional act or omission." *See* Ala. Code § 6-5-572 & 573 (Westlaw 2010).

C. THE CONSEQUENCES OF CLASSIFICATION

In a tort action, a great deal turns upon the degree of the defendant lawyer's culpability. The consequences of classifying the defendant's conduct as intentional, reckless, or negligent relate to such matters as: scope of liability, affirmative defenses, insurance coverage, vicarious liability, remedies, and discharge in bankruptcy.

1. Scope of Liability

The scope of a defendant's liability generally extends further in cases involving highly blameworthy conduct. *Cf. Restatement (Third) of Torts: Liability for Physical and Emotional Harm* § 33(b) (2010) (stating the rule in the context of physical harm). This is because where culpability is great, it is possible to impose extensive liability without offending the principle that liability should be proportional to fault. Not surprisingly, a lawyer who makes an intentional misrepresentation of fact may be held liable to a wider class of plaintiffs than a defendant who makes a merely negligent misstatement. (*See* Chapter 5.)

2. Defenses

Under generally applicable rules of contributory negligence, comparative negligence, and comparative fault, the plaintiff's negligence may act as a defense to a negligence claim, but not a claim based on intentionally tortious conduct. (*See* Chapter 7.) Whether the defense may be raised in an action alleging that a lawyer acted recklessly or is subject to strict liability depends on state law. In contrast, negligence on the part of the plaintiff is not a defense in a breach of contract claim.

The length of the statute of limitations applicable to attorney malpractice actions often depends upon the nature of the claim. For example, intentional tort claims for fraud or conversion may be subject to different statutes of limitations than claims for negligence or breach of contract. Because statutes of limitations vary by jurisdiction, it is impossible to generalize about whether certain causes of action have longer or shorter statutes of limitations than others. Note, however, that some states apply a single statute of limitations to actions against lawyers based on their professional conduct, regardless of the theories of liability alleged. *See, e.g., Harris v. City of St. Clairsville, Ohio*, 2006 WL 3791406, *6-*7 (S.D. Ohio).

3. Malpractice Insurance

Many lawyers carry malpractice insurance. A policy typically imposes two obligations on an insurer: a duty to defend a claim against the insured and a duty to indemnify losses resulting from the claim. Malpractice policies generally cover claims involving negligence, but exclude intentional torts from coverage. Coverage of other claims, such as actions for breach of contract or negligent misrepresentation, depends on the particular terms of the policy. Malpractice insurance is discussed in Chapter 11.

4. Vicarious Liability

Law firms, as employing entities, commonly face malpractice claims based on the tortious conduct of principals (partners or shareholders), lawyers employed by the firm (associates), or nonlawyer legal assistants (paralegals, secretaries, and administrative staff members). The principles of vicarious liability hold firms liable for harm caused by any person "who was acting in the ordinary course of the firm's business or with actual or apparent authority." *See Restatement (Third) of the Law Governing Lawyers* § 58(1) (2000).

Negligence frequently falls within the "ordinary course of the firm's business" because failure to exercise care is often incidental to acts intended to benefit the firm (*e.g.*, the drafting of documents for clients). In contrast, many intentional torts giving rise to malpractice claims (*e.g.*, sexual abuse of a client or embezzlement of money) lack any purpose on the part of the actor to benefit the firm, and to that extent are difficult or impossible to fit within even a generous definition of the "ordinary course of the firm's business." Some intentionally tortious conduct, such as over-billing of clients is intended to, and does, benefit a law firm by increasing revenues, and may be properly regarded as within the "ordinary course of the firm's business." Thus, firms are sometimes vicariously liable for the intentionally tortious conduct of principals and employees. Vicarious liability is discussed in Chapter 8.

5. Remedies

Proof of high culpability on the part of the defendant may have at least two significant advantages in terms of the remedies available to a malpractice plaintiff. First, subject to important statutory and constitutional limitations, the plaintiff may recover punitive damages in addition to compensatory damages. The proof required for a punitive damages award varies with the law of the relevant state. In general, only intentionally tortious conduct, or in some cases recklessness, will support a punitive award. Proof of mere negligence will never justify responsibility for punitive damages. (*See* Chapter 6.)

In addition, plaintiffs often seek not only damages, but forfeiture of attorney's fees. Loss of attorney's fees is a matter of discretion with the court, which will only be ordered where there is proof that the defendant committed a clear and serious breach of duty. (*See* Chapter 4.) In determining whether that threshold is met, courts consider several factors, including the culpability of the defendant's conduct. Forfeiture is more likely to be ordered, and more likely to be total rather than partial, if the defendant has engaged in intentional or reckless conduct, as opposed to negligent or innocent conduct. For example, a fee forfeiture is more appropriate if the plaintiff proves that the lawyer intentionally misused the client's confidential information for the lawyer's personal benefit, than if the lawyer negligently lost a file containing confidential client data.

6. Discharge in Bankruptcy

A lawyer who is the subject of an adverse malpractice judgment may sometimes escape liability for the award by filing for bankruptcy protection. In general, bankruptcy law offers debtors a clean start financially, except with respect to certain obligations that are exempted from discharge.

Whether a malpractice judgment is dischargeable is determined, in part, by the culpability on which it is based. Debts resulting from "willful and malicious injury by the debtor to another" are not dischargeable. 11 U.S.C.A. § 523(a)(6) (Westlaw 2010). Many intentional tort judgments fall within this category. For example, a malpractice judgment is likely to be nondischargeable if the plaintiff established that the lawyer deliberately cheated the client in distributing settlement proceeds. In contrast, if the error in paying out settlement funds was merely negligent, that form of liability may be dischargeable.

Further, debts arising from "money, property, [or] services *** obtained by false pretenses, a false representation, or actual fraud," or from "fraud or defalcation while acting in a fiduciary capacity, embezzlement, or larceny," are not dischargeable. 11 U.S.C.A. § 523(a)(2)(A) & (a)(4) (Westlaw 2010). Thus, whether the slate of obligation is wiped clean by bankruptcy with respect to a malpractice judgment based on misrepresentations in a tax shelter opinion letter may hinge upon whether the lawyer acted with *scienter* (knowledge of falsity or reckless disregard for the truth), and thus committed common law fraud (*see* Chapter 5), or whether the errors in the opinion letter resulted from mere negligence.

D. CLIENTS, PROSPECTIVE CLIENTS, AND NONCLIENTS

In suits against lawyers, the likelihood of success often varies according to the status of the plaintiff. Clients stand in the most favored position and are usually much more likely to prevail than nonclients. This is true because lawyers owe a wide range of duties to clients, but relatively few duties to nonclients. For example, a lawyer has a duty to exercise reasonable care to protect the interests of a client (*see*

Chapter 3), but no such general duty to a nonclient (*see* Chapter 5). However, clients and nonclients occasionally enjoy the same forms of protection from harm. A lawyer cannot deliberately deceive a person regardless of whether that person is a client. The law of fraud is discussed in Chapter 5.

Because important questions of liability turn upon whether one is a client or a nonclient, special rules apply to the formation of the lawyer-client relationship. (*See* Chapter 3 Part A.) Other rules address protection for prospective clients, those persons who seek legal representation, but never become clients. That would be true, for example, if, after an initial interview with a lawyer, a prospective client decided not to hire the lawyer or if the lawyer declined the representation. Questions arise as to what duties are owed to a prospective client. Not surprisingly, a lawyer owes a prospective client some, but not all, of the duties owed to a client. Those duties are discussed in Chapter 3 Part A.

E. MALPRACTICE VERSUS DISCIPLINE

Professional discipline and legal malpractice vary a great deal. First, in a disciplinary action, the designated prosecutorial authority commences an action alleging that the respondent lawyer violated applicable rules of professional conduct. If the prosecution proves its case, discipline is imposed to protect the public in general or the justice system from harm caused by that kind of improper conduct. A lawyer who has violated the disciplinary rules may, for example, be reprimanded, suspended from practice for a period of time, or, in extreme cases, disbarred. Because many disciplinary infractions are related to drug and alcohol abuse, bad work habits, or deficient knowledge of the law, a disciplined attorney may also be required to participate in a drug or alcohol treatment program, office management supervision, or remedial education. In some cases, disciplinary authorities may order restitution of money to an aggrieved client or third person. Thus, an attorney who has stolen client funds may be required to repay that amount to the client. However, the primary purpose of discipline is not to secure compensation for injured persons, but to police and protect the reputation of the profession and to safeguard the public generally by enforcing professional standards of conduct.

In contrast to discipline, a legal malpractice plaintiff usually seeks monetary redress for harm caused by the lawyer's misconduct. The representation of a malpractice plaintiff is commonly handled on a contingent fee basis by a lawyer in private practice. If the suit is successful, a lawyer with a contingent fee typically receives a percentage (perhaps one-third) of the resulting settlement or judgment. The fee may escalate depending on the point at which the matter is concluded. For example, the plaintiff's lawyer may be entitled to 25% if the matter is resolved before trial, 30% after the litigation commences, and 35% if the matter requires an appeal. In most states, disciplinary rules set forth specific requirements for documenting the terms of a contingent fee contract and accounting for the proceeds of that kind of representation. *See* Model Rules of Prof'l Conduct R. 1.5 (2010).

A state's codified rules of professional responsibility (often patterned on the American Bar Association's Model Rules of Professional Conduct) are the basis for determining whether discipline should be imposed. Those same rules may also play a role in malpractice litigation. (*See* Chapter 3 Part B.) However, the principles governing lawyers' civil liability are also drawn extensively from other bodies of law, such as the law of torts, agency, and contracts. In contrast, those bodies of law play a minimal role in disciplinary actions.

In some instances, a judge presiding over a malpractice case will decide that there is evidence of a breach of the jurisdiction's disciplinary rules that should be called to the attention of those charged with disciplinary enforcement. In that case, the court will send a copy of its opinion to those authorities, so that they may consider whether further action is appropriate. This type of referral may occur even if the plaintiff failed to recover damages in the malpractice action. *See, e.g.*, *Herrera v. Hark*, 2007 WL 1319448, *3 (N.J. Super. Ct. App. Div.).

F. THE RESTATEMENT (THIRD) OF THE LAW GOVERNING LAWYERS

Some of the provisions in the *Restatement (Third) of the Law Governing Lawyers* (2000) parallel rules set down in disciplinary codes. However, other parts of the *Restatement* address nondisciplinary matters that are generally not addressed in the Model Rules of Professional Conduct or parallel state codes, such as: formation and termination of an attorney-client relationship; principles of authority; basic rules of liability for negligence and breach of fiduciary duty; liability to nonclients; fees (including modification of fee agreements, fees in the absence of an agreement, and forfeiture); attorney-client privilege; and work product privilege.

The provisions in the *Restatement* are not the law anywhere until they have been adopted by a court or other legal authority. Nevertheless, the *Restatement* represents the considered wisdom of the country's most prestigious law reform organization. Even if a court has not adopted a *Restatement* section, the *Restatement* may serve as persuasive authority in a legal malpractice case. For practitioners, the *Restatement* also provides valuable guidance in addressing difficult issues that lawyers encounter.

CHAPTER THREE

NEGLIGENCE

A. DUTY TO EXERCISE REASONABLE CARE

Negligence is the most important cause of action in the field of lawyer liability. This is true, first, because the general principles of negligence are so well established and easily adaptable that they cover a wide range of the professional errors that cause harm to current or former clients. Second, as noted in Chapter 2, negligence sometimes has important advantages over other causes of action. For example, malpractice insurance typically covers negligence claims (*see* Chapter 11). Law firms and their principals are also routinely held liable for the negligent conduct of agents acting within the scope of a firm's business (*see* Chapter 8). These considerations mean that a malpractice judgment or settlement won by the plaintiff based on negligence is more likely to be collectible.

Nevertheless, the elements of a negligence cause of action, and the special rules that guide the application of negligence principles in cases against lawyers, may limit a lawyer's liability. As in other areas of the law, a negligence action against a lawyer has four elements: duty, breach, causation, and damages. A plaintiff may recover from a lawyer for negligence only if the plaintiff suffered damage that was caused (both factually and proximately) by the defendant's violation of a duty owed to the plaintiff. The action fails if any of the four elements of negligence is missing. This chapter explores the elements of duty, breach, and causation. The subject of damages is discussed in Chapter 6.

1. To Whom is a Duty Owed

In areas of tort law involving *physical* harm, a defendant often owes a duty of care to any person foreseeably endangered by the defendant's misfeasance. As Chief Judge Benjamin N. Cardozo famously wrote in *Palsgraf v. Long Island Railroad Co.*, 248 N.Y. 339, 162 N.E. 99, 100 (N.Y. 1928), a case involving physical injuries resulting from the explosion of a package, "the risk reasonably to be perceived defines the duty to be obeyed." However, lawyer malpractice rarely results in personal injury or property damage. In most cases, the harm is not physical, but *purely economic*. Because the economic consequences of negligence are often wide ranging, the law has traditionally been reluctant to recognize liability for negligence causing only economic harm. It is therefore not surprising that a lawyer does not owe a duty of care to every person who might foreseeably be affected by the lawyer's careless conduct. In fact, the scope of a lawyer's duties is rather tightly circumscribed.

Clearly, a lawyer owes a duty of care to a client (*see* Part A-1-a of this Chapter). Lawyers also owe certain duties of care to prospective clients, persons in the process of seeking legal advice, who might become clients (*see* Part A-1-b of this Chapter). Duties may also be owed by a lawyer to members of a class whose interests may be affected by class action litigation (*see* Part A-1-c of this Chapter). Nonclients have a difficult time stating a claim against a lawyer for negligence. Liability to nonclients is discussed in Chapter 5.

a. Three Kinds of Attorney-Client Relationships

Clients stand in the most preferred position when it comes to lawyer liability. They are entitled to have their lawyers exercise reasonable care to protect their interests from harm. Clients therefore usually have no difficulty establishing the duty element of a negligence cause of action, provided that the alleged negligence falls within the "scope of the representation," a concept that limits the extent of duty (discussed below in Part A-2).

The critical question, then, is who qualifies as a "client." At one level, the answer is simple. An attorney-client relationship is created only three ways: by judicial appointment, by express agreement, and by mistake. According to *Restatement (Third) of the Law Governing Lawyers* §14 (2000):

A relationship of client and lawyer arises when:

(1) a person manifests to a lawyer the person's intent that the lawyer provide legal services for the person; and either

(a) the lawyer manifests to the person consent to do so; or

(b) the lawyer fails to manifest lack of consent to do so, and the lawyer knows or reasonably should know that the person reasonably relies on the lawyer to provide the services; or

(2) a tribunal with power to do so appoints the lawyer to provide the services.

Thus, two of the three ways of establishing a lawyer-client relationship—court appointment and express agreement—are relatively formal and easy to recognize. However, the third type of attorney-client relationship—which is created by mistake—is subtle. To that extent, it is a more dangerous theory of legal liability.

(1) Court Appointment

Court appointment involves the judicial exercise of official power to instruct a lawyer to render legal services to an affected individual. Through a formal process the court notifies a lawyer that the tribunal has determined that the lawyer must act to protect the interests of a specific person or group. For example, a court may appoint a lawyer to represent an indigent individual accused of a crime. In these types of cases, there is little chance that a lawyer will not understand that there is a lawyer-client relationship. However, uncertainties about who qualifies as a client may arise when a lawyer is appointed by a court as counsel to represent a class in class action litigation (*see* Part A-1-c of this Chapter).

(2) Express Agreement

Formalities also mark an express agreement to create an attorney-client relationship. Typically, a person requests legal services, and the lawyer, by words or conduct, manifests a willingness to provide those services. Often the parties reach an agreement on the terms of compensation. Ideally, the obligations of the lawyer and client are embodied in a written employment contract. When a lawyer expressly consents to render legal services, a lawyer must recognize that duties follow the establishment of an attorney-client relationship. Of course, the parties to the agreement may misunderstand the scope of the lawyer's obligations to the client (*see* Part A-2 of this Chapter).

Sometimes the formalities leading to client status are a bit different because a person does not deal with the lawyer directly. For example, a request for legal services may be made through an agent. Thus, in *Smith v. Patout*, 956 So.2d 689 (La. Ct. App. 2007), the plaintiff gave a power of attorney to a woman who then retained a lawyer to represent several heirs, including the plaintiff. A Louisiana appellate court found that there was nevertheless an attorney-client relationship between the lawyer and the plaintiff. Even though the plaintiff had never directly dealt with the lawyer, there was an authorized request for legal services and the lawyer agreed to represent the plaintiff's interests.

(3) Inadvertent Clients

In contrast to attorney-client relationships established by court appointment or express agreement, a relationship arising from mistake may create obligations that come as an unwelcome surprise when the attorney faces a malpractice action. This is particularly true because in many instances there may be an attorney-client relationship even though no fee was agreed upon or paid. However, the attorney should not be totally surprised because, as discussed below, the putative client must have requested legal services. Nonetheless, the circumstances may be such that the lawyer did not expect to be exposed to liability for failure to protect the plaintiff's interests.

(a) Common Mistakes

Consider three common scenarios. First, some persons seeking legal advice may do so in casual settings. For example, a lawyer may be asked legal questions at some event, such as a party, a sporting event, a church gathering, or a shopping mall. In some instances, the person making the inquiry may be seriously seeking legal guidance and discussing a matter of great importance to the person. However, the lawyer, perhaps because of the casual setting, may fail to appreciate that fact, or may even give an evasive response which induces detrimental reliance. For example, a lawyer might incautiously say, "That's a good question; let met look into it," or "I need to think about that." If the lawyer forgets about the question or otherwise fails to get back to the person making the inquiry, the lawyer may have opened the door to liability. The putative client may believe that the lawyer has taken the matter under advisement and will provide direction if there is anything the person needs to do to protect his or her interests.

A second common scenario involves the ownership of entities. For example, suppose that several physicians hire a law firm to create a limited partnership that will own and operate an ambulatory surgery center in which the physicians will be limited partners. The law firm may believe that it represents the entity that will come into being (the limited partnership), or perhaps, during the period prior to the formation of the limited partnership, the unincorporated association that reflects the common, undifferentiated interests of the physicians vis-a-vis a proposed management group. Despite the law firm's understanding, an individual physician who becomes a limited partner in the new enterprise may later allege that he or she believed that the firm represented the physician's personal financial interests in the formation of the limited partnership venture.

Another example involves owners of a small, closely-held corporation asking a law firm to provide representation regarding certain issues of legal liability. Although the firm may believe that it represented only the entity, the owners of the closely-held corporation may allege that they believed that the law firm, which was in communication with them personally, was also hired to protect their individual ownership interests.

A third common scenario relates to entity constituents, such as the officers, directors, and employees of corporations. The constituent, as a result of regular dealings with the company's legal counsel, may view that lawyer as a trusted legal advisor. Constituents may believe that the lawyer is protecting their personal interests, and not just the interests of the corporation.

(b) Request for Legal Services

The *Restatement* is clear that in order for an attorney-client relationship to arise by reason of mistake, there must have been a request for representation. The putative client must have manifested to the lawyer "the person's intent that the lawyer provide legal services for the person." *Restatement (Third) of the Law Governing Lawyers* § 14(1) (2000).

This requirement is decisive in some cases. For example, in *International Strategies Group, Ltd. v. Greenberg Traurig, LLP*, 482 F.3d 1 (1st Cir. 2007), an investor in a corporate venture sued the corporation's lawyer for losses sustained when the venture failed as a result of unauthorized transfers of assets. In his efforts to recoup the corporation's losses, the lawyer had urged the investor not to sue the corporation by arguing that such litigation would disrupt negotiations to recover the missing funds, and that everyone would be better off if those efforts succeeded. In a subsequent suit by the investor against the lawyer (and the lawyer's present and former law firms), the First Circuit rejected an argument that the investor had become an "inadvertent" client of the lawyer. As its opinion explained:

> Courts interpreting *** [Massachusetts law] require concrete communication by the plaintiff requesting that the attorney represent him, or

explicitly seeking individualized legal advisement. For example, in *Robertson v. Gaston Snow & Ely Bartlett*, 404 Mass. 515, 536 N.E.2d 344, 351 (1989), the Massachusetts Supreme Judicial Court ("SJC") found no implied attorney-client relationship between a corporate officer and a law firm representing the corporation, where the officer never explicitly requested that the firm represent him regarding his employment status at the corporation after a reorganization. The SJC reached this conclusion even though the officer had previously been a client of the firm in regard to other matters, had numerous discussions with the firm about the corporate reorganization and his future employment with the corporation, and had requested and received a sample employment agreement from the firm. ***. The SJC concluded that an implied relationship cannot be formed without active communication from the plaintiff to the lawyer requesting legal representation or legal advice:

> In spite of several written and many oral communications between the plaintiff and the other participants, the plaintiff introduced no evidence of a specific reference to [the firm] as his personal counsel. His claim is essentially, therefore, that he thought that [the firm] represented him but that he failed to communicate his thought to anyone.

482 F.3d at 8. In *ISG*, the court found that the facts were even weaker than in *Robertson* because not only had there been no express request for legal services, but on at least two occasions the plaintiff had ac-

knowledged that it was not a client. In one letter, the plaintiff's director had stated "I appreciate that you act for *** [the corporation]" and in another he complained about "your treatment of us as third parties." 482 F.3d at 9.

(c) Reasonable Reliance

A key issue in inadvertent-client cases is whether the putative client reasonably relied on the lawyer to provide legal services. *See Restatement (Third) of the Law Governing Lawyers* § 14(1) (2000). That is, was it reasonable for the person to think that the lawyer was protecting the person's own interests? In many cases, this is a hotly contested issue of fact, making attorney-client relationship by mistake a dangerous theory of liability. The issue of whether it was reasonable for the plaintiff to believe there was an attorney-client relationship will ultimately be decided by a fact finder, typically a lay jury, which may sympathize more with the plaintiff than with the malpractice defendant.

There are many factors that might bear upon whether it was reasonable for a person seeking legal services to believe that an attorney-client relationship has been created. The fact finder may want to know: Was there a written contract of employment? Who did the agreement name as the "client?" To whom were the invoices for legal services addressed and delivered? Who paid the bills? Who was listed as the "client" in the firm's filing system and conflicts-checking database? What were the oral communications between the lawyer and the putative client? What statements were made in correspondence and other written communications with the putative client and others? To whom were letters and electronic messages addressed? What did the regarding line (*e.g.*, "Re: ***") of the letters say? Was the "client" a sophisticated person who was unlikely to misunderstand to whom representation was being provided? Did the plaintiff hire other lawyers, either in this instance or in other matters, to protect the plaintiff's interests? Did the lawyer ever appear in litigation on behalf of the putative client or tell a third party that the lawyer represented the putative client?

The *Restatement* indicates that, insofar as concerns the "rights of third persons," "[a] lawyer who enters an appearance before a tribunal on behalf of a person is presumed to represent that person as a client." *Restatement (Third) of the Law Governing Lawyers* § 25 (2000). However, the presumption does not apply to "litigation between lawyer and client, where the person seeking relief usually bears the burdens of persuasion and of coming forward with evidence." *Id.* § 25 cmt. d. Nevertheless, whether a lawyer appeared in court on behalf of a person would seem to be a factor relevant to the issue of whether there was an attorney-client relationship.

In some cases, it may be significant that the lawyer represented the "client" in other transactions. For example, *Geddes v. Campbell*, 2006 WL 3352182, *4 (Cal. Ct. App.), was a dispute arising in the context of complex business transactions. Based in part on the fact that the defendant-lawyer had written a letter stating that he represented the plaintiff in a subsequent, closely-related transaction, the court found there was a question of fact as to whether the defendant represented the plaintiff in an earlier transaction.

Under the mistake theory of attorney-client relationship, it is not enough that the plaintiff seeks legal services and reasonably believes that they are being rendered. The lawyer must also have known or had reason to know that the plaintiff was relying on the lawyer to provide those services. Thus, there is one question about the state of mind of the would-be client, and another about the state of mind of the lawyer. However, the latter matter is often not a great obstacle to a finding of liability. A jury willing to believe that it was reasonable for a person to have relied upon a lawyer to provide legal services will usually also be ready to find that the lawyer knew or should have known of that mistake and should have corrected it.

(d) Prevention

Sloppy business practices greatly increase the risk of a lawyer being held liable for failing to protect the interests of a person who claims client status under the mistaken relationship theory of liability. Employment agreements and other correspondence should clearly document who is, and who is not, being represented. Similarly, the owners and representatives of entities should be informed—again, preferably in writing—that they are not being personally represented (unless the lawyer intends to provide representation). When reliable *written* evidence disclaiming representation can be adduced in a malpractice suit, it is likely to be given great weight by the fact finder. Tangible evidence that the lawyer took steps to clarify the lawyer's role may be a critical factor in avoiding a finding that the plaintiff was a client. (See Chapter 10 for a discussion of non-engagement letters.)

By contrast, evidence that the plaintiff was *orally* advised at an earlier date that the plaintiff was not being represented is much less helpful. Often the plaintiff denies that the lawyer orally disclaimed representation. In a swearing-match between the parties, the lawyer's self-serving testimony may be unpersuasive. This may be true for no other reason than that it would have been easy for the lawyer to have documented the disclosure, thereby creating a more dependable piece of evidence. From the perspective of law and economics scholarship, it might be said that liability in these types of cases is likely to be imposed on the lawyer because the lawyer was the "cheapest cost avoider" in preventing a misunderstanding about who was being represented.

b. Prospective Clients

Persons seeking legal services sometimes never become clients. This is true, for example, if the person elects not to hire a lawyer or if the lawyer declines the representation. Nevertheless, in the course of determining whether an attorney-client relationship will be commenced, a person seeking legal services may entrust confidential information to a lawyer. Likewise, a lawyer may provide advice relevant to the person's interests, such as a preliminary assessment of the merits of a claim or defense. Therefore, it is not surprising that the law recognizes that lawyers owe some duties to prospective clients.

According to *Restatement (Third) of the Law Governing Lawyers* § 15 (2000):

> (1) When a person discusses with a lawyer the possibility of their forming a client-lawyer relationship for a matter and no such relationship ensues, the lawyer must:
>
> (a) not subsequently use or disclose confidential information learned in the consultation, except to the extent permitted with respect to confidential information of a client or former client ***;
>
> (b) protect the person's property in the lawyer's custody ***; and
>
> (c) use reasonable care to the extent the lawyer provides the person legal services.

This means, for example, that a lawyer may be subject to liability for telling a prospective client, without qualification, that a claim has no merit, if careful research and investigation of the facts would have led to a contrary conclusion. Similarly, if a lawyer misstates the applicable statute of limitations in advising a prospective client to seek other counsel, the lawyer may be subject to liability if the misstatement induces the person to delay the search for counsel until the claim is time-barred.

Certain duties relating to the important subject of conflicts of interest survive the termination of an attorney-client relationship. (*See* Chapter 9.) Similarly, information learned from a prospective, rather than actual, client may create conflicts of interest that disqualify the lawyer from representing certain persons in the future. The *Restatement* explains:

(2) A lawyer *** may not represent a client whose interests are materially adverse to those of a former prospective client in the same or a substantially related matter when the lawyer or another lawyer whose disqualification is imputed to the lawyer *** has received from the prospective client confidential information that could be significantly harmful to the prospective client in the matter, except that such a representation is permissible if:

(a) (i) any personally prohibited lawyer takes reasonable steps to avoid exposure to confidential information other than information appropriate to determine whether to represent the prospective client, and (ii) such lawyer is screened *** [from involvement in the representation]; or

(b) both the affected client and the prospective client give informed consent to the representation ***.

Restatement (Third) of the Law Governing Lawyers § 15 (2000). Note that this conflict of interest rule relating to former prospective clients (which contains a "significantly harmful" condition) is narrower than the conflict of interest rule applicable to former (actual) clients (*see* Model Rules of Prof'l Conduct R. 1.9 (2010)). This makes sense since a narrower range of duties is owed to a former prospective client than to a former client.

In dealing with prospective clients, limiting the scope of discussion may minimize the risks of future disqualifying conflicts of interest. Of course, regardless of whether an initial consultation is narrowly limited or wide ranging, a lawyer must track information related to the identity of a prospective client and the matters about which legal representation was discussed. Such records enable the lawyer to comply with conflict of interest rules, even if a conflict does not emerge until many years later. Systematic procedures for tracking information and identifying conflicts of interest are discussed in Chapter 10.

c. Class Members

A lawyer appointed to represent a group of persons in class action litigation has an attorney-client relationship with the named class representatives. The lawyer also owes certain legal and ethical duties to members of the class, at least until they opt out of the lawsuit. Thus, if a law firm represents, in housing litigation, a class defined as the tenants who resided in a building on a certain date, the firm has a duty to distribute the proceeds of a judgment or settlement only to members of the class, and not to other persons who may have resided in the building on earlier occasions. *See Taylor v. Akin, Gump, Strauss, Hauer & Feld,* 859 A.2d 142 (D.C. 2001).

However, if a potential class has not been certified as one suitable for aggregate litigation, the unnamed members of the putative class are not clients. In the usual case, those persons never requested legal services from the lawyer and no court appointed the lawyer to represent them. Thus, the potential class members do not fall within any of the three categories of attorney-client relationship discussed above (*see* Part A-1-a). *See generally* Vincent R. Johnson, "The

Ethics of Communicating with Putative Class Members," 17 *Rev. Litig.* 497 (1998).

2. Scope of Representation

A lawyer's duties to a client extend only as far as the scope of the representation. Thus, a lawyer who serves as general counsel to a corporation has a much greater range of potential liability than a lawyer hired by a corporation to handle only an isolated matter.

a. Defining the Scope of Representation

In assessing the scope of representation, it is useful to focus on what services the client requested and what services the lawyer agreed to provide. Statements in the lawyer-client employment contract about the contemplated legal work are highly relevant. However, other factors also must be taken into account. These factors include the history of dealings between the parties and whether the client employed different attorneys to handle other legal matters for the client. If the lawyer has served for a period of years as the sole, all-purpose counsel for a client, it is easier to conclude that a new matter of legal significance discussed with the lawyer was within an expanded scope of the representation, regardless of what the original lawyer-client contract stated. Similarly, if a business entity hires different lawyers from time to time, or hires multiple lawyers simultaneously to handle diverse matters, it may be difficult to prove that a new matter, even if it was called to the attention of the defendant lawyer, was within the scope of the defendant's representation of the plaintiff. The client may have mentioned the matter just to test the lawyer's reaction, before deciding whom to hire to handle the representation. Thus, it makes a difference whether the client is sophisticated, in terms of knowing how to retain or change lawyers, or inexperienced in dealing with lawyers, and therefore likely to depend on counsel to do whatever is necessary to protect the client's interests.

b. Changes in the Scope of Representation

The scope of representation may change during the course of a lawyer's employment. As time passes, a client may ask a lawyer to address matters that were not contemplated at the time the employment agreement was initially signed. Thus, testimony about an expanding range of representation may persuade jurors, even if the testimony differs from the written terms of the engagement. The failure to revise the original statements about the scope of representation may mean simply that the document was not updated, rather than that the scope of representation never changed.

In *Grochocinski v. Mayer Brown Rowe & Maw LLP*, 2007 WL 1875995, *5 (N.D. Ill.), the defendants argued that they were not responsible for alleged malpractice relating to litigation because their agreement with the client said that they were retained "only in connection with *** [the client's] formation and corporate activities." *Id.* at *7. However, a federal court in Illinois concluded that there was a basis for concluding that the defendants owed a duty of care with respect to the litigation because, in fact, they provided legal advice related to the lawsuit and an e-mail from one lawyer instructed the client to feel "free to contact *** me with any questions *** you might have regarding the current situation." *Id.*

c. Unreasonable Limits on the Scope of Representation

Relevant rules governing professional conduct afford lawyers and clients broad latitude in defining the scope of representation. *See Restatement (Third) of the Law Governing Lawyers* § 19 (2000). Such a limitation is valid if it is reasonable under the circumstances and the client gives informed consent. Model Rules of Prof'l Conduct R. 1.2 (2010). This means, for example, that the duties of a lawyer retained by an insurer to represent an insured may be limited to matters related to the insurance coverage. *See id.*

In *Lerner v. Laufer*, 359 N.J. Super. 201, 819 A.2d 471 (App. Div. 2003), a lawyer had a client sign a detailed statement acknowledging that the lawyer: was reviewing a property settlement agreement only to ensure that it reflected the terms of an earlier mediation; was not advising the client on the fairness of the deal; and had not investigated the divorcing couple's assets or liabilities. In a subsequent malpractice action, the court concluded that the lawyer did not breach the standard of care by performing no discovery or investigatory services related to the fairness of the agreement because the scope of representation had been limited to exclude those services. Relevant to whether the limited scope of representation was reasonable was the fact that there was no dispute relating to the client's "competence, her general knowledge of the family's financial and personal affairs, or the voluntariness of her actions in submitting to mediation." 359 N.J. Super at 219, 819 A.2d at 484.

However, a limitation on duty is invalid and unenforceable if the limitation unreasonably impairs the efficacy of a lawyer's services. Consider, for example, the case of a lawyer advising a client on a contract for the sale of goods to a foreign buyer. If the lawyer-client contract provides that the lawyer is not obliged to consider issues arising under international law, such as the Convention on the International Sale of Goods, that limitation may be so unreasonable that it may not limit the lawyer's liability for failing to address such issues.

In some cases, doubts about the scope of representation are resolved against the lawyer. For example, if a lawyer unsuccessfully represents a client at trial, and no agreement has been reached as to whether the lawyer will be responsible for appealing the adverse judgment, the lawyer must consult with the client about the possibility of appeal before relinquishing responsibility for the case. *See* Model Rules of Prof'l Conduct R. 1.3 cmt. (2010). A contract limiting the scope of representation is construed from the standpoint of a reasonable client. *See Restatement (Third) of the Law Governing Lawyers* § 19 cmt. c (2000).

d. Responsibility for Closely Related Matters

In a related vein, some cases hold that a lawyer's duties extend beyond the strict scope of representation and encompass closely related matters. For example, in *Geddes v. Campbell*, 2006 WL 3352182 (Cal. Ct. App.), the court held that if a lawyer represented an individual in connection with the sale of certain partnership property, and discovered by reading the partnership agreement that the individual owed certain fiduciary duties to others, the lawyer had a duty to advise the individual with respect to his fiduciary duties, regardless of the precise scope of the representation. The court explained:

> An attorney who undertakes one matter on behalf of a client owes a duty to consider and advise the client as to other related matters the client may be overlooking and which should be pursued to avoid prejudicing the client's interests. "[E]ven when a retention is expressly limited, the attorney may still have a duty to alert the client to legal problems which are reasonably apparent, even though they fall outside the scope of retention."

Id. at *5 (Cal. Ct. App.), *quoting Nichols v. Keller*, 15 Cal. App. 4th 1672, 1684, 19 Cal. Rptr. 2d 601 (1993).

However, other cases appear to be contrary. In *AmBase Corp. v. Davis Polk & Wardwell*, 8 N.Y.3d 428, 866 N.E.2d 1033, 834 N.Y.S.2d 705 (2007), the New York Court of Appeals held that a law firm that successfully represented a client in a tax protest had no duty to question whether an agreement between the client and a related company could have been interpreted to relieve the client of tax liability in the dispute with the Internal Revenue Service. The court wrote:

The retainer agreement states that AmBase has "engaged [Davis Polk] to represent [it] as agent for City Investing to resolve the tax issues currently before" the IRS. The plain language of the retainer agreement indicates that Davis Polk was retained to litigate the amount of tax liability and not to determine whether the tax liability could be allocated to another entity. Thus, the issue whether plaintiff was primarily or secondarily liable for the subject tax liability was outside the scope of its representation.

834 N.Y.S.2d at 709.

e. Termination of the Attorney-Client Relationship

Termination of the attorney-client relationship greatly contracts the scope of duties owed to a client. At the moment of termination, the client, who previously occupied the most preferred status, is transformed into a former client to whom only limited duties are owed. The most important of the surviving duties is continued confidentiality of client information. However, the array of duty is somewhat larger. According to *Restatement (Third) of the Law Governing Lawyers* § 33(2) (2000), after a lawyer-client relationship has ended, a lawyer must:

(a) observe obligations to a former client such as those dealing with client confidences ***, conflicts of interest ***, client property and documents ***, and fee collection ***;

(b) take no action on behalf of a former client without new authorization * * *;

(c) take reasonable steps to convey to the former client any material communication the lawyer receives relating to the matter involved in the representation; and

(d) take no unfair advantage of a former client by abusing knowledge or trust acquired by means of the representation.

(1) Post-Termination Loyalty

Cases occasionally assert that a lawyer owes a former client a continuing duty of loyalty. That is certainly not true in any broad sense. A past engagement is not transformed by termination of the representation into a lifetime of far ranging obligations. As the language quoted above from § 33 of the *Restatement* suggests, specific duties of loyalty are owed to former clients, such as preservation of confidences and avoidance of carefully defined types of conflicts of interest. Moreover, state law may impose other particular obligations. For example, in Texas, a lawyer representing a new client shall not question "the validity of the lawyer's [own] services or work product for *** [a] former client." Tex. Discip. Rules of Prof'l Conduct R. 1.09(a)(1) (2010). However, there is no general continuing duty of loyalty that requires a lawyer to broadly protect a former client's best interests.

Of course, lawyers may, and frequently do, feel *moral* obligations of loyalty to former clients, and often tailor their conduct in accordance therewith. Depending on the facts, solicitude for the interests of former clients may be appropriate and wholly laudable. Nevertheless, malpractice law is concerned with *legal* obligations, and there is no general, broad-ranging duty of loyalty to a former client that is enforceable in an action for negligence or under any other legal theory.

In *Torban v. Obermayer Rebmann Maxwell & Hippel*, 2007 WL 1827283 (N.J. Super. Ct. App. Div.), a lawyer revised the wills of a husband and wife to include trusts for tax-planning purposes. Although the lawyer advised the couple that all of the tax planning would be worthless unless they divided their assets, the couple, either intentionally or negligently, rejected that advice, and continued to own their assets jointly. Later, when the wife died, the couple's son, serving as executor, hired the lawyer to handle the administration of his mother's estate. After a fee dispute developed, the son alleged that the lawyer committed malpractice by failing to advise him and his father, after his mother death, about other steps his father could take to minimize estate taxes by disclaiming an interest in the mother's certificates of deposit. An appellate court in New Jersey rejected the malpractice claim. It found that the father's attorney-client relationship with the lawyer had terminated long before his wife's death, and that the attorney-client relationship between the son and the lawyer did not encompass advice about his father's estate planning, because the lawyer had been hired only to probate the mother's will. Therefore, the lawyer had no duty to provide the tax advice in question. This was true even though that information might have been useful to the son or his father and was in some sense related to the subject matter of the earlier representation. The lawyer's continuing duties to the father had greatly contracted because the attorney-client relationship with the father had ended. And the duties to the son were limited by the narrow scope of the new engagement, which did not include estate planning.

(2) Termination of Authority

A lawyer's authority to represent a client may end for any of several reasons. Authority terminates if the client discharges the lawyer; if the client dies or, in the case of an entity client, loses its capacity to function; or if the lawyer dies or becomes physically or mentally incapable of providing representation. Authority also ends if the lawyer is disbarred or suspended from the practice of law, or is ordered by a tribunal to cease representing the client. Likewise, authority terminates if the representation has ended as provided for by the contract or because contemplated services have been completed. *See Restatement (Third) of the Law Governing Lawyers* § 22 (2000).

However, *termination of authority* to act is not the same as *termination of representation*. Some of the named factors that bear on the issue of authority (*e.g.*, death of the client or lawyer) may also support the conclusion that the representation has ended. However, other considerations may be relevant. If a lawyer's engagement is limited to a specific matter, the attorney-client relationship normally terminates when the matter has been resolved. In contrast, if a lawyer has represented the client in many different matters over a period of years, the client may be justified in assuming that the lawyer will continue to serve on a continuing basis unless the lawyer gives notice of withdrawal. *See* Model Rules of Prof'l Conduct R. 1.3 cmt. 4 (2010).

Harkening back to the mistake theory of attorney-client relationship (*see* Part A-1-a-3 of this Chapter), it is useful to ask whether the person who was previously represented still reasonably believes that he or she is a client. If so, it may well be the case that the attorney-client relationship has not ceased, and that plenary duties are still owed to that person. Thus, lawyers should clearly communicate in writing the termination of the attorney-client relationship. Subsequent communications with former clients, such as newsletters, should avoid creating the impression of continuing representation.

B. BREACH OF DUTY

As the Michigan Court of Appeals explained in *Harris v. Farmer*, 2010 WL 395764 (Mich. Ct. App.):

An attorney is obligated to use reasonable skill, care, discretion, and judgment in representing a client and to act as would an attorney of ordinary learning, judgment, or skill under the same or similar circumstances ***. Although an attorney has the duty to fashion a strategy so that it is consistent with prevailing *** law, he does not have a duty to ensure or guarantee the most favorable outcome possible. ***.

Id. at *1.

Whether a lawyer breached a duty of care to the plaintiff is normally a question of fact for the jury (or for the court sitting as fact finder). However, in cases where fair minds could not differ, a court may rule as a matter of law that the defendant acted unreasonably. This may be true, for example, where a lawyer fails to file a lawsuit before the statute of limitations lapses.

Conversely, a court may sometimes rule as a matter of law that certain conduct was not negligence. In *Driftmyer v. Carlton*, 2007 WL 1229305, *14 (Ohio Ct. App.), the court found that the record contained no evidence of foreseeable harm to a man's estate based on his naming a Defined Pension Benefit Trust as the beneficiary of his life insurance policy. The estate therefore could not maintain an action for legal malpractice against the decedent's lawyer based on the lawyer's alleged failure to recommend the establishment of a separate trust to avoid estate taxation of the life insurance proceeds. *Driftmyer* is an apt reminder of the fact that negligence is the unreasonable failure to guard against *foreseeable* harm. If harm is not foreseeable, the failure to avoid it is not a breach of duty under negligence principles.

1. The Standard of Care

a. An Objective Measure

The law of negligence sets an objective standard for evaluating the conduct of a defendant lawyer. The question is simply whether the defendant did what a reasonably prudent lawyer exercising ordinary care would have done under the same or similar circumstances. Either the defendant measures up to that standard, or the defendant falls short.

(1) No Good Faith Defense

Because negligence is concerned with *conduct*, not *state of mind*, there is no good faith defense to a negligence claim. *See Cosgrove v. Grimes*, 774 S.W.2d 662, 664-65 (Tex. 1989). The issue is not whether the defendant tried his or her best, or undertook certain conduct in an effort to benefit the client, or honestly believed that the client's interests would be protected. Rather, the relevant inquiry is whether the defendant acted *reasonably*.

If the defendant acted reasonably, there is no liability for negligence. Thus, in the absence of an agreement to bring a retaliation claim, no matter how much or little it was worth, a lawyer is not liable for failing to assert such a claim where the undisputed facts indicate that it would not yield more than nominal damages. *See Cecala v. Newman*, 2010 WL 1936384, *1 (9th Cir.).

(2) Reasonable, Not Average

Note carefully that the standard of care does not require "average" performance, which would imply that lawyers in the less skillful part of the profession were necessarily negligent. *See Restatement (Third) of the Law Governing Lawyers* § 52 cmt. b (2000). The duty is not to be average, or better than average, but to be reasonable under the circumstances.

(3) Consumer Protection

An objective negligence standard makes sense from a consumer protection perspective. When any client walks into any law office, the client is guaranteed a certain objectively defined level of protection with respect to a host of important matters, such as protection of confidential information, avoidance of conflicts of interest, communication of material information, and diligence in researching legal and factual issues. By mandating the exercise of reasonable care, the law of negligence not only protects clients who do not know what risks should be considered in hiring a lawyer, it also makes the engagement of legal representation more efficient for sophisticated clients. Every client is assured, in the absence of an agreement to the contrary, that every lawyer comes with all of the "standard equipment" that is reasonably necessary for effective and ethical legal representation. This includes, for example, knowledge of the law, legal research skills, diligent work habits, good office practices, and conformance with professional ethics rules.

b. **Risk Balancing and Economic Analysis**

In the law of negligence generally, the standard of care is discussed in different ways. For example, rather than asking whether the defendant acted appropriately in the anthropomorphic terms of what a reasonably prudent person would have done, courts or scholars sometimes ask whether the risks outweighed the utility of the actor's conduct (*see Restatement (Third) of Torts: Liability for Physical and Emotional Harm* § 3 cmt. e (2010)). Or they consider whether the burden of prevention outweighed the gravity of the threatened loss viewed in light of the probability of that harm occurring (*United States v. Carroll Towing Co.*, 159 F.2d 169 (2d Cir. 1947)).

Interestingly, balancing tests and economic analysis seem to play almost no role in legal malpractice cases. Although the reason is not clear, courts and scholars rarely speak in those terms. The relevant inquiry in evaluating whether a lawyer acted appropriately is virtually always framed in terms of custom. That is, the question is whether the defendant exhibited the level of care that is customary among lawyers in the relevant geographic area. (*See* Part B-1 of this Chapter.)

The extent to which risk-utility calculations or other aspects of economic analysis apply (or do not apply) to legal malpractice claims has yet to be fully charted. Nevertheless, it is worth noting that such principles have occasionally played a role in *medical* malpractice litigation. In the famous and controversial case of *Helling v. Carey*, 83 Wash.2d 514, 519 P.2d 981 (Wash. 1974), the court employed a type of economic analysis in concluding that the defendant ophthalmologist was negligent in following the customary practice of not testing persons under forty years of age for glaucoma. The court found that the test, if properly administered, would have been relatively simple, inexpensive, and dependable, and that without the test, detection of the disease at that time was virtually impossible. Mindful of the "grave and devastating" nature of the potential harm to the plaintiff patient and of the slight burden that administering the test would have imposed, the court held that it was negligent as a matter of law not to give the test. In economic terms, the gravity of the threatened loss, viewed in light of its probability, significantly outweighed the burden of prevention (B < L x P).

Perhaps similar balancing-test arguments could be made in the legal malpractice context. For example, in *Hodges v. Carter*, 239 N.C. 517, 80 S.E.2d 144 (N.C. 1954), the lawyers representing the plaintiff in a case involving denial of insurance coverage for losses resulting from a fire were not liable for failing to predict that a long-observed practice for serving out-of-state insurance companies with process would be held invalid. However, it might have been argued that once it was known that the insurance companies were contesting the validity of the customary procedures, the defendant lawyers should not have gambled that the procedures would be upheld by the state high court. Instead, the lawyers should have reinitiated the suit within the approximately sixty days then available by serving process in a different manner, assuming that was possible. Viewed in terms of economic analysis, it was arguably negligent for the attorneys not to incur the slight burden of re-instituting the suit when doing so would have avoided great harm (loss of coverage) that, while unlikely (because the challenged practice was long-standing), was nevertheless a serious risk (because validity of the process had been contested). If the case had been argued in those terms, the result might have been different.

If there is a persuasive reason why balancing tests and economic analysis do not apply in the field of legal malpractice, it may relate to the need to ensure that lawyers have room to exercise judgment without fear of legal liability. (*See* Part B-2 of this Chapter.)

c. Specific Duties

It is difficult to identify what specific obligations are encompassed by the duty of care because virtually every aspect of a lawyer's performance could be treated as a subcategory. A lawyer's duty of reasonable care extends to all aspects of the client's representation, including, for example, interviewing, counseling, research, drafting, advocacy, litigation, and dispute resolution. However, at a general level, there are at least two overarching obligations encompassed by the duty of reasonable care: competence and diligence. *See Restatement (Third) of the Law Governing Lawyers* § 52 cmt. b (2000). Competence and diligence are discussed in the following sections. Certain specific obligations, such as the duty of candor (*see* Chapter 4 Part C), are discussed in other parts of the text.

(1) Competence

Competence entails many things, including both knowledge and professional skills. Required knowledge may concern applicable law, legal institutions, ethical restrictions, and to some extent, human nature. The professional skills that are necessary for competent representation may relate to such routine matters as research, writing, interviewing, counseling, advocacy, dispute resolution, and office management.

(a) Duty to Recommend a Specialist

On appropriate facts, the duty of competence may require a lawyer to refer a potential client to a specialist if the proposed representation entails a need for greater knowledge or skills than are typically possessed by an ordinary practitioner. *Restatement (Third) of the Law Governing Lawyers* § 52 cmt. d (2000).

In *Dennerline v. Atterholt,* 886 N.E.2d 582 (Ind. Ct. App. 2008), a lawyer, despite lack of relevant experience, agreed to represent a complex insurance trust. He did not consult anyone for advice, nor did he conduct research into applicable laws. He failed to advise the trust about the legal ramifications of operating without a certificate of registration from the state Department of Insurance. Further, the lawyer did not "even think about" a mandatory provision in the trust agreement requiring termination of the trust if it became insolvent. Ultimately, the lawyer and his law firm were held liable for nearly $18 million in losses.

(2) Diligence

Diligence requires timely attention to the client's affairs and reasonable persistence in addressing obstacles. Diligence also requires a lawyer to perform whatever tasks are appropriate to the representation. The degree of diligence required of a reasonably prudent attorney varies according to many factors, including the importance of the matter, the instructions of the client, applicable deadlines, the costs entailed, customary practice among other lawyers, and the press of competing obligations which affect the time available. If a client instructs a lawyer to draft a complex will and trust within a day because the client is gravely ill, and the instrument turns out to be invalid, the time limitation under which the lawyer was acting will be a relevant factor in determining whether reasonable care was exercised. *Restatement (Third) of the Law Governing Lawyers* § 52 illus. 1 (2000).

2. Exercise of Judgment

To say that lawyers are held to an objective standard of care normally defined by reference to customary professional practice is not to suggest that there is only one way to practice law and that anything else is negligence. Indeed, most legal assignments entail a degree of factual and legal complexity that makes it reasonable for the lawyer to use any of several different approaches to serving the client's needs. Therefore, the application of negligence principles to legal malpractice issues must allow room for an attorney's exercise of discretion.

For example, an "appellate attorney is not required to raise every claim of arguable legal merit in order to be an effective counsel." *Kandalaft v. Peters*, 2007 WL 1138395, *3 (Mich. Ct. App.). Thus, decisions relating to which issues to raise, or whether to appeal rather than seek reconsideration of an adverse finding, will ordinarily not form the basis for a malpractice action. *Id*.

Similarly, a lawyer may exercise caution by advising a client to be more concerned about the potential ramifications of felony convictions, including the loss of liberty, than about the possible civil consequences of not cooperating with the client's employer. *See Hopp & Flesch, LLC v. Backstreet,* 123 P.3d 1176, 1185 (Colo. 2005). This is nothing more than a reflection of the type of judgment commonly exhibited by lawyers who need to counsel clients about the risks of making potentially incriminating statements.

a. Room for Discretion

A lawyer is negligent only if the lawyer does what no reasonably prudent lawyer could do, or fails to do what every reasonably prudent lawyer must do. Between those broad extremes, there is a wide field of discretion. Some lawyers would handle a matter one way and others would handle it another way. The mere fact that someone else would have done differently than did the defendant is merely evidence of a divergence of opinion or practice. The duty of competence "does not require a lawyer, in a situation involving the exercise of professional judgment, to employ the same means or select the same options as would other competent lawyers in the many situations in which competent lawyers reasonably exercise professional judgment in different ways." *Restatement (Third) of the Law Governing Lawyers* § 52 cmt b (2000). To establish negligence, the evidence must show that no reasonably prudent lawyer could have done what the defendant did. That is, the evidence must show that the defendant's choice was unreasonable.

For example, it would be unreasonable for a lawyer not to call an expert witness in a case requiring expert testimony. However, lawyers typically have discretion in deciding how many experts to call in support of a client's case. Similarly, a defense lawyer may normally elect, without risk of negligence liability, to cross-examine the plaintiff's expert, rather than introduce opposing expert testimony.

To establish the standard of care in legal malpractice cases, it is insufficient for experts to testify that they, personally, would have handled the matter differently than did the defendant. That is not the question. The issue is not whether someone (an expert or anyone else) could or would have done differently, but rather whether any lawyer exercising reasonable care could have done what the defendant did.

b. The "Mere Error of Judgment" Fallacy

Judgment calls by lawyers are often not actionable. Thus, "decisions made involving trial tactics or litigation strategy are generally not subject to attack in an action for legal malpractice." *Harris v. Farmer*, 2010 WL 395764, *2 (Mich. Ct. App.).

In *Harris*, the plaintiff argued that defendant lawyer was negligent in failing to subpoena or present certain witnesses and documents. Citing precedent protecting lawyers' exercise of discretion and other evidence that was presented at trial, the Michigan Court of Appeals held that summary disposition was properly granted in favor of the lawyer.

In efforts to capture the idea that lawyers are not liable under negligence law for the *reasonable* exercise of discretion, opinions sometimes (over)state that a "mere error of judgment" does not give rise to liability. That, of course, is an imprecise and unnecessarily misleading way to formulate the rule. If an error of judgment is reasonable, there is no liability. However, if the choice made by a lawyer was the type of unreasonable choice that no lawyer could make, the fact that the lawyer was exercising judgment does not insulate the lawyer from liability. The essential question is whether the lawyer acted reasonably, not whether the lawyer's conduct involved a choice between competing alternatives.

Because reasonableness is often a disputed fact question, the judgment rule rarely resolves a malpractice claim early in the litigation. For example, in *General Nutrition Corp. v. Gardere Wynne Sewell, LLP*, 2008 WL 4411951(W.D. Pa.), a law firm advised a client that it would have limited liability for damages if it terminated a contract. However, when the client was sued after it terminated the agreement, a court held that the client was liable for millions of dollars in consequential damages because the contract predominantly involved a sale of *services*, rather than *goods*. Because that was true, the Uniform Commercial Code did not apply to preclude an award of consequential damages. In a subsequent malpractice action by the client against the law firm, alleging that the client had received improper legal advice, the law firm moved to dismiss on the ground that its advice to the client was an exercise of judgment. The firm argued that there was some basis for it to have concluded that the contract involved a sale of goods subject to the UCC. A federal court nevertheless refused to dismiss the claim. The court quoted an earlier decision stating:

Although a lawyer is not expected to be infallible, he or she is expected to conduct that measure of research sufficient to allow the client to make an informed decision. In order for a lawyer to advise a client adequately, he or she is obligated to scrutinize any contract which the client is to execute, and thereafter must disclose to the client the full import of the instrument and any possible consequences which might arise therefrom.

Id. at *2. The *General Nutrition* court reasoned that the complaint properly pleaded that the law firm "breached this standard in numerous respects, for example, by assigning labor and employment attorneys to a contract case and by conducting inadequate factual and legal research." The court concluded that these issues were fact-intensive and that the discovery process must run its course before the applicability of the "judgment rule" could be determined.

In some states, the "attorney judgment rule" is an affirmative defense. *See Bowman v. Gruel Mills Nims & Pylman, LLP*, 2007 WL 1203580, *4 (W.D. Mich. 2007). In those jurisdictions, the defendant must prove that the conduct in question was a permissible exercise of discretion.

In *Bloomberg v. Kronenberg*, 2006 WL 3337467, *3 (N.D. Ohio 2006), a federal court concluded that "Ohio has explicitly refused to adopt the professional judgment rule." Presumably, that means that in Ohio the focus is on whether a lawyer acted reasonably, not on whether the lawyer was choosing between alternatives.

c. Not Every Error is Negligence

Not every error by a lawyer amounts to negligence. Even reasonably prudent lawyers make mistakes. Sometimes the law is so confused or underdeveloped that it is not possible to predict the resolution of an unsettled question or even fully understand the import of a decision that has already been made. A lawyer must act reasonably in consulting legal authorities and in interpreting their meaning. A lawyer must consider debatable issues of importance. However, the fact that the lawyer is wrong does not mean that the lawyer was negligent, if the lawyer exercised reasonable care in arriving at a decision and counseling the client.

d. Novel Theories, Trends in the Law, and Other Jurisdictions

There is a duty to be aware of novel theories of liability and defenses, trends in the law, and out-of-state precedent, but only to the extent that a reasonably prudent lawyer would be cognizant of those developments. For example, in *Darby & Darby, P.C. v. VSI Int'l, Inc.*, 95 N.Y.2d 308, 739 N.E.2d 744, 716 N.Y.S.2d 378 (2000), the New York Court of Appeals held that a law firm had no duty to inform its clients about possible "advertising liability" insurance coverage for their patent infringement litigation expenses. The court noted that the basis for liability was a novel theory which, at the time, had been rejected by courts in the two states most relevant to the litigation, and was largely unrecognized by courts elsewhere. In not calling the theory to the attention of its clients, the law firm, therefore, acted reasonably and in a manner consistent with the law as it existed at the time of the representation.

3. Expert Testimony

Expert testimony plays an important role in almost every legal malpractice lawsuit. Not surprisingly, a considerable body of law has developed relating to the necessity for, and legal sufficiency of, such evidence.

a. Necessary to Establish the Standard of Care

Although juries are usually charged with determining whether a lawyer breached a duty of care to a malpractice plaintiff, the persons sitting on juries normally have no specialized knowledge about the responsibilities of members of the legal profession. Consequently, expert testimony is generally necessary to guide the jury in understanding the standard of care as applied to the facts of the case. Indeed, so important is such assistance that the introduction of expert testimony is normally an essential step in securing an award of damages. *See Restatement (Third) of the Law Governing Lawyers* § 52 cmt. g (2000).

For example, it is beyond the ken of the jury whether a lawyer breached the standard of care by failing to raise on appeal issues related to double jeopardy, jury instructions, jurisdiction, and verdict consistency. *See Moore v. Crone*, 114 Conn. App. 443, 970 A.2d 757, 760 (2009). Where such complex matters are at issue, expert testimony must be adduced to prove what the standard of care required.

(1) Exception for Obvious Negligence

Only in the rarest cases—where even laypersons must know that the lawyer acted improperly—is expert testimony unnecessary. Courts have held, for example, that expert testimony was not required where a client suffered a default judgment because his lawyer did "absolutely nothing to protect him" (*Paul v. Gordon*, 58 Conn. App. 724, 728, 754 A.2d 851 (2000)); where the defendant engaged in an adulterous affair with a client's wife (*see Pierce v. Cook*, 992 So. 2d 612, 618 (Miss. 2008)); and where, despite a client's instruction to the defendant lawyer to appeal a judgment, notice of appeal was not timely filed (*see Global NAPs, Inc. v. Awiszus*, 457 Mass. 489, 930 N.E.2d 1262 (2010)).

Similarly, in *Guyton v. Hunt*, 2010 WL 2885944 (Ala. Civ. App.), an Alabama appellate court ruled that "an attorney's failure to notify a client of a [court's] ruling on a motion in time for the client to timely file an appeal constitutes a breach of the standard of care that is so apparent that expert testimony is not required." *Id.* at *5. In an earlier case, the Alabama Supreme Court had ruled that expert testimony was not necessary in a malpractice action where the defendant lawyer had allegedly lied to a client about his experience by falsely stating that he had represented other clients in previous breast implant litigation. *See Valentine v. Watters*, 896 So.2d 385, 395 (Ala. 2004).

In *Dowell v. Nelissen*, 2010 WL 2384617 (Iowa Ct. App.), an Iowa appellate court held that a layperson could recognize that not filing a request to modify child support, which had been agreed upon by the plaintiff client and his ex-wife, and not informing the plaintiff of that inaction, failed to meet the standard of reasonable care. As the court explained, "[b]asic deficiencies in legal representation do not require illumination by an expert." *Id.* at *3.

(2) Expert Affidavit Requirements

In an effort to promptly dispose of frivolous claims, a number of jurisdictions have enacted expert affidavit requirements that apply to legal malpractice actions. A plaintiff must file an affidavit of merit by an expert within a specified period of time after the commencement of litigation, or else the suit will be dismissed.

Shamrock Lacrosse, Inc. v. Klehr, Harrison, Harvey, Branzburg & Ellers, LLP, 2010 WL 2346341 (N.J. Super. Ct. App. Div.), was a malpractice action based on a lawyer's failure to ensure that renewal fees for a patent were paid. A New Jersey court found that the state's affidavit requirement applied to claims against law firms, as well as to claims against individual lawyers, and that this was true even though the firms were located out of state. However, the court vacated an order dismissing the plaintiff's claims based on lack of an affidavit because the law on these issues was unsettled and in conflict at the time the affidavit should have been filed.

Even where expert affidavit requirements are imposed, there may be exceptions. An affidavit generally is not required in the rare malpractice case where expert testimony is unnecessary. For example, in *Whalen v. DeGraff, Foy, Conway, Holt-Harris & Mealey*, 53 A.D.3d 912, 863 N.Y.S.2d 100 (2008), the plaintiff argued that the defendant firm was liable for malpractice because the outside lawyer it employed to file a notice of claim with an estate had failed to do so. In ruling that the law firm was liable for negligent supervision of the outside lawyer, a New York appellate court held that no affidavit was necessary. It was undisputed that the defendant law firm knew of the deadline for filing the notice of claim and took no steps whatsoever to ensure that the claim was filed. Therefore, the plaintiff was entitled to summary judgment as a matter of law.

Noncompliance with an affidavit requirement may not bar claims against lawyers that are rooted in obligations other than those created by the professional standard of care. Thus, in *Stoecker v. Echevarria*, 408 N.J.Super. 597, 975 A.2d 975 (App. Div. 2009), a New Jersey court affirmed dismissal of a legal malpractice claim because an affidavit was filed too late, but allowed a fraud claim related to a real estate transaction to go forward.

b. Admissibility of Expert Testimony

Trial courts perform an important gate-keeping function in determining who is qualified to testify as an expert. In general, the witness must be well acquainted, by study or experience, with the matters at issue. Under these circumstances, it is appropriate for a jury to rely on the expert's guidance because the testimony is informed and arguably trustworthy.

There are more than a million lawyers in the United States, and presumably not all of them are qualified to testify as legal ethics experts simply by reason of the fact that they have been licensed to practice law. Nevertheless, some lawyers are indeed ethics experts because they have studied (or perhaps helped to draft) the relevant standards of conduct, served on grievance committees, taught courses, lectured on malpractice prevention, or served as law firm in-house ethics counsel. Not surprisingly, law professors who teach courses on attorney professional responsibility frequently appear as experts in lawyer malpractice litigation. Generally, such faculty members are so well versed with respect to the standards of conduct for lawyers that their testimony might aid a jury in understanding what a lawyer was required to do when faced with certain facts.

Many malpractice cases involve questions of legal ethics, such as whether certain facts created a conflict of interest or had to be disclosed to a client. Legal malpractice cases also raise issues of conduct that are not related to legal ethics. For example, the question may be whether the duty of reasonable care requires a lawyer to include a noncompetition provision in a contract between family members (*see Russo v. Griffith*, 147 Vt. 20, 510 A.2d 436 (1986)) or to ensure that a company hired to pay a structured settlement is bonded (*see Williams v. Lakin*, 2007 WL 1170597 (N.D. Okla.)). Those types of cases require special expertise not related to ethics, so it is likely that someone other than an ethics expert should testify to support those aspects of a plaintiff's claim. In many legal malpractice cases, there are multiple experts on each side of the litigation.

c. Geographic Frame of Reference

Whether a lawyer's conduct complied with the standard of care can only be determined in context, an important part of which is the geographic frame of reference.

(1) State-based Standards

As a general rule, lawyers are judged by a state-wide standard, because substantive law often varies from state to state, and so do the ethics rules that govern attorney conduct. Taking this approach, the Vermont Supreme Court, in *Russo v. Griffith*, 147 Vt. 20, 510 A.2d 436 (Vt. 1986), held that an out-of-town expert's testimony sufficiently supported a negligence claim because even though the expert was not from the same locality as the defendant, the expert was acquainted with the standard of care in the state.

Out-of-state experts sometimes testify in legal malpractice cases. All that is necessary is that the expert be sufficiently familiar with the law of the jurisdiction that the expert's testimony will assist the jury in understanding the case. Virtually all state ethics rules are based, to some extent, on the American Bar Association's model codifications. So, too, the American Law Institute's *Restatement (Third) of the Law Governing Lawyers* (2000) reflects legal principles that are endorsed by the law of many jurisdictions. Therefore, it is not surprising that an expert well acquainted with the ABA Model Rules of Professional Conduct and the *Restatement*, and the types of issues addressed in law school professional responsibility courses, might be found capable of assisting a jury in understanding the standard of care, even if the expert does not reside in the state whose law governs the dispute.

(2) Federal Issues

Some areas of the law are national in scope, such as federal tax law, federal securities law, bankruptcy law, and patent law. When a case involves issues relating to these sources of law, it makes sense that the frame of reference should be national. Of course, a single case may raise multiple issues, some of which are state-based and others of which are federal. Whether a lawyer practicing federal tax law in Pennsylvania has a conflict of interest might properly be determined with reference to the Pennsylvania ethics rules, but whether particular advice for minimizing tax liability was reasonable might more appropriately be determined by reference to what lawyers practicing federal tax law throughout the United States would regard as acceptable conduct.

(3) International Law Practice

The growing internationalization of law practice raises many questions about how the standard of care should be defined when a lawyer's work involves international treaties or the law of other nations, or when the lawyer is located in a foreign county or serves foreign clients. As of yet, there is no clear consensus on these types of questions. Nevertheless, these issues are sure to be litigated in coming years.

In one recent case, Austrian clients alleged (unsuccessfully) that an American law firm had negligently provided erroneous advice. The advice related to the structure of an investment in the securities of a Russian natural gas concern, and to the risk of criminal prosecution if the investment structure was to be deemed illegal. *See GUS Consulting GMBH v. Chadbourne & Parke LLP*, 2010 WL 2518538 (N.Y. App. Div.).

In *DiStefano v. Greenstone*, 357 N.J. Super. 352, 815 A.2d 496 (App. Div. 2003), a U.S. lawyer failed to "sustain contact" with an Italian law firm that he was using to handle an international tort claim for the plaintiff, who had been injured in Italy. As a result, the claim was not timely filed and became time-barred. In a subsequent malpractice action, the U.S. lawyer was held liable for the full value of the lost claim, attorney's fees in the malpractice action, and other expenses.

(4) No Locality Rule

Perhaps the most important consideration relating to geographic frame of reference is that the standard of care not be defined in purely local terms. Embracing a locality rule raises two concerns. The first is that it may be difficult or impossible for a plaintiff with a meritorious case to recruit an expert from the town or region in which the defendant practices. In a given locality, there may be a small number of lawyers, and those lawyers may be reluctant or unwilling to testify against one another. This is the "conspiracy of silence" problem. The second concern relates to encouragement of good practices.

Setting the standard of care at the local level undercuts the incentives that tort law can provide for lawyers to avoid liability by keeping pace with legal knowledge and evolving notions of professional conduct in other geographic areas. The standard of care should be framed in geographic terms that protect consumers of legal services by tending to ensure that lawyers are not insulated from liability when practitioners in a particular area lag behind others in terms of knowledge, skills, and procedures. Fortunately, courts have rarely applied a locality rule for measuring the performance of lawyers charged with malpractice. The standard of care is ordinarily set at the state or national level. *See generally Restatement (Third) of the Law Governing Lawyers* § 52 cmt. b (2000).

d. The Role of Legal Malpractice Experts

Expert witnesses play a special role in legal malpractice litigation. Their job is neither zealous advocacy of a party's interests, nor determining who should win the lawsuit. Rather, the duty of an expert witness is to assist the judge and jury in understanding how the law governing lawyers applies to the facts of a dispute giving rise to a malpractice claim.

(1) Duties and Compensation

Ethics experts in legal malpractice litigation typically review voluminous amounts of material, such as pleadings, discovery answers, depositions, underlying documents, and court decisions relating to the case. They study this information to fully understand the facts from which the dispute arises and to identify and be prepared to discuss relevant issues. Other types of experts perform similar tasks. For example, an expert on damages may need to examine the facts of the dispute to construct a model for determining what consequential damages were caused by alleged negligence.

Deciphering handwritten notes made by attorneys or others during the course of representation is often maddeningly tedious, but sometimes holds the key that allows an expert to understand what was really going on at a particular point in time. Ethics experts may also need to research the holdings of other cases or the writings of scholars because malpractice lawsuits frequently raise questions to which the answers are less than clear, even when viewed from an expert's perspective. All of this work takes a great deal of time. Because experts are normally paid by the hour, and contingent fees are forbidden (*see* Model Rules of Prof'l Conduct R. 3.4 cmt. 4 (2010)), litigating a malpractice claim can be an expensive proposition.

It is possible to minimize the expenses of expert testimony by engaging an expert to testify based solely in response to hypothetical questions, rather than based on review of the facts of the case. For example, a lawyer can hire an expert to testify in response to a simple list of questions, such as "Is there a conflict of interest if a lawyer persuades a client to invest in a business the lawyer owns without disclosing that ownership interest to the client?" Surprisingly, expert testimony based on hypothetical questions seems to be a practice rarely used in legal malpractice litigation. Presumably, the lawyers litigating malpractice cases find it more effective to present expert witnesses who are well acquainted with the dispute and can testify about what was required by the particular circumstances of the case.

In the usual case, the law firm that hires a malpractice expert, as well as the client on whose behalf the expert serves, is liable for the payment of the expert's fees. *See Restatement (Third) of the Law Governing Lawyers* § 30 & cmt. b (2000).

(2) Independence Versus Partisanship

Although experts who appear in malpractice litigation are selected and paid for their time by the parties on whose behalf they work, experts are not merely partisans. A testifying expert has a duty to the court and to the justice system to honestly answer questions under oath, even if those answers may hurt the side of the case that has engaged the expert.

An expert's credibility may be challenged on many grounds, such as general qualifications, inadequate devotion of time to the case, or lack of access to critical documentary materials. Opposing counsel may also challenge an expert's credibility if the expert's testimony is inconsistent with what the expert has previously stated in publications, such as law review articles, or before tribunals on other occasions.

Ordinarily no attorney-client relationship exists between a legal malpractice expert and the party on whose behalf the expert has been retained. Because this is true, the conflict of interest rules contained in attorney disciplinary rules generally do not apply to the expert because the expert is not "representing" a client. Nevertheless, experts, as agents or subagents, have certain duties to their principals (the clients for whose benefit they have been hired). For example, an expert must treat information learned in the course of working on the case confidentially, unless the information has become a matter of public record or common knowledge, or some other consideration permits revelation or use. *See generally* ABA Formal Op. 97-407 (1997). Moreover, in a limited range of cases, it might be argued that a lawyer who previously served as an expert witness has a conflict of interest that materially limits the representation of a subsequent client due to obligations of continuing confidentiality owed to the person for whom the lawyer served as an expert. *See* Model Rules of Prof'l Conduct R. 1.7(a)(2) (2010). Conflicts of interest are discussed in Chapter 9.

(a) Non-Testifying Experts

A distinction is drawn between testifying experts (with which this discussion is concerned) and non-testifying experts, who act as consultants or co-counsel. Non-testifying experts may have an attorney-client relationship with the individual on whose behalf their guidance is sought. (*See* Part A of this Chapter.) In that case, the expert is subject to the duties and restrictions normally imposed on lawyers representing clients. *See* ABA Formal Op. 97-407 (1997). Of course, the scope of a consulting expert's duties may be limited, and therefore the conduct of the expert will be judged with reference to the narrowness of the engagement.

(3) Honesty and Effectiveness

In most malpractice cases, there are multiple competing versions of the facts that are supported by the testimony of the various witnesses. Typically, some versions of the facts favor the plaintiff and others favor the defendant. Rarely will an expert be in a position to testify that, regardless of which set of facts the jury accepts, the lawyer acted appropriately (or inappropriately). Rather, intellectual honesty and candor to the court normally oblige an expert to admit that if the jury makes certain findings, the other side wins on particular issues. Indeed, a lawyer will have no credibility with the jury, and will be subject to relentless (and well deserved) cross-examination, if the expert fails to concede points that must be conceded. For example, if an expert is asked to assume that the jury will find that the defendant lawyer knowingly made a false statement of material fact to a client, the expert cannot opine that the lawyer complied with the standard of care. Intentional deception about an important matter is never consistent with a lawyer's obligations. (*See* Chapter 5 Part B.)

In many cases, there is a dispute about whether an attorney-client relationship existed between the plaintiff and defendant who are now the parties to the malpractice litigation. If an attorney-client relationship did exist, it may be clear that the lawyer breached obligations to the client. If there was no attorney-client relationship, it may be equally clear that there was no breach. An expert's testimony must reflect these realities. Knowing and admitting what must be conceded is part of the job of an honest and effective expert.

(4) Testimony on Causation

The principal focus of a legal malpractice expert's work relates to establishing the standard of care and whether it was breached. However, in many jurisdictions, the law permits experts to testify about causation and damages as well.

(a) Sometimes Permitted

In some states, expert testimony about the harm caused by malpractice is allowed. *See Restatement (Third) of the Law Governing Lawyers* § 52 cmt. g (2000). However, whether an expert persuades a jury as to what losses resulted from unprofessional conduct probably depends upon the nature of the malpractice.

For example, suppose that a lawyer breached a duty of candor by failing to tell a client that the client was entrusting funds to a person the lawyer knew to have been previously convicted of, and incarcerated for, a felony involving financial fraud. The expert may firmly believe that the client would not have entrusted money to the former felon, and that the funds would not have been lost, had the lawyer disclosed the information to the client. A court might permit such testimony on causation of damages because it does not seem particularly speculative. On those facts, a judge may allow the testimony to assist the jury.

In other cases, it is harder for an expert to trace the lines of factual and proximate causation that run between breach of duty and alleged damages. Assume that a lawyer has serious conflicts of interest that are undisclosed and that the transaction in which the lawyer is assisting a client (say, acquisition of certain assets) fails. Although the expert may offer convincing testimony about the conflicts of interest, it may be difficult for the expert to persuade a judge or jury that the expert, based on professional knowledge and experience, knows to a reasonable degree of certainty that, but for the breach of the conflicts rules: the defendant lawyer would have withdrawn; an independent lawyer without conflicts would have been hired; better advice or assistance would have been provided by the new, unconflicted lawyer; and the plaintiff would have been able to consummate the purchase of assets on acceptable terms. In some jurisdictions, such testimony may be permitted because the expert helps the jury to understand the case by connecting the dots between breach of duty and damages. However, in other cases, the testimony may be rejected as impermissible speculation by the expert.

Factual causation is normally established in a legal malpractice action by applying a demanding "but for" test that requires the plaintiff to prove that the harm would not have occurred if the defendant had not been negligent. (*See* Part C of this Chapter.) However, in some jurisdictions, claims for breach of fiduciary duty are actionable upon a lesser showing that the defendant lawyer's conduct need only have been a "substantial factor" in producing harm to the plaintiff. (*See* Chapter 4 Part B.) A court applying the "substantial factor" rule to the facts in the undisclosed conflicts of interest example, mentioned above, might extend greater latitude to an expert testifying about causation issues.

(b) Sometimes Required

Some jurisdictions not only permit expert testimony on causation in legal malpractice cases, they require it, in most instances, because whether a lawyer's breach of duty causes harm is beyond the ken of the average layperson. For example, in *Estate of Sicotte v. Lubin & Meyer, P.C.*, 157 N.H. 670, 959 A.2d 236 (N.H. 2008), a law firm charged a one-third contingent fee for representing a minor without indicating that a court would ordinarily not approve a fee in excess of twenty-five percent, except "upon good cause shown." The firm also did not disclose, as required by state law, that the client had a right to be represented on a non-contingent fee basis. The Supreme Court of New Hampshire dismissed the resulting malpractice claim because the plaintiff failed to produce expert testimony on whether the alleged breaches of duty caused damage.

Similarly, in *Primis Corp. v. Milledge*, 2010 WL 2103936 (Tex. App.), a default judgment was entered against the plaintiff in a suit to confirm an arbitration award. In a subsequent malpractice action, the plaintiff alleged, and the trial court found, that the defendant law firm was negligent in connection with the plaintiff's efforts to overturn the default judgment. However, the trial court also determined that the plaintiff failed to prove that the law firm's negligence caused damage. The Texas Court of Appeals agreed because no expert testimony was introduced on that issue. According to the appellate court, the plaintiff was required to prove that, with the assistance of reasonably prudent counsel, a court would have vacated or modified the arbitration award. This causation inquiry was beyond the common understanding of the triers of fact. Therefore, expert testimony was necessary to prove causation.

Some courts strongly reject the idea that expert testimony on causation is ordinarily required in a malpractice case. Thus, in *Bloomberg v. Kronenberg*, 2006 WL 3337467, *6 (N.D. Ohio 2006), a federal court in Ohio stated that "the overwhelming weight of authority indicates that although an expert certainly *may* testify regarding the issue of proximate cause in a legal malpractice cause of action, such testimony is not required."

e. Reliance on Ethics Rules

(1) Directly Relevant Standards

In forming their opinions, legal malpractice experts often rely on the text of relevant disciplinary rules. Thus, an expert will probably consider either Rule 1.8 of the Model Rules of Professional Conduct, or more likely the parallel disciplinary rule of the state whose law governs the dispute, when opining on whether a lawyer took unfair advantage of a client in purchasing property from the client. Such rules directly address what a lawyer should do when engaging in business transactions with clients. For example, a Nevada ethics rule, which is identical in relevant part to ABA Model Rule 1.8, provides that "[a] lawyer shall not enter into a business transaction with a client *** unless: (1) The transaction and terms on which the lawyer acquires the interest are fair and reasonable to the client and are fully disclosed ***; (2) The client is advised in writing of the desirability of seeking and is given a reasonable opportunity to seek the advice of independent legal counsel on the transaction; and (3) The client gives informed consent ***." Nev. Rules of Prof'l Conduct R. 1.8(a) (2010). In these types of cases, the terms of a disciplinary rule are highly relevant to any assessment of what the standard of care requires. *See generally* Douglas R. Richmond, "Why Legal Ethics Rules are Relevant to Lawyer Liability," 38 *St. Mary's L.J.* 929 (2007).

Many courts do not object to an expert's reference under oath, by title, number, or text, to disciplinary rules bearing upon the issues in a malpractice case. Moreover, even courts that do not permit citation to specific provisions usually permit an expert to use the language of a disciplinary rule in testifying about the standard of care. *See, e.g., Tilton v. Trezza,* 12 Misc. 3d 1152(A), 819 N.Y.S.2d 213, 2006 WL 1320738 (Sup. Ct. 2006).

(2) Ignorance of Ethics Rules

While experts' reliance on ethics rules is a common practice regarded as generally acceptable, ignorance or disregard of the disciplinary rules is another matter. An "expert" who does not know what state disciplinary rules require might not be permitted to testify if the judge determines that the expert's opinion is not sufficiently informed to be likely to assist the jury. For example, one malpractice case arose from legal representation of a medical limited partnership in matters that involved a peer review process. A lawyer who was an ethicist at a prestigious university, and who was a highly regarded expert in medical peer review procedures, was not permitted to testify about the malpractice standard of care applicable to determining whether the defendant lawyers had acted properly. This was true because the expert admitted that he was unacquainted with the state's disciplinary rules governing lawyers.

In addition, if an expert is permitted to take the stand, testimony that ignores the terms of a relevant ethics rule may be found to be unpersuasive. *See Sealed Party v. Sealed Party*, No. Civ. A. H-04-2229, 2006 WL 1207732, at *11 n.32 (S.D. Tex.).

(3) Inconsistency with Ethics Rules

Testimony of an expert that departs from what the disciplinary rules require may be found to be so subjective as to provide no reliable basis for a jury determination that the defendant lawyer breached the standard of care. For example, in *Lerner v. Laufer*, 359 N.J. Super. 201, 819 A.2d 471 (App. Div. 2003), a lawyer agreed with a client to a limited scope of representation relating to the client's divorce. Despite assertions to the contrary by the client's expert in a subsequent malpractice case, a New Jersey appellate court held that the lawyer had no duty to discuss with the client the client's feelings of guilt, or how guilt might have affected the property settlement to which the client had agreed. The court found that the expert's report failed to establish "an authoritative or recognized standard of care" that rose above provisions in the state's disciplinary rules which allow a lawyer and client to limit the scope of representation.

819 A.2d at 483. The court found that any obligation the lawyer had to explore the client's guilt feelings appeared to be "personal" to the expert. 819 A.2d at 484.

(4) Other Sources of Guidance

Of course, there are sources of guidance other than disciplinary rules that experts should take into account. Case law, advisory ethics opinions, or scholarly writings may amplify or clarify what disciplinary rules say. Those sources may make a convincing case for why a particular rule may set an appropriate standard for discipline, but not for malpractice. An expert may freely consider these kinds of authority, and may sometimes espouse an opinion at odds with language in the state's disciplinary rules. For example, suppose that, unlike the ABA Model Rules (*see* Model Rules of Prof'l Conduct R. 1.6(b)(4) (2010)), a state's disciplinary rule on confidentiality does not address whether a lawyer may disclose client information to a third party in the course of seeking ethics advice relating to the representation. An expert might nevertheless reasonably opine that such disclosure does not violate the standard of care because other authorities recognize the propriety of such disclosures. Of course, an expert whose opinion departs from the terms of a disciplinary rule in stating the standard of care should expect to be called upon in cross-examination to defend that position.

f. Expert Witness Liability

Although expert testimony may harm persons involved in the litigation, experts normally cannot be sued because of the widely-recognized judicial proceedings privilege (sometimes called the litigation privilege). The privilege bars a civil action for damages against persons participating in litigation (*e.g.*, judges, jurors, and witnesses). (*See* Chapter 7 Part G.) However, the privilege, as it applies to expert witnesses, may have limits. At least in theory, an expert who fails to review crucial documentary evidence, or does so carelessly, should no more be immune from suit than a lawyer who fails to prepare adequately for trial. *Mattco Forge, Inc. v. Arthur Young & Co.*, 5 Cal. App. 4th 392, 6 Cal. Rptr. 2d 781 (1992), held that an action by a client against its own expert was not barred by the litigation privilege. However, there is little precedent to support a theory of expert witness liability for negligence.

4. Specialists, Novices, and Laypersons

According to a number of cases, lawyers who specialize in a particular area of the law are held to a higher standard of care than lawyers who do not specialize. Conceptually, this has appeal because those with talent should be encouraged to use it wisely. Nevertheless, the difficulties of implementing a higher standard of care for specialists (or for others) deserve consideration.

a. The Need for a Point of Reference

In practice, it is easiest to hold specialists to a higher standard if there is some clear point of reference that can be used to articulate what a specialist knows or does that is different from, and presumably superior to, what an ordinary practitioner would know or do. For example, some states have certification processes by which lawyers earn the right to call themselves specialists. These credentialing processes typically involve either educational requirements and/or demonstrations of proficiency through examinations, performance standards, or peer review. If that is the case, the standard of care for a certified specialist could be established by producing expert testimony from another certified specialist, or by reference to the principles that are taught or tested in the credentialing process (assuming those principles are distinguishable from what ordinary lawyers know or do).

b. De Facto Specialists

It may be difficult to discern the applicable standard of care if specialization, in a *de facto* sense, means simply that a lawyer has devoted a percentage of his or her practice to a particular kind of work for a period of years. Would a plaintiff have to adduce expert testimony from another lawyer who devoted a similar percentage of practice to the same type of work for about the same number of years? Could an expert who has specialized in an area of the law for twenty years opine on what type of care should have been exercised by a defendant lawyer who has specialized in the same area for one year, five years, ten years, or thirty years?

If *de facto* specialists are held to a higher standard of care, what about other groups that could be treated similarly? Should there be a higher standard of care for lawyers practicing in large law firms, or graduates of Ivy League law schools, or lawyers who have earned post-doctoral LL.M. degrees? It is easy to see why tort law has normally eschewed fracturing the standard of care into a myriad of different measures. In the absence of a clear point of reference (such as a certification process) for articulating what the higher standard entails, the preferable course may be the one that minimizes complexity. Lawyers—regardless of where they graduated from law school, what courses they took, what degrees they earned, or what kind of firm they practice in—should be held to the standard of conduct of an ordinary, reasonably prudent lawyer under the same or similar circumstances. Rather than changing the standard of care, *de facto* specialization might simply be treated as a factor relevant to whether ordinary care was exercised.

c. Representations of Greater Competence

The *Restatement* does not directly address whether specialization changes the standard of care, or is merely a circumstance relevant to whether the lawyer has acted in conformance with the usual standard of ordinary care under the circumstances. In discussing lawyers who claim to be experts or specialists, the commentary says that "a lawyer who represents to a client that the lawyer has greater competence *** is *held to that higher standard.*" *Restatement (Third) of the Law Governing Lawyers* § 52 cmt. d (2000) (emphasis added). However, that language is part of a comment entitled "[s]imilar circumstances," the first sentence of which says that "A lawyer's representations or disclaimers and qualifications may *constitute circumstances* affecting what a client is entitled to expect from the lawyer." *Id.* (emphasis added).

Note that holding specialists to a higher standard might not necessarily be an advantage to malpractice plaintiffs. A plaintiff may prefer to rely on an ordinary standard of care if establishing the higher standard complicates the presentation of the malpractice case, or if finding a qualified expert to testify about the higher duty of care is difficult.

d. Disclosure of Inexperience

At the other end of the spectrum, new members of the legal profession are ordinarily held to the same standard of care as those with experience. There is no "learners permit" for the practice of law that absolves novices from liability for mistakes that could have been avoided through the exercise of reasonable care.

One exception to this rule is where the novice discloses to the client the novice's lack of knowledge or experience. If a client could reasonably consent to being represented by such a lawyer, the disclosure of limitations and client consent may lower the applicable standard of care, at least temporarily.

The *Restatement* says that an agreement limiting the duty that a lawyer owes to a client is permissible if the client is adequately informed and the terms of the limitation are reasonable. *See Restatement (Third) of the Law Governing Lawyers* § 19 (2000). Moreover, "disclaimers and qualifications may constitute circumstances affecting what a client is entitled to expect from the lawyer." *Id.* at § 52 cmt. d. However, an illustration in the *Restatement* adds that a general waiver of the duty of competence would be invalid. *Id.* § 19 illus. 3.

e. Malpractice by Laypersons

A layperson who practices law can be sued for legal malpractice. It is no defense to liability for the layperson to argue that he or she was never admitted to the practice of law.

For example, in *Buscemi v. Intachai*, 730 So.2d 329 (Fla. Dist. Ct. App. 1999), the defendant, a financial planner who had a legal education but was not admitted to the bar, was sued for mishandling legal issues related to the investment of guardianship funds. The defendant had told the plaintiff that he "would comply with the Supreme Court of Florida rules and regulations," and charge a cheaper fee than a lawyer. 730 So. 2d at 2. A Florida appellate court held that, whether a person is a lawyer or not, one who undertakes to give legal advice, must exercise due care.

Similarly, in *Webb v. Pomeroy*, 8 Kan. App. 2d 246, 655 P.2d 465 (1982), a layperson, whose brother was a lawyer, was sued for malpractice related to real property conveyancing instruments. The Kansas Court of Appeals ruled broadly that a person "in the same position as a regularly admitted practicing attorney" is "bound to the same degree of knowledge, skill, dedication, and ethical conduct as *** [a] member of the bar." 655 P.2d at 468.

There are few reported cases holding nonlawyers liable for legal malpractice. This may change as nonlawyers are increasingly permitted to represent persons before state and federal agencies, or take on a wider range of law-related tasks for businesses. However, it is possible that the law may develop in a way that does not hold all nonlawyers to the standard of performance for lawyers, but instead liable under contract principles requiring simply that they must deliver what they promise. *See generally* Thomas D. Morgan, "Professional Malpractice in a World of Amateurs," 40 *St. Mary's L.J.* 891, 903 (2009). This might not be too far different from liability under tort principles which, as noted above, say that a lawyer and client may define the scope of the representation (*see* Part A-2 of this Chapter) and that disclosures of inexperience may lower the standard of care (*see* Part B-4-D of this Chapter). Even under a contract standard, a person who impersonates a lawyer, or otherwise expressly or implicitly represents that he or she can deliver the same quality of services as a lawyer, might be judged by reference to the standard of care for lawyers.

5. Lawyers with Disabilities

There are numerous unanswered questions regarding the malpractice liability of lawyers with disabilities. One issue is whether an undisclosed disability (*e.g.*, dyslexia or inability to focus in noisy situations) affects the standard of care. In many areas of tort law, physical disabilities are taken into account in determining whether the defendant acted as a reasonably prudent person. *See Restatement (Third) of Torts: Liability for Physical and Emotional Harm* § 11(a) (2010). Thus, a person who is blind is required to exercise the same degree of care as a reasonably prudent person who is blind. However, mental disabilities, such as poor judgment, low intelligence, or even insanity, are generally ignored. *Id.* § 11(c). The difficulties of applying these rules to learning disabilities are apparent because it is often less than clear whether such disabilities can be categorized as exclusively or predominantly physical or mental.

For consumer protection reasons, it is arguable that a lawyer's *undisclosed* disability of any kind should not play any role in a legal malpractice action. Such lawyers should be held to the same standard of care as any reasonably prudent attorney. This view would seem to be consistent with the position of the *Restatement (Third) of the Law Governing Lawyers*, which, as noted above, provides that an agreement limiting the duty that a lawyer owes to a client is permissible *if the client is adequately informed* and the terms of the limitation are reasonable. *See Restatement (Third) of the Law Governing Lawyers* § 19 (2000).

6. Negligence *Per Se* in Legal Malpractice

In ordinary negligence actions, a plaintiff may be able to take a shortcut in establishing breach of duty. In a majority of jurisdictions, an unexcused violation of a legislative enactment may conclusively prove that the defendant acted unreasonably. This is called negligence *per se*, meaning negligence "in itself." Proof of the unexcused violation obviates the need for a "totality of the circumstances" inquiry into the facts surrounding the defendant's conduct. The unexcused violation of the legislative enactment conclusively proves breach of the duty of reasonable care. (Note, however, that in a minority of states, violation of a standard-setting legislative enactment is only (a) presumptive evidence of negligence or (b) some evidence from which negligence may be inferred. In those jurisdictions, a detailed inquiry into the facts may still be necessary to determine whether the presumption of unreasonable conduct is rebutted by other evidence or whether the permissible evidence of negligence that the violation constitutes is sufficiently strong to warrant a finding of unreasonableness in light of competing facts.)

a. How Statutes Set the Standard of Care

A legislative enactment may set the standard of care for a civil cause of action for either of two reasons. The first reason is that the enactment contains language making clear that one of the remedies for breach of its requirements is a civil suit for damages. The second reason that an enactment may set the standard of care is that, even though it is silent as to civil liability, a court determines that it is an appropriate indicator of whether the defendant acted reasonably. In making that assessment, a court considers whether the enactment was intended to protect the class of persons of which the plaintiff was a member from the type of harm that occurred. *See Restatement (Third) of Torts: Liability for Physical and Emotional Harm* § 14 (2010). If the answer is yes on both accounts, a court may treat the statute as setting the standard of conduct of a reasonably prudent person, provided there are no good reasons to the contrary. For example, a court might decline to hold that a legislative enactment sets the standard of care if it is obsolete or vague. Likewise, the court should not hold that a statute sets the standard of care if there is evidence that the legislature intended other penalties, such as criminal or administrative fines, to be the exclusive remedy for a violation or intended that a violation of the enactment, by itself, not trigger liability for negligence.

b. Statutes Disclaiming a Civil Cause of Action

State disciplinary rules typically contain a provision, similar to one found in the Model Rules of Professional Conduct, which states that a violation of a disciplinary rule does not automatically give rise to a cause of action against a lawyer or create a presumption that a legal duty has been breached. *See* Model Rules of Prof'l Conduct Scope Note (2010). It is clear from this type of provision that the drafters of the relevant enactment did not intend for a violation of the rules to support a negligence *per se* argument.

Similarly, the rules adopted by the Securities and Exchange Commission pursuant to the federal Sarbanes-Oxley Act, which impose various duties on lawyers, expressly indicate that they do not create a private right of action against a lawyer or law firm. 17 C.F.R. § 205.7 (Westlaw 2010). Again, it seems clear that a negligence *per se* argument is foreclosed.

However, it is not true that disciplinary rules and Sarbanes-Oxley regulations play no role in legal malpractice actions. A violation of their provisions does not establish a shorthand route to a finding that the defendant acted unreasonably. Nevertheless, a plaintiff may still argue that the defendant was negligent under the usual "totality of the circumstances" test, one of the relevant factors being that the defendant violated applicable rules. So too, an expert testifying in support of the plaintiff's case may base an opinion about the standard of care in part on what legislative enactments state about the lawyer's duties, even if those enactments do not create a negligence *per se* shortcut.

c. Restatement Position on Statutory Standards

Summarizing the relationship between rules governing lawyer conduct and the standard of care in malpractice litigation, the *Restatement* explains:

Proof of a violation of a rule or statute regulating the conduct of lawyers:

(a) does not give rise to an implied cause of action for professional negligence or breach of fiduciary duty;

(b) does not preclude other proof concerning the duty of care *** or the fiduciary duty; and

(c) may be considered by a trier of fact as an aid in understanding and applying the standard of *** [care or fiduciary duty] to the extent that

(i) the rule or statute was designed for the protection of persons in the position of the claimant and

(ii) proof of the content and construction of such a rule or statute is relevant to the claimant's claim.

Restatement (Third) of the Law Governing Lawyers § 52(2) (2000).

d. Statutes Imposing Duties Not Unique to Lawyers

Some legislative enactments applicable to lawyers may support a negligence *per se* argument. For example, a few jurisdictions have laws expressly requiring lawyers, among others, to reveal confidential information to prevent child abuse. Under this type of law, a victim who suffers harm might persuasively argue that a lawyer who failed to make a report is liable for abuse that could have been prevented because the statute was intended to prevent that type of harm to the class of persons of which the plaintiff was a member. However, no case has yet imposed this type of tort liability. *See* Lisa Hansen, "Attorneys' Duty to Report Child Abuse," 19 *J. Am. Acad. Matrim. Law.* 59, 75-77 (2004).

Many states have passed security breach notification laws which require database possessors (like law firms) to protect the personal information of data subjects (like present and former clients) from unauthorized access. Database possessors must also notify data subjects when the security of their personal information has been breached. Some of these laws expressly provide for civil liability for damages. *See, e.g.*, Cal. Civ. Code § 1798.84 (Westlaw 2010) (allowing an injured customer to "institute a civil action to recover damages"). Other state laws are silent on the issue of civil liability. However, in those jurisdictions, a court might conclude that a lawyer was negligent *per se* based on an unexcused violation of these statutory obligations. *See generally* Vincent R. Johnson, "Cybersecurity, Identity Theft, and the Limits of Tort Liability," 57 *S.C. L. Rev.* 255 (2005).

7. Informed Consent in Legal Malpractice

The doctrine of informed consent is well established in the medical malpractice field. With limited exceptions, the doctrine requires a physician to disclose to a patient the material risks of, and available alternatives to, a course of treatment. The failure to make such disclosures and obtain the patient's consent is actionable negligence if that breach causes harm. This is true regardless of whether the physician otherwise exercised care in treating the patient.

Clients, like patients, have a right to exercise extensive control over their own affairs, including their legal representation. *Cf. Restatement (Third) of the Law Governing Lawyers* §§ 21-22 (2000). Consequently, there is no reason why the informed consent doctrine should not apply as readily to legal malpractice cases as it does in suits against physicians.

Until recently, the term "informed consent" only occasionally appeared in court opinions dealing with legal malpractice. However, the underlying idea is well established. A lawyer has a duty to communicate to a client material information relating to the client's case. *See id.* § 20; Model Rules of Prof'l Conduct R. 1.4 (2010). Failure to keep a client reasonably informed is a breach of a lawyer's duties. (*See* Chapter 4 Part C.)

In *Bowman v. Gruel Mills Nims & Pylman, LLP*, 2007 WL 1203580, *5-*6 (W.D. Mich.), a malpractice action, a federal court considered the obligations imposed by the Michigan counterpart to Model Rule 1.4. It concluded that regardless of whether a lawyer's decision not to press ERISA claims in a retirement benefit dispute was a protected exercise of professional discretion, that choice, as a key strategic decision, needed to be discussed with the client.

The language of "informed consent" is now becoming better established in the law of lawyer professional responsibility than was previously true. The most recent major revision of the Model Rules of Professional Conduct so frequently used the term "informed consent" that the drafters specifically defined those words. The term "informed consent" signals agreement to a proposed course of conduct manifested by a person whose lawyer has communicated adequate information and explanation about the material risks of and reasonably available alternatives to that course of conduct. *See* Model Rules of Prof'l Conduct R. 1.0(e) (2010). While the term "informed consent" may take on a slightly different meaning in the malpractice context than it has in lawyer discipline, courts are likely to increasingly discuss lawyers' obligations in terms of "informed consent." This means that greater attention will be focused on whether or not material risks and alternatives were disclosed.

With respect to lawyers' liability for negligence, three issues relating to informed consent are likely to warrant attention and debate. The first concerns "materiality," since even in the medical malpractice field, only *material* risks and alternatives need to be disclosed. The term "materiality" has diverse meanings in different areas of the law. In many instances, it means simply that the matter is of such weight and moment that a reasonable person would take it into account in making a decision. Considering that the purpose of the informed consent doctrine is to enable clients to decide their own affairs, courts should interpret the term "material" in a manner that does not frustrate the purposes of the rule. Nevertheless, the term has limits. For example, a lawyer is not liable for failing to advise a client to assert a claim for insurance benefits for which the client is not eligible. *See Abbo v. Perkins*, 2007 WL 949760, *6 (Ohio App. 2007). One way to explain this result is to say that the undisclosed information was not "material."

Second, exceptions to informed consent obligations should be recognized in the law of legal malpractice. In medicine, a physician need not disclose a risk if it ought to be known by everyone or is in fact known to the patient; if there is an emergency and the patient is incapable of determining whether treatment should be administered; or if full disclosure would be detrimental to the patient's care and best interests. These exceptions are narrowly construed so that they do not undercut the policies behind the informed consent doctrine. Presumably, similar exceptions will apply to informed consent rules in the legal malpractice field.

Third, it is important to remember that failure to obtain informed consent is merely evidence of breach of duty. A plaintiff suing for negligence must still prove that the breach of duty caused damages. *(See* Part C.) In medical malpractice law, a large majority of courts hold that, in proving causation in an informed-consent case, the appropriate inquiry is whether a reasonable person (as opposed to the specific plaintiff) would have made a different decision if the undisclosed matter had been called to attention. Courts may follow this approach in legal malpractice cases. Phrasing the inquiry in reasonable-person terms minimizes the risk that self-serving testimony by the plaintiff will distort the assessment of whether the nondisclosure did, in fact, cause damage.

However, some courts may take a different approach. In *Smith v. O'Donnell*, 288 S.W.3d 417 (Tex. 2009), the Texas Supreme Court allowed an executor to bring a malpractice claim against a law firm which allegedly provided bad advice to the decedent. In dicta the court stated that, "Of course, if the evidence demonstrates that *** [the decedent] would have ignored *** [the law firm's] advice no matter how competently provided, the malpractice claim will fail for lack of proximate causation." *Id.* at 421.

Consider this example: a client alleges that the defendant lawyer failed to advise the client about the risks of submitting a dispute to arbitration, rather than trying a case in a court. Among the undisclosed risks are the fact that the arbitrators are not strictly bound by substantive law and that there is very little opportunity for judicial review of an unfavorable arbitration decision. In a legal malpractice action alleging lack of informed consent, the plaintiff will have to establish that the undisclosed matters were material and unknown to the plaintiff, that a reasonable person would not have agreed to arbitration if that information had been disclosed, and that a court of law would have rendered a decision more favorable to the client. Consequently, the plaintiff in an informed consent case faces many obstacles.

C. CAUSATION

As suggested above, a plaintiff suing a lawyer for negligence must always prove that the lawyer's unreasonable conduct caused harm. The usual inquiry into causation has two aspects. Factual causation requires that the defendant's conduct be significantly linked to the damages the plaintiff alleges, and proximate causation requires that it be fair to hold the defendant responsible for damages factually caused. Factual and proximate causation are discussed in the following sections.

1. Factual Causation

No matter how serious a lawyer's negligence, causation of damages is not presumed. If a new associate with no experience and inadequate supervision makes serious errors in trying a case, the plaintiff must still prove that those errors adversely impacted the result. *See Alexander v. Turtur & Associates, Inc.*, 146 S.W.3d 113 (Tex. 2004).

Similarly, even if a law firm is negligent in failing to prevent a lawyer from sexualizing a lawyer-client relationship, a client cannot recover damages for losses incidental to an adverse arbitration ruling without proving that, except for the negligence, those losses would not have occurred. *See Cecala v. Newman*, 2007 WL 2530369, *6 (D. Ariz.).

In a recent case filed in a New York federal court, the plaintiff alleged that a lawyer committed malpractice by including in a patent application eleven pages of plagiarized content. One issue in the dispute was whether the request for a patent was denied because of the plagiarism or because the Patent and Trademark Office concluded that the technology in question was not patentable in light of the prior work of other scientists. Only if the former is true would the alleged malpractice be actionable.

a. The "But For" Test

Legal malpractice cases are governed by the same factual causation principles that apply in other areas of tort law. *See Restatement (Third) of the Law Governing Lawyers* § 53 (2000). Thus, the well-known "but for" test is the most common method of proving factual causation. Under that test, the plaintiff must show that but for the negligence of the defendant, harm would not have occurred. For example, "[i]n an action alleging that an attorney failed to perfect an appeal, the plaintiff must prove that he or she would have been successful on appeal if the appeal had properly been perfected." *Universal Underwriters Ins. Co. v. Judge & James*, Ltd., 372 Ill. App. 3d 372, 865 N.E.2d 531, 538 (2007).

If a plaintiff wishes to recover damages resulting from a business transaction that allegedly failed as a result of a lawyer's negligence, the plaintiff must show that but for the lawyer's errant conduct the transaction would have succeeded and the losses would not have been suffered. Likewise, if the plaintiff alleges that a lawyer's failure to disclose relevant information to the client caused a lawsuit not to settle and eventually precipitated a disastrous jury verdict, the plaintiff must convince the jury that, but for the nondisclosure, there could have been a meeting of the minds on an acceptable settlement amount. If such evidence is adduced, the plaintiff can then recover the difference between the lesser amount for which the case would have settled and the amount of the jury verdict.

(1) Difficult to Establish

"But for" causation is often difficult to establish. For example, in *Faber v. Herman*, 731 N.W.2d 1 (Iowa 2007), a divorcing couple had agreed that the wife was entitled to half of the husband's retirement benefits. However, the husband's lawyer erred, first, by drafting a stipulation that sought to implement the agreement by means not permitted by law (an immediate payment from the retirement fund based on present value), and, second, by failing to advise his client of the further steps he had taken to correct the first error (a delayed payment of a percentage of the husband's retirement benefits). Nevertheless, the Iowa Supreme Court held that the lawyer's malpractice did not cause damages because the husband had agreed to an even division of retirement benefits and that was what was ultimately achieved.

In another case, the plaintiff alleged that but for a law firm's failure to provide proper tax advice "it would not have had to maintain the multi-million dollar loss reserve on its books, creating the appearance that it had a negative net worth, which caused it to lose business opportunities and incur monetary damages." *AmBase Corp. v. Davis Polk Wardwell*, 8 N.Y.3d 428, 866 N.E.2d 1033, 834 N.Y.S.2d 705, 710 (2007). However, the New York Court of Appeals found that the plaintiff failed to establish factual causation of damages. The loss reserve had been in place for years before the law firm was hired and was still carried on the books after the law firm advised the plaintiff that there was a very strong case that it had no liability for the taxes in question.

(2) Proving an Alternative Would Have Occurred

Proving causation often requires a plaintiff to show that an alternative sequence of events would have occurred but for the defendant's breach of duty. Moreover, persuasion by a preponderance of the evidence is required. The mere fact that another sequence of events might have occurred is insufficient to establish factual causation. Rather, it must be shown that, more likely than not, but for the lawyer's negligence, a different series of events would have taken place.

Bristol Co., LP v. Osman, 190 P.3d 752 (Colo. Ct. App. 2007), was a suit based on a law firm's alleged failure to provide proper advice about the defense of laches. A Colorado appellate court found that the portions of the plaintiff's complaint addressing causation were insufficient to support a damages award because the allegations were purely hypothetical and speculative. The complaint did not identify an actual harm, but merely "a harm that might have occurred had events unfolded differently." 190 P.3d at 758.

However, the mere fact that an alternative sequence of events involves several variables does not necessarily preclude proof of causation, if each of those variables is susceptible to proof. In *Geddes v. Campbell*, 2006 WL 3352182, *7 (Cal. Ct. App.), a California court found that causation was not "beyond the realm of proof" or a matter of speculation where it was necessary for the plaintiff to show that, if the defendant lawyer had advised the plaintiff to make certain disclosures to a third party, the plaintiff would have followed that advice and the third party would have agreed to a release of liability. Presumably, the plaintiff could testify about whether he would have followed the advice; the defendant could challenge that testimony or introduce contrary evidence; and the jury could resolve the issue, one way or the other. As to whether the third-person would have signed a release, the court noted simply that the person "could be questioned about whether he would have signed such a release had he known what he allegedly did not know." *Id.* at *8.

Christensen & Jensen, P.C. v. Barrett & Daines, 613 Utah Adv. Rep. 3, 194 P.3d 931 (Utah 2008), was a legal malpractice case that arose from a dispute which gave rise to a landmark punitive damages ruling. In the underlying case, multiple jointly-represented co-clients rejected a $150 million settlement offer. Ultimately, they recovered a total of about only $10 million after the United States Supreme Court articulated new standards, which now greatly constrain punitive damages awards (*see* Chapter 6). In the malpractice case, the plaintiff (one of the former co-clients) argued first that the $150 million settlement offer would have been accepted by the co-clients if it had been better explained, and second that the plaintiff could have settled his claim individually if he had not been represented by lawyers who had a conflict of interest by representing multiple co-clients. The Utah Supreme Court rejected both arguments, finding that on neither ground could the plaintiff prove that the malpractice defendants' conduct caused damage. The $150 million settlement offer had been conditioned by the defendant in the underlying case on all co-clients joining in a request for the state supreme court to vacate an opinion which contained findings that defendant had nationally engaged in a pattern of abusive business practices over a period of many years. The settlement offer was further conditioned on the state supreme court's vacatur of the opinion in question. In the malpractice case, the Utah Supreme Court found that the causation standards for negligence, breach of fiduciary duty, and even breach of contract were essentially the same as applied to the facts of the dispute. Thus, in order to recover, the plaintiff needed to show that, but for the breach, the plaintiff would have benefitted. However, the court concluded that the plaintiff was unable to make this showing. There was undisputed evidence that the co-clients had entered into an agreement requiring unanimity for acceptance of any settlement offer. The co-clients other than the plaintiff were adamant that they would not have settled on the terms proposed by the defendant in the underlying suit because they were more interested in preserving the disputed opinion and its findings than they were in money. Finally, there was no evidence that the defendant would have settled with the malpractice plaintiff separately.

(3) Prior Judge and Jury May Not Testify

If malpractice is alleged to have impacted an earlier trial, it is reasonable to consider whether it would be possible to ask the judge or jurors from the earlier case if their decisions would have been different but for the malpractice. However, this is not permitted. For reasons of judicial ethics, the judge in the earlier proceeding is not allowed to testify in the malpractice lawsuit. Testimony by the former judge would be unduly prejudicial because the prestige of the judge's judicial office would be aligned with one of the parties in the malpractice litigation. For different reasons, generally relating to impracticality, finality, and the integrity of jury deliberations, jurors from the first proceeding are also not allowed to testify about whether they would have decided the underlying case differently if the lawyer had not been negligent.

(4) The "But For" Test and Multiple Tortfeasors

In cases involving multiple tortfeasors, the "but for" will be conducted with respect to each tortfeasor. Whether each tortfeasor is then liable for the entire harm, as opposed to just a portion of the harm, is discussed later in connection with the subject of joint and several liability. (*See* Chapter 7 Part E.)

Suppose that Lawyer #1 negligently omits important provisions from a contract, and that successor counsel, Lawyer #2, negligently fails to discover the omission at a time when it would have been possible to reform the instrument at minimal costs to the

client. If the client becomes liable under the contract
for onerous amounts as a result of the omitted provisions, the client can successfully sue either lawyer or
both. But for Lawyer #1's omission of the provisions,
the client never would have become liable under the
contract. But for Lawyer #2's negligence, the omission
would have been discovered, the contract would have
been reformed, and the client would not have incurred
contractual liability. The negligence of each lawyer is
a factual cause of the plaintiff's harm.

(5) Independently Sufficient Causes

Authorities widely recognize that even if the "but
for" test cannot be met, the defendant's conduct is a
factual cause of the plaintiff's harm if the defendant's
conduct was independently sufficient to cause the
harm. *Cf. Restatement (Third) of Torts: Liability for
Physical and Emotional Harm* § 27 (2010). This rule
applies to legal malpractice cases.

Consider the following scenario: Lawyer #3 and
Lawyer #4 are each asked to draft separate provisions
for a complex document. Each lawyer does so negligently, and each act of negligence is sufficient to
render the document entirely invalid, causing losses
to the client. Lawyer #3 does not escape liability
because Lawyer #4's conduct would have precipitated
the same losses, and vice versa. Because each lawyer's
conduct was independently sufficient to cause the
invalidity of the document, each lawyer will be held
responsible even though it cannot be said that either
was a "but for" cause of the damages.

b. "Trial within a Trial" Analysis

Establishing factual causation requires the plaintiff to prove what would have happened if the facts had been different. In a malpractice lawsuit, this process is commonly referred to as a "trial within a trial." The expression is particularly apt when the alleged malpractice relates to an underlying litigation claim, because the first lawsuit must be presented within the context of the malpractice action to gauge what the result would have been but for the defendant lawyer's negligence. For example, a malpractice plaintiff may allege that, but for the lawyer's negligence, the plaintiff would have secured a more favorable result in an earlier action. In that case, "[a]ll the issues that would have been litigated in the previous action are litigated between the plaintiff and the plaintiff's former lawyer, with the latter taking the place and bearing the burdens that properly would have fallen on the defendant in the original action." *Suder v. Whiteford, Taylor & Preston, LLP*, 413 Md. 230, 992 A.2d 413, 420 (2010) (quoting *Restatement (Third) of the Law Governing Lawyers* § 52 cmt. b (2000)). In *Suder*, the Maryland Court of Appeals held that the malpractice defendant was not precluded from raising defenses which were never asserted in an earlier trial which gave rise to the malpractice claim. 992 A.2d at 421.

In *Aquino v. Kuczinski, Vila & Assoc.*, P.C., 39 A.D.3d 216, 835 N.Y.S.2d 16 (2007), the plaintiff alleged that the defendant-attorney failed to file her slip-and-fall case before the statute of limitations expired. The court held that the defendant-attorney was entitled to summary judgment because the "plaintiff failed to introduce any evidence that the casino either created the dangerous condition, or had actual or constructive knowledge of it." 835 N.Y.S.2d at 20. Absent such evidence, the plaintiff could not prove that she would have prevailed on the underlying premises liability claim.

(1) Factual Complexity

One practical consequence of the "trial within a trial" process is that legal malpractice cases can be exceedingly complex. This is particularly true if the underlying matter involves a sophisticated area of law practice that is ordinarily difficult to understand even without the added issues of a legal malpractice claim. This may be true, for example, in a case where the lawyer represented a subsidiary in a dispute with the subsidiary's parent corporation. In that situation, malpractice liability may turn on careful assessment of the actions, statements, and expectations of numerous entity representatives and stakeholders.

In some cases, holding a trial within a trial requires the presentation of many witnesses and documents, prolonging the malpractice trial with little hope of keeping the jurors focused until a verdict can be reached. Even then, if all the evidence is presented, the jury may not fully comprehend the matter. Faced with these realities, some cases settle because it is unlikely that a better result will be forthcoming if the litigation is allowed to run its course.

In order to minimize the complexity of the trial within a trial process, it may make sense to sever the underlying action for a separate trial. Procedures in some states permit this. *See, e.g.*, Ala. Code § 6-5-579 (Westlaw 2010).

(2) Tortious Spoliation of Causation Evidence

Sometimes a lawyer's negligence results in the loss of evidence needed by a client to prove that the lawyer's conduct caused damages. For example, in *Fontanella v. Marcucci*, 89 Conn. App. 690, 877 A.2d 828 (2005), *certification granted in part*, 275 Conn. 907, 882 A.2d 670 (2005), *certification withdrawn* (Mar. 13, 2006), a boy was injured in an auto accident as the result of allegedly defective seatbelts. However, before the seatbelts were inspected properly, the boy's mother sold the car to her insurer, allegedly on the advice of their attorney. The car was subsequently destroyed, making the seatbelt evidence unavailable.

A judge may address spoliation procedurally by instructing the jury that it may infer that the lawyer's negligence caused damage or by shifting to the lawyer the burden of disproving causation.

For example, suppose that a lawyer deceives a client for a period years about performing work to investigate the facts of the client's case. *See Jerista v. Murray*, 185 N.J. 175, 883 A.2d 350, 366 (2005). By the time the deception is discovered, it may be too late to assemble the essential witnesses and documents. In these types of cases, if the client sues the lawyer it is unfair to require the client prove that the underlying claim would have been won. A spoliation inference or presumption may be an appropriate remedy for this kind of misconduct, at least where the spoliation was culpable, unexcused, and clearly injurious to the client.

Some states permit an independent tort action based on intentional or negligent spoliation of evidence. However, the trend of recent decisions favors using spoliation inferences or presumptions when that is feasible. The jury is told that it may infer, or in the absence of evidence to the contrary is required to presume, that the missing evidence would have been favorable to the plaintiff.

Of course, a lawyer who wrongfully destroys evidence is subject to disciplinary sanctions, as well as malpractice liability. *See* Karen Sloan, "Ohio Supreme Court Suspends Lawyer for Destroying Documents and Lying About It," www.law.com, Aug. 30, 2010.

(3) Legitimate Destruction of Potential Evidence

Lawyers discard things all the time, such as notes, hardcopy documents, e-mail messages, and electronic files. Prohibiting destruction of such material would essentially transform law offices into over-stocked warehouses for information that might rarely be used. Therefore, lawyers must be allowed to destroy material pursuant to a carefully crafted document retention policy. Such a policy can help protect lawyers from spoliation claims because the policy may explain why it was reasonable, rather than negligent, to discard certain papers or electronic files. Of course, when it is foreseeable that a dispute might call for information pertaining to a client, ordinary policies on document retention must give way to more careful implementation of the duty to preserve client information and property.

c. Loss of a Chance

Loss of a chance is not a theory of factual causation, but rather a different way of looking at damages. The chance of securing a successful result is regarded as something important, the loss of which is a kind of damage itself. If that is true, proving factual causation is simple: all that the plaintiff must show is that, but for the defendant's tortious conduct, the valuable chance would not have been lost.

Many states have accepted "loss of a chance" arguments, generally in the context of medical malpractice. *See Matsuyama v. Birnbaum*, 452 Mass. 1, 890 N.E.2d 819, 828 n. 23 (Mass. 2008). For example, assume that a doctor negligently fails to read an x-ray that revealed cancer, and that during the period that the cancerous condition goes undetected, the plaintiff's chances of survival decline from 40% to 10%. Most persons would regard the lost chance of survival as an important loss, and some states permit recovery. This may be true even if, as in the posited scenario, the patient was already more likely than not to die at the time that the initial x-ray was taken. In the subsequent action, the doctor's negligence is a "but for" cause of the lost chance of survival, rather than of the death.

Courts and scholars sometimes bristle at the mere mention of "loss of a chance" as a legitimate rationale for recovery. They fear that the doctrine is an unwise step down an ill-advised path that might lead to theories of "probabilistic causation" that lie far afield from the certainties of the "but for" rule. Few cases have *expressly* endorsed the loss of a chance theory in the legal malpractice context. Nevertheless, the *Restatement* opines that "a plaintiff who can establish that the negligence or fiduciary breach of the plaintiff's former lawyer deprived the plaintiff of a substantial chance of prevailing and that, due to that misconduct, the results of a previous trial cannot be reconstructed, may recover for the loss of that chance in jurisdictions recognizing such a theory of recovery in professional-malpractice cases generally." *Restatement (Third) of the Law Governing Lawyers* § 52 cmt. b (2000).

There are many cases where a lawyer's negligence does indeed cause the loss of an important chance, such as where a lawyer neglects to relay a settlement offer or plea bargain that might have been accepted. In malpractice actions arising from these types of disputes, some decisions effectively recognize the loss of a chance doctrine without using the term. For example, in *Vahila v. Hall,* 674 N.E.2d 1164 (Ohio 1997), the Supreme Court of Ohio held that, in order to succeed in a malpractice action, the plaintiffs were not required to show that they would have prevailed in certain civil, criminal, and administrative proceedings absent the negligence of their lawyers. The court wrote:

> [W]e reject any finding that the element of causation in the context of a legal malpractice action can be replaced *** with a rule of thumb requiring that a plaintiff *** prove in every instance that he or she would have been successful in the underlying matter(s) giving rise to the complaint.

***. A strict "but for" test *** ignores settlement opportunities lost due to the attorney's negligence.

674 N.E.2d at 1168-69 (internal quotations omitted).

Note, however, that in some cases, a plaintiff may have framed malpractice allegations in terms that require the plaintiff to prove that, but for the defendant's malpractice, a better result would have been obtained. Thus, "when a plaintiff premises a legal-malpractice claim on the theory that he would have received a better outcome if his attorney had tried the underlying matter to conclusion rather than settling it, the plaintiff must establish that he would have prevailed in the underlying matter and that the outcome would have been better than the outcome provided by the settlement." *Environmental Network Corp. v. Goodman Weiss Miller, L.L.P.*, 893 N.E.2d 173, 175 (Ohio 2008).

d. Shifting the Burden of Proof on Causation

Occasionally, courts have shifted the burden of proof on the issue of causation to the malpractice defendant. *See* Ronald E. Mallen & Jeffrey M. Smith, *Legal Malpractice* § 31:17 n. 36 (2009 ed.) (noting a "significant minority" of jurisdictions). Shifting the burden of proof particularly makes sense if the lawyer's alleged malpractice is of a type that would naturally deprive the plaintiff of evidence relating to causation.

Under Louisiana law, a client's proof that a lawyer's negligence caused the loss of the opportunity to assert a claim creates an inference that the lost opportunity caused damages. The burden then shifts to the lawyer to establish that the client could not have succeeded on the original claim. *See Prince v. Buck*, 969 So.2d 641, 643 (La. Ct. App. 2007).

In *Gamer v. Ross*, 49 A.D.3d 598, 854 N.Y.S.2d 160 (2008), lawyers were hired to handle personal injury actions against a landowner and an independent contractor after a boy, while in-line skating, tripped over wires and debris located on a public sidewalk. After the actions were decided adversely to the plaintiffs, the plaintiffs sued their lawyers for malpractice. The plaintiffs alleged that the lawyers were negligent in failing to conduct proper discovery. The lawyers sought summary judgment on the ground that the plaintiffs could not have succeeded in the underlying actions inasmuch as they adduced no evidence that the landowner or independent contractor caused the dangerous condition. In affirming an order denying the lawyers' request for summary judgment, a New York appellate court wrote:

> [T]his argument fundamentally misconstrue[s] the central theory of the plaintiffs' case, *viz.*, that the defendants were negligent in failing to conduct proper discovery that would have uncovered facts sufficient to prevent the dismissal of the underlying actions. As the moving parties, the defendants bore the initial burden of establishing that the missing discovery would not have prevented the dismissal of the underlying actions. "This burden cannot be satisfied merely by pointing out gaps in the plaintiff[s]' case" ***.

854 N.Y.S.2d at 162.

In many jurisdictions, there is as yet little precedent for shifting the burden of proof on causation to a legal malpractice defendant.

2. Proximate Causation

The requirement of proximate causation is a policy-based inquiry into fairness. The rule holds that even if the defendant factually caused the plaintiff's harm, the defendant will not be accountable if it would be unfair to impose responsibility.

a. In General

There are many different ways of talking about fairness. Thus, as in other areas of tort law, a malpractice defendant's conduct may be found not to be a proximate cause of a loss that was unforeseeable or not within the risks that made the defendant's conduct tortious. *Cf. Restatement (Third) of Torts: Liability for Physical and Emotional Harm* § 29 (2010). It also may be impossible or unfair to impose liability if many intervening forces contributed to the production of the loss. Thus, it may be said that "[a] proximate cause is one that produces an injury through a natural and continuous sequence of events unbroken by any effective intervening cause." *Cleveland v. Rotman*, 297 F.3d 569, 573 (7th Cir. 2002).

Consider the recent economic "meltdown" of American financial institutions. Lawyers presumably contributed to the marketing of the sub-prime loans and financial "derivatives" that many persons say were an important cause of the crisis. If those lawyers are sued for malpractice by the entities they represented, by the successors of those entities (*see* Chapter

5 Part A), or by investors or lenders who suffered losses, one defense may be lack of proximate causation. The argument, presumably, would be that a collapse of the American economy on a scale approaching the Great Depression was so unforeseeable and had so many contributing causes, that it would be unfair to hold particular lawyers liable for resulting damages. Of course, whether that is a good argument depends upon how one reads legal history. There are literally thousands of cases addressing the issue of proximate causation in tort law generally, and many addressing it specifically in the context of lawyer liability.

Even courts that frame proximate causation in terms of foreseeability do not require strict foreseeability of harm. Otherwise many blameworthy tortfeasors would escape liability. Rather, fairness simply requires that the defendant should have foreseen, in loose terms, harm to the class of persons of which the plaintiff is a member, and the general type of harm that in fact occurred. Differences in the manner of occurrence are generally irrelevant, as is the fact that the harm may have been greater than expected.

Some decisions have saved a lawyer from liability based on lack of proximate causation. In *TIG Ins. Co. v. Giffin Winning Cohen & Bodewes, P.C.*, 444 F.3d 587, 592 (7th Cir. 2006), the Seventh Circuit determined that huge expenses incurred in fighting a discovery motion were not recoverable by an insurer in its legal malpractice action against a law firm hired to represent its insured because it was unforeseeable that a failure to produce documents would "spawn a million-dollar bill for attorneys fees."

b. Superseding Causation and Shifting Responsibility

The proximate causation inquiry in legal malpractice cases may also require consideration of the doctrines called "superseding causation" and "shifting responsibility." Intervening causes are actions or forces that contribute to the production of the plaintiff's harm. Sometimes intervening causes break the chain of proximate causation, in which case they are called "superseding causes." In contrast, "shifting responsibility" concerns the question of whether someone else's failure to act saves an antecedent tortfeasor from liability. Occasionally, but not often, an omission breaks the chain of proximate causation.

The operative principles in this area are much the same as they are in any tort case raising issues of proximate causation. If the act or omission was foreseeable or part of the risks that made the defendant's conduct tortious, it probably will not preclude a finding of proximate causation. However, a few points deserve special mention.

(1) Intervening Negligent Conduct

Even if intervening conduct is negligent, it usually does not prevent a finding of proximate causation. Taking an example from the physical injury context, suppose that a driver negligently strikes a pedestrian, who then receives deficient medical care in the emergency room. The driver is likely to be held to be a factual and proximate cause of both the initial injuries sustained in the collision and the aggravated injuries resulting from the negligent medical treatment. As to the latter component of damages, the reasoning is likely to be that one of the risks to which the driver subjected the pedestrian was the risk of negligent medical care in an emergency room. Put somewhat differently, negligently deficient medical care is a foreseeable risk, not because it is so common that it is probable, but because it is not so rare or bizarre that it should save the driver from liability for aggravated injuries that would not have been incurred but for the driver's negligence.

The same principles apply in the field of legal malpractice. Think back to the example, above, where Lawyer #1 negligently omits important provisions from a contract, and another lawyer, Lawyer #2, negligently reviews the document and fails to discover the omission at a time when it would have been possible to reform the instrument. Lawyer #2's negligent actions do not prevent Lawyer #1 from being found to be a proximate cause of losses resulting from the lack of key provisions in the document. (Of course, Lawyer #2's negligence is also a proximate cause of the harm, since that was precisely the harm that was foreseeable if Lawyer #2 failed to exercise care in reviewing the document.)

(2) Failure by the Client to Discover Malpractice

In general, American tort law is reluctant to allow a tortfeasor to escape liability merely because someone else subsequently failed to prevent threatened harm from occurring. Thus, a subsequent omission, even if negligent, usually does not break the chain of causation. *See Restatement (Second) of Torts* § 452 (1965).

A person who causes an auto accident is liable for injuries resulting from the victim's loss of blood or exposure to bad weather, even if someone else could have stopped to render aid and assistance before those consequences developed. Similarly, if a lawyer inadvertently omits a critical residuary clause from a will, the lawyer may be found to have proximately caused harm to intended beneficiaries, even though the client reviewed the will before signing it and had an opportunity to detect the omission. *See Young v. Williams*, 285 Ga. App. 208, 645 S.E.2d 624, 626 (2007).

(3) Subsequent Counsel's Failure to Act

Notwithstanding the general rule on omissions, the law sometimes holds that even if one person set the stage for harm to occur, the responsibility for preventing that harm shifted to another person. Generally, these are cases where the antecedent tortfeasor has done everything possible to prevent the risk of harm from coming to fruition or where the other person's failure to act is so unforeseeable, bizarre, or abnormal that it would be unfair to hold the initial tortfeasor liable.

Consider an example from the physical injury context. Suppose that a store sells a defective portable heater and upon learning of the danger undertakes a massive recall campaign advising the public of the danger and offering a substantial cash bonus to purchasers who allow the store to deliver a free replacement. If a child's parents fail to return their heater after repeatedly receiving notice of the recall and its favorable terms, and the child is injured when the heater catches fire, it might be argued that the store is not liable because responsibility for preventing the harm shifted to the parents. That is, if the store did everything reasonable to recall the defective product and the parents' refusal of the substantial cash bonus and delivery of a free replacement was essentially unforeseeable, the store may escape liability based on lack of proximate causation.

In the legal malpractice context, these types of issues arise in cases where one lawyer, who acted negligently, is replaced by a second lawyer who then fails to avert the harm by identifying the problem and taking effective action. In many situations, the second lawyer's omission does not save from liability the lawyer who initially set the stage for harm to occur.

Consider a variation of the example discussed above, assuming that after Lawyer #1 omits important terms from a document, successor counsel, Lawyer #2, does not review the document at all and therefore fails to discover the deficiency and seek reformation of the document. It seems quite unlikely Lawyer #2's omission will save Lawyer #1 from liability. On the stated facts, there is no reason to say that the first lawyer did everything that could be done to prevent the harm from coming to pass, nor is there any reason to think that Lawyer #2's omission was so unforeseeable or extraordinary that it would be unfair to hold Lawyer #1 responsible for harm caused by the missing provisions.

An important variation of the subsequent omission problem concerns failure to file suit before the statute of limitations elapses. Assume, for example, that in declining representation of a prospective client, Lawyer #5 incorrectly advises the client that the statute of limitations is longer than it actually is. Does the client's failure to seek new counsel before the claim is time barred prevent Lawyer #5 from being liable? Probably not. Dilatory inaction is foreseeable. Or suppose that before the period for filing elapses, the client consults Lawyer #6, who declines to take the case, or hires Lawyer #7, who then neglects to file suit before it is too late. In those situations, do subsequent events break the chain of causation so that Lawyer #5 is not liable for the untimely filing of the case? Does it make any difference whether Lawyer #6 or Lawyer #7 knows what Lawyer #5 said about the statute of limitations deadline?

Some cases have focused on whether there is a new attorney on board and a fair opportunity to file the action before the statute of limitations elapses. Those decisions "appear to have taken the position *** that when the duty of care shifts from the original attorney to the successor, so does the liability, provided that the successor had the opportunity to undo or avert the harm precipitated by the actions or omissions of the original attorney." *Lopez v. Clifford Law Offices, P.C.*, 362 Ill. App. 3d 969, 841 N.E.2d 465, 475, 299 Ill. Dec. 53 (2005). However, even if that is the case, there is reason to distinguish situations where the client merely had the opportunity, never exercised, to engage substitute counsel before the claim became time barred. Thus, in *Lopez,* the Illinois Appellate Court held that a client's consultation with possible successor counsel, who declined to take the case before the statute of limitations expired, was not sufficient to absolve from liability a law firm which incorrectly advised a prospective client about the statute of limitations when the firm declined representation. 841 N.E.2d at 476.

CHAPTER FOUR

BREACH OF FIDUCIARY DUTY

A. LAWYERS AS FIDUCIARIES

When a lawyer's performance is examined under the law of negligence, it is clear that there is room for the professional exercise of discretion. A lawyer need only act reasonably in order to avoid liability. So long as a lawyer does not make a choice beyond the range of reasonable prudence, responsibility for damages will not be imposed. (*See* Chapter 3 Part B.)

However, the lawyer-client relationship is not a mere arms-length transaction, but rather a relationship of trust and confidence. As a matter of law, the lawyer serves as the client's fiduciary. This means that lawyers must always act with clients' interests in mind, and those interests must come first.

1. A Different Reference Point

Does fiduciary duty law allow lawyers the same room for the professional exercise of discretion that is accorded by negligence law? This is an important question because the sound exercise of judgment in the face of uncertainty and complexity is the quintessence of good lawyering. However, judgment can only be exercised if it is permissible for a lawyer to choose between alternatives. The answer to the question depends on how the standard of care for breach of fiduciary duty is framed, and how far that standard governs.

2. Fiduciary Duty Versus Negligence

The language of fiduciary duty is demanding. Fiduciary principles speak, for example, not of *reasonable* prudence and *ordinary* care, but of the *utmost* good faith, *complete* fair dealing, and *full* disclosure. At face value, the language of fiduciary duty appears to require more of a lawyer than the law of negligence. Consequently, it may afford less room for the exercise of judgment. If that is so, and if fiduciary principles are allowed to sweep too broadly in determining the obligations of lawyers, there is a risk that by imposing a more demanding standard for performance they will render negligence law largely irrelevant. With that demise, the latitude for the exercise of discretion would logically contract or disappear.

a. Disloyalty Versus Lack of Care

The key to understanding the proper role of fiduciary principles in the governance of lawyer conduct is to ask whether the matter at issue involves a question of loyalty, and not just competence or skill. If so, fiduciary principles apply, for those norms exist to ensure that obligations of trust are neither betrayed nor ignored. In contrast, if loyalty is not an issue, then it is likely that negligence principles are sufficient to protect clients from unnecessary harm. Negligence law applies to many aspects of modern life, and it usually provides an appropriate mechanism for balancing competing interests and creating incentives that minimize unnecessary harm.

Issues relating to conflict of interest, confidentiality, and candor frequently involve questions of loyalty, and are examples of matters where it is appropriate to presume that fiduciary principles apply. In contrast, issues relating to knowledge of substantive law, correct drafting of documents, and adequate trial preparation often raise questions of competence and skill, rather than loyalty. To that extent, they may more properly be resolved by reference to negligence principles.

Of course, there are cases where the same course of professional conduct can raise issues of both competence and loyalty. A lawyer may violate conflict of interest rules not merely because the lawyer chooses to sacrifice the interests of a client to competing interests, but because the lawyer ignores what the rules require or fails to appreciate that they apply to particular facts. A loyal lawyer does not violate the conflicts rules, but neither does a competent one. Thus, in some situations, a plaintiff may properly allege that certain lawyer conduct constitutes both a breach of fiduciary duty and the tort of negligence.

However, some courts have gone to great lengths in distinguishing negligence from breach of fiduciary duty. For example, in *Lee v. Brenner, Saltzman and Wallman*, 2007 WL 1600052 (Conn. Super. Ct. 2007), lawyers purportedly represented a medical practice group and several of its physicians individually, in violation of applicable conflict of interest rules. In a subsequent malpractice action, one of the physicians asserted a variety of claims, including, among others, legal malpractice and breach of fiduciary duty. A Connecticut court struck the breach of fiduciary duty claim because there was no evidence that the lawyers were dishonest or disloyal. Thus, the court distinguished between conflicts of interest arising from the lawyer's own interests, and conflicts arising among the interests of clients. Only the former, the court found, is sufficient to establish a breach of fiduciary duty. The court concluded that "the plaintiff's allegations that a conflict of interest existed between the defendants' representation of the Group and its representation of the Group's individual members *** [did] not give rise to a breach of fiduciary duty because the allegations do not suggest that the defendants were involved in fraud or self-dealing of any kind." *Id*. at *4.

The principal advantage of suing for breach of fiduciary duty in comparison to negligence is that obligations are often articulated in more demanding terms. This makes it easier for a fact finder to conclude that the lawyer fell short of what fiduciary principles require. Beyond that significant distinction, actions for breach of fiduciary duty and negligence have certain similarities and some important differences.

b. Similarities to Negligence

Breach of fiduciary duty is not a strict liability tort. A plaintiff alleging fiduciary breach must show that the defendant lawyer acted negligently, recklessly, or intentionally in violating fiduciary principles. Absent proof of culpability, there is no liability for breach of fiduciary duty.

For example, suppose that a former corporate client has changed names so frequently that, in the exercise of reasonable care, the lawyer could not have detected a conflict of interest. On those facts, the lawyer is not liable for breach of fiduciary duty even if the lawyer engaged in conflicting representation during the period in which the relevant facts were unknown.

Thus, an action for breach of fiduciary duty cannot be distinguished from negligence on the ground that culpability is not required. A suit against a lawyer for breach of fiduciary duty requires at least as much culpability as a suit for the tort of negligence.

Moreover, the culpability of a fiduciary breach determines whether defenses based on the plaintiff's conduct (contributory negligence, comparative negligence, or comparative fault, depending on the state) may be asserted by the lawyer-defendant (*see* Chapter 7). If a client claims that a lawyer breached a fiduciary duty based on *negligent* failure to prepare settlement documents in a timely manner because the lawyer's needs were placed ahead of the client's, the client's own *negligent* failure to promptly inform the lawyer that an agreement was reached and that documentation was needed may constitute a total or partial defense according to state law.

Further, both negligence and breach of fiduciary duty actions generally require expert testimony to establish the standard of care (*see* Chapter 3 Part B). Typically, the same expert will testify as to whether particular conduct, such as the lawyer's practices in handling client property, constituted negligence, breach of fiduciary duty, or both. An expert claiming acquaintance with the standard of care generally can be assumed to be prepared to talk about a lawyer's duty of reasonable care under negligence law, as well as the lawyer's fiduciary obligations.

No useful distinction can be drawn between negligence and breach of fiduciary duty with respect to statutes of limitations. Different limitation periods may apply to the two actions. However, which statute is longer depends on the law of the jurisdiction. It is not possible to generalize. Moreover, in some jurisdictions, the same statute of limitations governs all legal malpractice claims, regardless of the theory of liability asserted. (*See* Chapter 7 Part C.)

c. Differences from Negligence

The most important distinctions between negligence and breach of fiduciary duty claims against lawyers concern proof of causation, disclosure obligations, and fee forfeiture. Those subjects are discussed in the following sections.

B. THE "SUBSTANTIAL FACTOR" TEST FOR FACTUAL CAUSATION

If a legal malpractice plaintiff wishes to recover damages, the plaintiff must prove that a lawyer's negligence or breach of fiduciary duty caused harm. However, some states hold that the demanding "but for" test for factual causation, which is a basic part of a negligence cause of action (*see* Chapter 3 Part C), does not apply to claims for breach of fiduciary duty. In those states, it is enough for a plaintiff to show that the defendant's conduct was a "substantial factor" in producing the harm for which damages are sought. Because "but for" causation is often difficult to prove, the relaxed "substantial factor" standard, if applicable, makes it considerably easier for the plaintiff to establish that the defendant should be required to pay damages for breaching fiduciary duties.

For example, it may be hard for a jury to conclude that, "but for" an undisclosed conflict of interest amounting to breach of fiduciary duty, a lawyer's efforts to negotiate a corporate merger would have been successful. However, depending on the strength of the conflict, it may be possible for the fact finder to determine that the conflict was a "substantial factor" in the failure of negotiations.

Some states apply the more lenient "substantial factor" rule only to cases involving *intentional* breaches of fiduciary duty (*cf. Restatement (Third) of the Law Governing Lawyers* § 49 cmt. e (2000)). Other states also apply the rule to *negligent* breach of fiduciary duty. However, certain states do not embrace any type of "substantial factor" standard, and require proof of "but for" causation in breach of fiduciary duty cases.

In *Estate of Re v. Kornstein Veisz & Wexler*, 958 F. Supp. 907 (S.D.N.Y. 1997), a case involving both negligence and breach of fiduciary duty claims, the plaintiff alleged that certain debatable advocacy tactics had caused the plaintiff to be defeated in arbitration. The court found that the evidence was insufficient to establish "but for" causation, and therefore dismissed the negligence claim. However, the court further determined that certain potential conflicts of interest caused the defendants' otherwise defensible tactical decisions to take on a more troubling gloss, which suggested that divided loyalties had contributed to the plaintiff's arbitration defeat. The defendants' motion for summary judgment on the breach of fiduciary duty claim was therefore denied because, under applicable law, the plaintiff was only required to show that the alleged breach of fiduciary duty was a "substantial factor" in the loss at arbitration.

C. DISCLOSURE OBLIGATIONS

What must a lawyer tell a client? This question arises thousands of times every day in law offices. If the law of negligence governs, the answer is clear. The lawyer must keep the client reasonably informed about the status of the matter, must respond to reasonable requests for information, and must provide the information reasonably necessary to enable the client to make informed decisions about the representation. *See Restatement (Third) of the Law Governing Lawyers* § 20 (2000). In other words, a lawyer must act reasonably in communicating with the client.

For example, if a lawyer learns that "precious stones" listed on a balance sheet for millions of dollars are rented, and not owned, the lawyer has a duty to tell the client that the stones are not a legitimate asset, particularly if that means that the client is insolvent. *See Dennerline v. Atterholt,* 886 N.E.2d 582, 588 (Ind. Ct. App. 2008).

1. "Absolute and Perfect Candor"

Fiduciary duty law sometimes sets a higher standard than the law of negligence. Indeed, incautious language in certain fiduciary duty cases purports to impose on lawyers an obligation of "absolute and perfect candor." Surely this is not an accurate statement of a lawyer's disclosure obligations—at least not in every circumstance. If lawyers were routinely subject to actions for damages based on anything falling short of "absolute and perfect candor," they would be compelled to forego the exercise of judgment about the significance of information and to pass on to clients every fact learned in the course of representation, no matter how dubious, redundant, trivial, or useless. *See* Vincent R. Johnson, "Absolute and Perfect Candor" to Clients, 34 *St. Mary's L.J.* 737 (2003).

One area where legal precedent effectively requires total candor is when lawyers engage in business transactions with clients. As explained later (*see* Chapter 9), the law is highly suspicious of such dealings because of their potential for lawyer abuse. Absent "absolute and perfect candor" courts are unlikely to uphold business transactions between lawyers and their clients.

The reason that a high degree of candor is required in the context of business transactions is because the interests of lawyer and client are adverse. Whenever there is such adversity, there is reason to think that the lawyer may be less than fully faithful to the client or protective of the client's interests. Consequently, the heightened disclosure obligations under fiduciary duty law are not restricted to business transactions. They apply to other situations where the interests of lawyers and clients are at odds. This is why a lawyer must inform a client when the lawyer's negligent conduct gives the client a substantial malpractice claim. *See Restatement (Third) of the Law Governing Lawyers* § 20 cmt. c (2000); *see also* Benjamin P. Cooper, "The Lawyer's Duty to Inform His Client of His Own Malpractice," 61 *Baylor L. Rev.* 174, 214 (2009). (*See* Chapter 11).

Of course, special ethics rules already govern disclosure obligations in certain contexts where the interests of lawyer and client are adverse. For example, the disciplinary rules dealing with conflicts of interest spell out in detail what types of disclosures are required to obtain informed consent. *See, e.g.*, Model Rules of Prof'l Conduct R. 1.7 cmt. 18, R. 1.1(e), and R. 1.1, cmt. 6 (2010). Similarly, the rules already clearly specify what a lawyer must tell a client about the terms of a contingent fee agreement. *See id.* R.1.5. There is no reason to substitute an amorphous "absolute and perfect candor" standard for these types of well developed principles that were undoubtedly formulated with lawyers' fiduciary obligations in mind.

To the extent that a rule of "absolute and perfect candor" defines a lawyer's disclosure obligations, it should be limited to contexts where the interests of lawyer and clients are adverse *and* where specific guidance as to what is required of a lawyer has not yet been articulated. Moreover, the culpability requirement of fiduciary duty law means that, even if, there is clear adversity between lawyer and client, liability should not be imposed for nonnegligent nondisclosure. Though some cases use the phrase "absolute and perfect candor," their holdings usually can be explained on the ground that the lawyers who were ultimately held liable were negligent or even more blameworthy. Cases never impose liability for nonnegligent failure to communicate information.

2. How Negligence Duties and Fiduciary Duties Mesh

It is possible to summarize the disclosure obligations of lawyers as follows: (1) In a broad range of situations, a lawyer is subject to a duty of reasonableness, which is to say the law of negligence. (2) In situations where the lawyer's and client's interests are adverse, as in the case of a business transaction between them, a lawyer has heightened disclosure obligations, which sometimes approach "absolute and perfect candor." (3) If applicable ethics rules (*e.g.*, the rules dealing with fees, client funds and property, and conflicts of interest) specify what must be disclosed, those provisions will be regarded by many as defining what is called for under general negligence and fiduciary principles. Finally, (4) liability should never be imposed on a lawyer for nondisclosure without proof of culpability.

3. Limits on Disclosure Obligations

Several factors limit the disclosure obligations of lawyers. These limits apply regardless of whether negligence or fiduciary duty principles govern.

A lawyer is generally under no duty to disclose facts outside the scope of the representation (*see* Chapter 3 Part A) or information that is immaterial (*see* Chapter 5 Part B). In addition, there is usually no obligation to tell a client what the client already knows. Thus, in *Grochocinski v. Mayer Brown Rowe & Maw LLP*, 2007 WL 1875995, *10 (N.D. Ill.), a federal court in Illinois ruled that a bankruptcy trustee could not recover from lawyers for their allegedly negligent failure to disclose the risk that a third person would file suit. This was true because the bankrupt entity was already well aware that there was a risk of such litigation.

There is also never an obligation to disclose to one client what a lawyer is obliged to keep private about the representation of another client. So, too, a lawyer and client ordinarily can tailor disclosure obligations, just as they may agree on other aspects of the representation. Consequently, there is normally no duty to disclose to a client information which the client has agreed need not be transmitted. These various factors which limit the disclosure obligations of lawyers frequently play a role in malpractice litigation.

D. FEE FORFEITURE

Every client who is unhappy with a lawyer would like to recover any fees already paid to the lawyer, as well as be excused from paying any balance still due. Reflecting this reality, malpractice plaintiffs increasingly seek fee forfeiture. *See* Jeff A. Webb & Blake W. Stribling, "Ten Years After *Burrow v. Arce*: The Current State of Attorney Fee Forfeiture," 40 *St. Mary's L.J.* 967 (2009).

1. To Prevent Unjust Enrichment

Damages and forfeiture are different remedies, but are frequently asserted together in a legal malpractice action. A claim for damages is a request for compensation for harm caused by the lawyer's misconduct. Fee forfeiture, in contrast, is essentially a request for a refund, or for forgiveness of nonpayment, because the client did not get what was bargained for, namely representation by a lawyer faithful to important duties. Forfeiture is a restitutionary remedy designed to prevent unjust enrichment of the lawyer.

The difference between damages and forfeiture is the difference between loss and gain. Damages are measured by what the plaintiff lost; forfeiture, as a form of restitution, is measured by what the defendant improperly gained. *See generally Restatement (Third) of Restitution & Unjust Enrichment* § 49 (Tent. Draft No. 5, 2007).

If a client is seeking a return of fees that have already been paid, the claim is sometimes called a request for fee "disgorgement." However, the term "forfeiture" is increasingly used to cover any loss of fees by a lawyer, regardless of whether those fees have yet been paid.

In response to a request for fee forfeiture, a lawyer may seek a declaratory judgment that outstanding amounts are owed. Thus, a malpractice plaintiff who does not prevail on a claim for fee forfeiture is sometimes ordered to pay amounts due under the attorney-client contract. *See AmBase Corp.*

v. Davis Polk & Wardwell, 8 N.Y.3d 428, 866 N.E.2d 1033, 834 N.Y.S.2d 705, 708 (2007).

2. Causation of Harm is Not Required

Importantly, fee forfeiture is available even if the plaintiff is unable to prove that the lawyer's tortious conduct caused damages. The fact that fee forfeiture may be awarded even if damages are not proved is a significant remedial consideration. This is true because proving that malpractice was a factual and proximate cause of harm is often difficult or impossible. The fees paid to a lawyer, particularly if the representation was complex or extended over a long period of time, may be so great that it may be worth bringing a malpractice action to obtain forfeiture, even if it might not be possible to show that the lawyer's breach of duty caused damages.

3. Clear and Serious Breach of Duty

The *Restatement* recognizes that total or partial fee forfeiture may be appropriate in cases involving a "clear and serious violation of duty." *See Restatement (Third) of the Law Governing Lawyers* § 37 (2000). Among the factors that are relevant to the issue of forfeiture are "the gravity and timing of the violation, its willfulness, its effect on the value of the lawyer's work for the client, any other threatened or actual harm to the client, and the adequacy of other remedies." *Id*. Some courts also emphasize that, because "the central purpose of the equitable remedy of forfeiture is to protect relationships of trust by discouraging agents' disloyalty," an additional factor that must be given great weight in determining whether fees should be lost is "the public interest in maintaining the integrity of attorney-client relationships." *Burrow v. Arce*, 997 S.W.2d 229, 244 (Tex. 1999).

With respect to fee forfeiture, there are roles to be played by both jury and judge. The jury normally decides disputed questions of fact, relating, for example, to the culpability of the lawyer's breach of duty. The judge then determines whether forfeiture is appropriate, and if so, what amount of fees should be lost by the lawyer.

In *Chen v. Chen Qualified Settlement Fund*, 552 F.3d 218 (2d Cir. 2009), the Second Circuit denied all compensation to a lawyer who had secured a multimillion dollar settlement of claims arising from birth-related injuries to a young child named David. The lawyer had submitted to the court an unexplained request for attorney's fees in excess of the statutory maximum allowed in medical malpractice cases. The court found that the evidence indicated that the lawyer had made "only limited inquiries into David's condition and the nature and extent of David's future medical needs" and "offered none of the documentation and reports necessary for the court to determine whether the settlement proposed by the parties was reasonable." 552 F.2d at 227. The appellate court concluded that "it was not an abuse of discretion for the district court to determine that *** [the lawyer] had inadequately represented his client." *Id.*

4. Is Breach of Fiduciary Duty Required?

Without dispute, a clear and serious breach of *fiduciary duty* can trigger the powerful remedy of fee forfeiture. However, whether *negligence* not amounting to breach of fiduciary duty is sufficient to warrant total or partial loss of a fee is an open question in many states.

The relevant portions of the *Restatement*, discussing what constitutes a "clear and serious violation of duty," indicate that "the source of the duty can be civil or criminal law, including, for example, the requirements of an applicable lawyer code or the law of malpractice." *Restatement (Third) of the Law Governing Lawyers* § 37 cmt. c (2000). This language seems to allow the possibility that negligence not involving disloyalty may, on appropriate facts, support an award for forfeiture.

Support for the proposition that mere negligence, not amounting to breach of fiduciary duty, is sufficient to cause loss of attorney's fees can be found in *DiStefano v. Greenstone*, 357 N.J. Super. 352, 815 A.2d 496 (App. Div. 2003). In *DiStefano*, an American lawyer failed to "sustain contact" with an Italian law firm that he was using to handle an international tort claim for the plaintiff. As a result, the claim was not timely filed and became time-barred. There was no evidence that the failure to sustain contact was the result of disloyalty to the plaintiff. Therefore, the case involved mere negligence. In a subsequent malpractice action against the American lawyer, the fundamental question was whether the plaintiff could recover the full value of the lost claim ($90,000) or only a reduced amount ($60,000) reflecting reduction for the one-third contingent fee the client would have had to pay if the claim had been timely prosecuted and successful. The court surveyed New Jersey law and found that it stood for the proposition that a "negligent attorney is precluded from recovering his attorney fee." 357 N.J. Super. at 357, 815 A.2d at 499. The court therefore allowed the plaintiff to recover the full value of the lost claim ($90,000) with no reduction for the amount that would have gone to the defendant attorney under the fee agreement if the representation had not been negligent. (Interestingly, the court, in departure from the "American rule," also allowed the plaintiff to recover compensation for attorney's fees incurred in prosecuting the malpractice action, noting that the result was not a windfall because the plaintiff had to "endure two lawsuits." 357 N.J. Super. at 357-58, 815 A.2d at 499-500.)

Nevertheless, a plaintiff's ability to call the lawyer's breach a violation of fiduciary principles appears to be important to the success of a forfeiture claim. Most of the cases ordering forfeiture involve breaches of fiduciary duty. Moreover, the *Restatement* commentary cautions that "forfeiture is generally inappropriate when the lawyer has not done anything willfully blameworthy." *Restatement (Third) of the Law Governing Lawyers* § 37 cmt. c (2000). "Willfully blameworthy" conduct would seem to amount to disloyalty, and therefore constitute breach of fiduciary duty. In addition, "willfully blameworthy" conduct is something more than mere negligence. The language tends to suggest that what is required is a type of aggravated malfeasance approaching recklessness or perhaps even intentionally tortious conduct.

The decisions on fee forfeiture often emphasize that forfeiture is especially appropriate in cases involving serious breaches of trust and disloyalty. Consequently, evidence of a breach of fiduciary duty, as opposed to mere negligence that does not involve disloyalty, places a client seeking fee forfeiture in a stronger position to persuade a court that the lawyer's loss of all or part of a fee is appropriate.

E. AIDING AND ABETTING A BREACH OF FIDUCIARY DUTY

Lawyers can be liable not only for breaching their own fiduciary duties, but for aiding and abetting other persons in their breaches of fiduciary duties. At one level, this is not surprising because aiding and abetting liability is a well-established, generally non-controversial theory of tort responsibility. *See Restatement (Second) of Torts* § 876(b) (1979). At a different level, however, holding a lawyer liable for aiding and abetting another's breach of fiduciary duty is not only surprising but alarming. This is because the theory has the potential to greatly expand the range of persons to whom lawyers may be accountable in damages. Many clients, such as corporate officers and directors, business partners, trustees, guardians, executors, and majority shareholders owe fiduciary duties to others. This theory says that, on an appropriate set of facts, a lawyer may be liable to persons standing in a fiduciary relationship with any of these kinds of clients, even though those third persons never stood in an attorney-client relationship with the lawyer.

1. A Dangerous Theory of Liability

At least four things make aiding and abetting a breach of fiduciary duty a dangerous theory of lawyer liability. The first is that the relevant legal principles are not well developed. This makes it difficult for lawyers to intelligently assess the risks and plan accordingly. Second, "aiding and abetting" claims are often factually complex, typically requiring analysis of various players and diverse areas of the law from which fiduciary duties arise. To this extent, claims against lawyers for aiding and abetting breaches of fiduciary duty are more expensive to defend, unpredictable, and difficult to manage. Third, in many respects, the law of fiduciary duty is phrased in highly demanding terms (*e.g.*, "utmost good faith" and "complete fair dealing") with few clear markers for understanding the extent of obligations (*see* Part A of this Chapter). If it is easy for the fiduciary-client to fall short of obligations to others, it may also be easy for a lawyer to become liable to a third person for aiding and abetting a client's breach of fiduciary duty. Finally, a lawyer's fear of liability to a nonclient for aiding and abetting may dilute the lawyer's loyalty to the fiduciary-client.

Claims for aiding and abetting breaches of fiduciary duty are now a common feature of what might be called "entity implosion" litigation. For example, in the 2001 collapse of Enron, then one of the world's largest companies, Enron's lawyers were sued on many theories, including aiding and abetting breaches of fiduciary duty. Eventually, some of the law firms paid huge settlements to various plaintiffs. The same was true of the suits against lawyers in the 1990s that followed the Saving and Loan Crisis. In the malpractice cases filed following the 2008-09 Wall Street "meltdown," plaintiffs are suing lawyers, asserting that they aided and abetted breaches of fiduciary duty by the officers and directors who ran the failed financial institutions.

2. Two Very Different Varieties

The first thing to understand about claims for aiding and abetting breach of fiduciary duty is that there are two very different varieties of the claim. In one case, the claim is asserted against the lawyer by the lawyer's own client. Typically, the client is an entity, and the lawyer is alleged to have aided and abetted fiduciary breaches by constituent representatives of the entity, such as officers and directors. This is the stronger variety of the claim because lawyers owe numerous duties to their clients. There is nothing shocking about saying, for example, that a lawyer cannot assist an officer or director in harming the lawyer's entity client. Indeed, in many cases, it might be possible to forego the language of "aiding and abetting" and simply argue that the lawyer's conduct was a violation of the lawyer's own fiduciary obligations to the plaintiff client.

The second variety of aiding and abetting claim is one asserted by a non-client. Because there is no privity between the lawyer and non-client, and typically no basis for saying the lawyer personally had any legal duty to the non-client, this is the weaker variety of claim. In this type of case, the fiduciary being aided by the lawyer is normally the lawyer's client (or a representative of the lawyer's client). In that case, it may be argued that there is a privilege to represent one's client without competing obligations to third persons, and that the privilege should defeat the aiding and abetting breach of fiduciary duty claim. These kinds of privileges are discussed below (*see* Part E-6 of this Chapter). Note, however, that this kind of privilege has no role in the first type of aiding and abetting claim discussed above. In that case, the plaintiff *is* the lawyer's client.

3. Tort Principles on Aiding and Abetting

Under general tort principles, aiding and abetting liability does not require proof of an express or tacit agreement on the part of the aider-abetter to participate in a wrongful activity in violation of the plaintiff's rights. Rather, what is necessary is that the aider-abetter knowingly provide substantial assistance to one engaged in tortious conduct. For this reason, the aiding and abetting theory of tort liability is sometimes called "concerted action by substantial assistance." *Halberstam v. Welch*, 705 F.2d 472, 477 (D.C. Cir. 1983).

Although courts differ in articulating the elements of lawyer liability for aiding and abetting a breach of fiduciary duty, the requirements are usually simple. Generally, the plaintiff must prove: (1) that the fiduciary breached a fiduciary obligation to the plaintiff; (2) that the breach caused damages; (3) that the lawyer knew that fiduciary obligations were being breached; and (4) the lawyer nevertheless provided substantial assistance to the fiduciary, thereby contributing to the breach.

Aiding and abetting a breach of fiduciary duty is an intentional tort in the sense that it must be shown that the defendant lawyer knew that the person being assisted was committing a breach of fiduciary duty. *Cf. Restatement (Third) of Torts: Liability for Physical and Emotional Harm* § 1 (2010) (discussing intent). Presumably, this classification carries with it all of the consequences that attach to an intentional tort, including the inapplicability of defenses based on the plaintiff's own negligent conduct. (*See* Chapter 2 Part C.)

4. Circumstantial Evidence of Knowledge

A lawyer's knowledge of a fiduciary's breach of duty can be proved either by direct evidence (*e.g.*, e-mail messages clearly indicating what the attorney knew) or by circumstantial evidence. In the latter case, indirect evidence is pieced together to draw a conclusion as to what the defendant-lawyer must have known. For example, a lawyer's acceptance of a valuable gift from a fiduciary, who was known to the lawyer to have longstanding financial problems, may provide the basis for a jury to conclude that the lawyer knew that fiduciary obligations were being violated and that the fiduciary was profiting. *See Chem-Age Industries, Inc. v. Glover*, 652 N.W.2d 756 (S.D. 2002).

In the *Enron* case, there was no direct evidence of any particular attorney's knowledge of wrongful conduct by Enron officers. However, despite the lawyers' denial of actual knowledge, circumstantial evidence suggested that the lawyers knew that fiduciary obligations were being betrayed. *See* Report of Neal Batson, Court-Appointed Examiner, app. C, at 1-2, *In re Enron Corp.*, No. 01-16034 (Bankr. S.D.N.Y. Nov. 4, 2003).

5. Substantial Assistance

De minimis non curat lex—the law does not concern itself with trifles. It is therefore not surprising that aiding and abetting liability will only be imposed on a lawyer who provides *substantial* assistance that contributes to a fiduciary breach.

The word "substantial" has different meanings in diverse areas of the law. On some occasions, a requirement of a "substantial" contribution sets a more demanding level of proof than on others. There are some court decisions that suggest that for a professional's assistance to be "substantial," for purposes of aiding and abetting liability, there must be something more than the rendition of routine professional services. *See Witzman v. Lehrman, Lehrman & Flom*, 601 N.W.2d 179, 189 (Minn. 1999) (involving accountants). Whether other courts will follow the same path is doubtful. Routine legal services often entail knowledge of the law, critical evaluation of the facts, and the exercise of professional judgment. Such services undoubtedly can make a "substantial" contribution to a fiduciary's performance (or breach) of duties to others. If a lawyer renders routine legal services to a fiduciary whom the lawyer knows is breaching fiduciary obligations, courts may refuse to allow the lawyer to escape responsibility on the ground that the lawyer did not "substantially" contribute to the breach.

Presumably, the "substantial assistance" requirement is concerned with ensuring that a lawyer made a real contribution to the plaintiff's harm. If what the lawyer did was minimal, irrelevant, duplicative, and of little efficacy, there may be good reason not to impose responsibility for aiding and abetting a breach of fiduciary duty. However, in other areas of the law, mere moral support that deliberately emboldens a tortfeasor in perpetrating wrongful conduct is sufficient to support a finding of aiding and abetting liability. *See generally Restatement (Second) of Torts* §876 cmt. d (1979). There is little justification for allowing a lawyer to escape responsibility on the ground that a contribution was insubstantial, if the lawyer knew what was at stake and acted in ways that effectively encouraged the fiduciary to betray important duties.

6. Privileges and Defenses

As mentioned above, a lawyer sued by a nonclient may attempt to defeat an aiding and abetting claim by arguing that recognition of such a claim would conflict with the lawyer's obligations to a client. Because a lawyer owes a duty of undivided loyalty to a client (as authorities often say), the lawyer's representation of the client should not be fettered by a theory of liability that recognizes competing obligations to a nonclient. Arguably, recognizing such a claim distorts the representation of a client who is serving as a fiduciary.

Of course, any such argument has limits. It is well recognized that a lawyer may not assist a client in conduct that is criminal or fraudulent. *See, e.g.*, Model Rules of Prof'l Conduct R. 1.2(d) (2010). Such forms of conduct can often be cast as breaches of fiduciary duty. Therefore, lawyers should not be protected from aiding and abetting liability if they knowingly assist clients in criminal or fraudulent conduct. Moreover, the lawyer-client relationship should not shield a lawyer from liability for conduct that falls outside the scope of representation. Duties to a client generally extend no further than the scope of the representation (*see* Chapter 3 Part A).

Mindful that a liability risk may create conflicts of interest for lawyers, some courts have recognized a privilege that may defeat a nonclient's claim against a lawyer for aiding and abetting a breach of fiduciary duty. For example, in *Reynolds v. Schrock*, 341 Or. 338, 142 P.3d 1062, 1069 (Or. 2006), the Supreme Court of Oregon endorsed a strong qualified privilege that protects lawyers from liability for conduct within the scope of representation that is not motivated by the lawyers' "own self-interest and contrary to their clients' interest," and that does not involve assisting clients in crime or fraud.

It is unclear whether other courts will follow the lead of the Oregon Supreme Court. Moreover, in other areas of tort law, courts have held that certain matters, not mentioned in *Reynolds*, such as bad faith, ill will, vindictiveness, or excessiveness, can destroy a qualified privilege. *See Restatement (Second) of Torts*

§ 603-04 (1977). Thus, it remains to be seen what role qualified privileges will play in the law governing lawyer liability for aiding and abetting breaches of fiduciary duty.

Some decisions have avoided the privilege issue by holding broadly that a nonclient cannot "bring a cause of action for 'aiding and abetting' a breach of fiduciary duty, based upon the rendition of legal advice to an alleged tortfeasor client." *See Span Enterprises v. Wood*, 274 S.W.3d 854 (Tex. App. 2008) (quoting *Alpert v. Crain, Caton & James, P.C.*, 178 S.W.3d 398, 407 (Tex. App. 2005)).

As mentioned above, privileges are likely to be irrelevant in cases where the plaintiff is a client and the lawyer is alleged to have aided an officer or director in breaching duties to the client. In such situations, imposing liability on the lawyer would not threaten to divert the lawyer from attention to the interests of the client, but would instead reinforce the performance of obligations the lawyer already owes to the client.

7. Implications for Corporate Policy Making

Subjecting a lawyer to liability for aiding and abetting corporate officers and directors in conduct that may later be viewed as a breach of fiduciary duty has implications for how lawyers perform the role of corporate counsel. This is true because prudent lawyers will want to minimize their liability exposure to claims asserting this theory.

Suppose, for example, that a lawyer for a corporation is assisting a corporate division manager in
closing an asset sale, and that the lawyer knows that
the manager, without authority, has made certain
guarantees to the purchaser. If the purchaser later
successfully sues the corporation to enforce those
guarantees, the corporation may seek to hold the
lawyer accountable. With the benefit of hindsight, the
making of unauthorized guarantees that could trigger
legal liability may be viewed as a breach of fiduciary
duties owed by the division manager to the corporation. Further, the work of the lawyer, perhaps in
transmitting those assurances to the purchaser or
embodying them in a document, may be viewed as
aiding and abetting the division manager's breach of
fiduciary duty. Rather than risk liability under this
theory, the lawyer, upon becoming aware that the
division manager lacked authority to make the
guarantees, might refuse to provide further assistance
for the transaction. This may be true even if the
manager insisted that making the guarantees was in
the best interests of the corporation and unlikely to
give rise to corporate liability. Indeed, the lawyer
might not only refuse to assist the transaction, but
might elect to report the matter to persons with
greater authority in the corporation—that is, go "over
the head" of the division manager in an effort to force
the manager to take a different course. *See* Model
Rules of Prof'l Conduct R. 1.13 (2010).

Perhaps this is not a bad result. Corporations
might be better off if lawyers asked more questions
about what their clients' representatives were doing
before carrying out orders. In fact, it is possible to ask

whether the Wall Street meltdown and the collapse of major investment banks in 2008-09 could have been avoided if lawyers had taken a more active role in challenging dubious practices, such as the marketing of subprime loans and incomprehensible financial derivatives or the use of bonus compensation arrangements which created disoriented incentives. *See* Terry Carter, "How Lawyers Enabled the Meltdown: And How They Might Have Prevented It," *A.B.A. J.*, Jan. 2009, at 34.

Not long ago, the established wisdom in many quarters of the legal profession was that corporate lawyers were not supposed to second guess the policy decisions of duly authorized representatives of corporate entities, such as officers and directors. However, it is sometimes easy to recast a policy decision as a breach of fiduciary duty. For example, the sale of an asset for a modest price may later be labeled as a breach of fiduciary duty by those who disagreed with the decision. The argument would be that disposing of property for inadequate consideration is a breach of fiduciary obligations.

Exposing lawyers to claims for aiding and abetting breach of fiduciary duty is likely to cause lawyers to scrutinize the conduct of their corporate clients more closely than once was the case. This is an important change in the world of corporate lawyering, but it is a change consistent with the temper of the times. The rules enacted by the Securities and Exchange Commission pursuant to the federal Sarbanes-Oxley Act (Sarbanes-Oxley Act of 2002, Pub. L. No. 107-204, 116 Stat. 745) and subsequent amendments to the Model Rules of Professional Conduct (*see* Model

Rules of Prof'l Conduct R. 1.13 (2010)) now provide, in an increased range of circumstances, for "up the ladder" reporting of information learned by a lawyer about unlawful conduct or breaches of duty that could harm the interests of corporate clients. The purpose of such requirements is to ensure that those at the top of the corporate ladder have the information that is needed to ensure that the corporations act lawfully and that corporate interests are protected from harm that can be caused by the unfaithful or ill-advised conduct of entity constituents.

F.   INTRA-FIRM FIDUCIARY DUTIES

Lawyers owe fiduciary duties not only to their clients, but to the law firms for which they work. The broad contours of these obligations are sketched below.

1. Duties of Partners and Other Firm Principals

Under *common law* principles, members of a law partnership are fiduciaries and owe important fiduciary obligations to one another. A partner may not prefer his or her economic interests to those of other partners. More specifically, a partner may not injure the partnership by establishing a competing enterprise. A partner also must disclose to the other partners facts concerning economic opportunities that relate to the partnership's business.

Some fiduciary duties can even survive the termination of a partner's relationship with a law firm. In *Friedman Siegelbaum, LLP v. Pribish*, 2009

WL 910326, *8 (N.J. Super. App. Div.), a New Jersey appellate court affirmed a judgment holding a former non-equity partner, who assured his former firm of his willingness to assist in the collection of accounts receivable, liable for breach of fiduciary duty based, in part, on failure to turn over money that had been collected.

Of course, common law principles are only the starting point for thinking about partners' obligations. The common law has been superseded or supplemented by statutes in many states patterned on the Uniform Partnership Act and the Revised Uniform Partnership Act. Moreover, many lawyers now practice law in limited liability partnerships and limited liability companies. (*See* Chapter 8.) Therefore, when talking about partners' duties, it is essential to consult pertinent legislative enactments in the relevant jurisdiction to determine whether and to what extent they alter the common law fiduciary obligations of partners and principals in other forms of business associations.

A firm's partnership agreement or other operating agreement may also define the duties of partners, members, or other principals. Of course, disputes often arise over the meaning of such documents. *See, e.g.*, Nate Raymond, "Former Chadbourne Attorney Claims Partnership Agreement Permits Him to Keep Compensation," www.law.com, Sept. 8, 2010.

There are at least two areas where partners may be charged with violating fiduciary obligations to one another. The first concerns expulsion, or, as it is sometimes called, "de-equitization." Lawyers who are forced out of a partnership sometimes assert claims for breach of fiduciary duty, as well as related claims for fraud, breach of contract, promissory estoppel, or unjust enrichment. *See, e.g.*, Nate Raymond, "Aging Divorce Lawyer Sues Former Partners for \$26 Million," *Nat'l L.J.*, Aug. 31, 2010. The second area, which is discussed below (*see* Part F-3 of this Chapter), involves a partner's voluntary withdrawal from a firm. A departing partner may seek to take along firm clients, thus depriving the firm of a future source of revenue. The departing lawyer's solicitation of those clients may involve conduct that is an alleged breach of fiduciary obligations to the firm.

2. Duties of Associates

Under common law principles, associates are agents who have fiduciary obligations to the firm for which they work. There is an overarching duty of loyalty which requires an associate to act loyally for the law firm's benefit in all matters connected with the firm. *Cf. Restatement (Third) of Agency* § 8.01 (2006). More specifically, an associate may not improperly benefit from the associate's relationship with the firm (*id*. § 8.02); act on behalf of an adverse party (*id*. § 8.03); divert or usurp business opportunities, or otherwise compete with the firm (*id*. § 8.04); or misuse the firm's property or confidential information (*id*.§ 8.05). Of course, conduct consented to by a law firm is not a breach of an associate's fiduciary duties (*id*.§ 8.06).

An associate has an obligation to the law firm to exercise care, competence, and diligence in law firm matters (*id*. § 8.07). An associate must also act only within the associate's scope of actual authority and must abide by the law firm's instructions (*id*. § 8.08).

The same type of departure-based client solicitation that creates issues when partners leave the firm may also arise when an associate moves to another firm or starts a new law office. (*See* Part F-3 of this Chapter.)

Unfortunately, there is some divergence between legal obligations and practice. Postings by associates on websites like Above the Law might be construed as breaches of fiduciary duty. *See generally* Susan Saab Fortney, "Leaks, Lies, and the Moonlight: Fiduciary Duties of Associates to Their Law Firms," 41 *St. Mary's L.J.* 595 (2010).

Receipt of an undisclosed commission, bonus, or gift from a third party for performing duties owed to the firm constitutes a breach of fiduciary duty. *Cf. Kinzbach Tool Co. v. Corbett-Wallace Corp.*, 138 Tex. 565, 160 S.W.2d 509 (1942). This is true even if there is no showing that the firm has been damaged.

Similarly, referring a potential firm client to another law firm in exchange for a commission is impermissible. However, fiduciary obligations are not absolute. An associate who recommends that a client engage different counsel because that is in the best interest of the client is not liable for the fee lost by the associate's firm, provided that the associate did not profit in some way based on the diversion of business. *See Brewer v. Johnson & Pritchard, P.C.*, 73 S.W.3d 193 (Tex. 2002).

An associate who fails to disclose to a law firm that he does not have a law degree, and who thereby steals money by collecting a lawyer's salary, is liable to the firm for the improper receipt of benefits. *See* "Fake Lawyer to Pay Firm Restitution," *Nat'l L.J.* at 16 (Oct. 15, 2007).

3. Movement Between Law Firms

It was once the case that most lawyers stayed with the same firm for life. Today, that degree of loyalty and continuity is the rare exception. Lawyers are highly mobile, typically changing firms several times in a career.

A question of tremendous practical importance is whether a lawyer can invite a client the lawyer served at one firm to transfer the client's business to the lawyer at the next firm. The answer to the question demands careful consideration, because client solicitation in the context of moving between law firms raises issues of potential liability under disciplinary, tort, and fiduciary duty principles. Fortunately, certain once-disputed points are now the subject of consensus. Thus, the *Restatement* provides that:

> Absent an agreement with the firm providing a more permissive rule, a lawyer leaving a law firm may solicit firm clients:
>
> (a) prior to leaving the firm:
>
> (i) only with respect to firm clients on whose matters the lawyer is actively and substantially working; and
>
> (ii) only after the lawyer has adequately and timely informed the firm of the lawyer's intent to contact firm clients for that purpose; and

(b) after ceasing employment in the firm, to the same extent as any other nonfirm lawyer.

Restatement (Third) of the Law Governing Lawyers § 9(3) (2000).

Although a few states continue to take a harsh view of departure-based client solicitation, a lawyer who acts in conformity with the *Restatement's* view is unlikely to be liable for breach of fiduciary duty or tortious interference with contract or prospective advantage. Professional discipline is also unlikely because prohibitions on solicitation normally exempt communications with one's own present or former clients. *See* Model Rules of Prof'l Conduct R. 7.3 (2010) (permitting contact with a person who has "a family, close personal, or prior professional relationship with the lawyer").

4. Post-Employment Restrictive Covenants

With respect to departure-based solicitation of clients, the most important principle is that clients have the right to decide who will provide representation. Not surprisingly, agreements between lawyers purporting to determine who "owns" which client, or banning departing lawyers from competing with the former firm, are invalid. *See generally* Vincent R. Johnson, "Solicitation of Law Firm Clients by Departing Partners and Associates: Tort, Fiduciary, and Disciplinary Liability," 50 *U. Pitt. L. Rev.* 1, 111-16 & n.226 (1988).

CHAPTER FIVE

DUTIES TO NONCLIENTS

A. MODERN NONCLIENT LITIGATION

Lawyers may be liable to nonclients on a variety of theories. Indeed, nonclient claims pose some of the greatest malpractice risks. Highly publicized cases often involve nonclients seeking to recoup losses resulting from failed investments and business transactions. Suits by shareholders and creditors are not uncommon. In malpractice cases like those resulting from the failure of major corporations, nonclient plaintiffs have recovered millions of dollars under an array of legal theories.

Often the stakes are high. In one recent case, a New York law firm, which previously represented the Stanford Financial Group, was sued by investors as the result of an allegedly fraudulent $7 billion scheme related to the sale of certificates of deposit by a Caribbean bank. In another suit, an American firm with offices on three continents was sued in Wisconsin for $150 million for allegedly assisting a client to squeeze a broker out of a supply chain contract.

This chapter examines the theories of nonclient liability that pose risks to lawyers and law firms. The chapter also considers the challenges that nonclients encounter in suing lawyers they never employed to provide legal services.

1. The Privity Obstacle

It is still true, and probably always will be, that nonclients have a harder time than clients holding lawyers accountable for the losses they sustain. The explanation for this reality concerns the issue of legal duty. Discussions of that subject are often cloaked in the language of "privity." In the law of legal malpractice, "privity" means that there was an attorney-client relationship between the defendant and the plaintiff (or the plaintiff's predecessor in interest), and that the lawyer therefore owed the plaintiff a broad array of legally enforceable obligations. *See* Chapter 3 Part A. In the absence of privity, a lawyer has only limited duties to potential plaintiffs.

In *Shoemaker v. Gindlesberger*, 118 Ohio St. 3d 226, 887 N.E.2d 1167 (Ohio 2008), two of the decedent's three children alleged that a lawyer had improperly drafted a will and a deed that allowed the decedent to retain an interest in a farm which had been transferred to the third child. As a result, the two other children suffered damages in the form of increased estate taxes and did not share evenly in their mother's assets, as their mother had intended. In rejecting their malpractice claim, the Ohio Supreme Court explained:

> The strict privity rule ensures that attorneys may represent their clients without the threat of suit from third parties who may compromise that representation. ***. Otherwise, an attorney's

preoccupation or concern with potential negligence claims by third parties might diminish the quality of legal services provided to the client if the attorney were to weigh the client's interests against the possibility of third-party lawsuits.

887 N.E. 2d at 1171.

2. Exceptions to Privity

Jurisdictions sometimes describe themselves as "strict privity" states in an effort to capture the idea that it is difficult—indeed, sometimes exceedingly difficult—for a nonclient to recover damages. Yet even where "strict privity" is the rule, nonclients can successfully assert certain malpractice claims.

Indeed, nonclients sometimes prevail on a dozen different theories of liability. Of course, there is no magic in the number twelve. Courts and legislatures may recognize new nonclient causes of action or reject theories of liability that were once found to be meritorious.

In thinking about the theories of liability which do not depend on privity, it is somewhat useful, for purposes of memory, to group the causes of action into categories. The first three exceptions concern the law of misrepresentation. Thus, lawyers may be liable to nonclients for fraud (*see* Part B), for negligent misrepresentation (*see* Part C), and for statutorily defined deceptive trade practices (*see* Part D).

Three other exceptions relate more or less directly to fiduciary obligations. A lawyer may be responsible for harm caused to a nonclient by knowingly aiding and abetting a client or third person's breach of fiduciary duties to the nonclient (*see* Chapter 4 Part E); by failing to exercise care while representing a fiduciary client (*see* Part E); and, under some circumstances, by failing to protect property or funds in the lawyer's possession that belongs to a nonclient (*see* Part F).

A third trio of exceptions to the privity requirement concern claims by persons whose interests were once actually or apparently aligned with the interests of the lawyer or the lawyer's client. Consequently, certain actions may be brought against a lawyer by a former prospective client (*see* Chapter 3 Part A), by an intended third-party beneficiary of legal services for a client (*see* Part G), or by a lawyer's former co-counsel (*see* Part H).

Two other theories of liability to nonclients relate to persons whose interests were always adverse to the defendant lawyer. Thus, a lawyer may be liable to a litigation opponent for malicious prosecution or malicious use of process (*see* Part I). Similarly, a lawyer hired to collect a sum of money may be civilly liable for violating applicable provisions of debt collection laws (*see* Part K).

Finally, lawyers are sometimes liable to nonclients under state or federal securities laws (*see* Part J). (Other statutes may also give a nonclient the ability to pursue a civil action.)

As noted above, liability to former prospective clients and to persons alleging that the defendant lawyer aided or abetted a breach of fiduciary duty are discussed elsewhere in this book. The other ten main theories of nonclient liability are explored below.

3. Statutory Limits on Nonclient Liability

In efforts to protect lawyers from malpractice liability to persons who were never their clients, some state legislatures have passed laws purporting to limit the theories under which responsibility may be imposed. For example, an Arkansas law limits liability to persons not in privity to "conduct that constitutes fraud or intentional misrepresentation" or conduct where the lawyer "was aware that a primary intent of the client was for the professional services to benefit or influence the particular person bringing the action." Ark. Code. Ann. § 16-22-310 (Westlaw 2010).

Although such laws undoubtedly set important limits on the malpractice liability of attorneys, the limits may be less expansive than might first appear. Federal laws, such as the Fair Debt Collection Practices Act (*see* Part K) and federal securities laws (*see* Part J), create bases of liability to nonclients which states are not free to supersede. Moreover, it remains unclear whether state legislation, such as the Arkansas statute quoted above, overrides every other form of nonclient liability under state law, such as a lawyer's liability for malicious prosecution or malicious use of process (*see* Part I) or pursuant to state securities laws.

4. Successors in Interest

Lack of privity is typically not an obstacle to a malpractice action brought by certain successors in interest to clients. As discussed below, this category includes bankruptcy trustees, estate executors and administrators, business entities resulting from corporate mergers, and receivers.

a. Bankruptcy Trustees and Estate Administrators

If a client files for bankruptcy protection or dies, the client's trustee in bankruptcy or estate representative stands in the shoes of the client. Lack of privity therefore does not bar the trustee or representative from bringing a malpractice action related to a lawyer's prior representation of the client. The trustee or estate representative is regarded as a successor in interest with essentially the same rights as the client. Indeed, once a person with a malpractice claim declares bankruptcy, the bankruptcy trustee is the only party with standing to pursue the malpractice claim. *See Douglas v. Delp*, 987 S.W.2d 879, 882 (Tex. 1999). Similarly, courts usually hold that claims on behalf of a decedent or the decedent's estate must be brought by the executor or administrator of the estate. *See, e.g., Fleischman v. Horton*, 2006 WL 3541780, *2 (W.D. Okla. 2006).

In *Smith v. O'Donnell*, 288 S.W.3d 417 (Tex. 2009), the executor of the estate of a husband brought a malpractice claim against a law firm which allegedly provided the husband with bad advice while he was serving as the executor of his wife's estate. The Texas Supreme Court held that it made no difference whether the alleged malpractice related to estate planning or occurred outside of the estate-planning context. The executor was permitted to sue. To hold otherwise, the court wrote, would "place us alone among the states, and would unnecessarily immunize attorneys who commit malpractice." *Id.* at 421.

If a bankruptcy trustee abandons a legal malpractice claim, the person whose debts are discharged in bankruptcy sometimes has a right to prosecute the malpractice action, provided that the claim is not time-barred. *See Newman v. Enriquez*, 171 Ohio. App. 3d 117, 869 N.E.2d 735 (2007).

b. Mergers and Sales of Assets

If entities merge, the successor entity may assert the rights of predecessor entities. The attorney-client relationship, and hence privity, is deemed to transfer.

However, a true merger must be distinguished from a mere sale of assets. In the latter case, there is no effort to continue the pre-existing operation, and the purchaser of the assets does not acquire client status.

c. Receivers

By statute, receivers appointed to liquidate insolvent companies may assert malpractice claims against the lawyers who represented the failed institutions. *Cf. Dennerline v. Atterholt,* 886 N.E.2d 582 (Ind. Ct. App. 2008). Thus, in the wake of the Savings and Loan Crisis in the late 1980s and early 1990s, the federal Resolution Trust Corporation initiated numerous suits against the lawyers who represented the defunct S&Ls.

B. FRAUD ON CLIENTS AND NONCLIENTS

In many respects, fraud is the most important theory under which lawyers may be liable to nonclients. This is true for several reasons. First, every state recognizes an action for fraud, so there is plenty of precedent to draw upon in crafting actions against lawyers. Second, numerous states have held lawyers liable to nonclients for fraud, and no state has ever ruled that a lawyer may deliberately defraud a person merely because of the lack of privity. Third, because legal work involves language, there is abundant material to cull in search of misstatements. Finally, fraud is seriously wrongful conduct, and a lawyer found to have acted fraudulently may be liable not only for compensatory damages (perhaps generously calculated by the jury because of the defendant's bad conduct), but punitive damages, too (*see* Chapter 6).

1. A Primer on the Law of Fraud

In the course of human history, there has been no shortage of fraudulent conduct. Not surprisingly, there is an immense amount of case precedent dealing with the subject, and equally voluminous scholarship exploring the intricate rules and distinctions that have emerged from the courts. A full examination of the law of fraud could easily consume an entire law school course. The following discussion merely sketches the subject, focusing on actions against lawyers.

a. Common Law Remedies and Other Consequences

At the outset, it is important to keep in mind the range of consequences that flow from fraud. In addition to a tort action for damages, fraud may trigger other remedies. Possible consequences include, forfeiture of attorneys fees (*see* Chapter 4 Part D), invalidation of a contract (*see Restatement (Second) of Contracts* § 7 cmt. b (1981)), and a suit for restitution in which recovery is based not on what the plaintiff lost (damages), but on what the defendant improperly gained (unjust enrichment) (*see* Chapter 6 Part C).

In addition, conduct that might be actionable as common law fraud sometimes forms the basis for an action that is rooted in statutory obligations. For example, in *Banco Popular North America v. Gandi*, 184 N.J. 161, 876 A.2d 253 (N.J. 2005), a bank alleged that a lawyer participated in a civil conspiracy to violate the Uniform Fraudulent Transfers Act. The New Jersey Supreme Court held that the lower court properly refused to dismiss the conspiracy count because the allegations indicated that the lawyer had counseled the client to transfer his assets to defraud a creditor and had facilitated the transfer.

Aside from civil liability, a lawyer's perpetration of fraud may also result in professional discipline. Under Model Rule 8.4, a lawyer commits professional misconduct if the lawyer engages "in conduct involving dishonesty, fraud, deceit or misrepresentation." Model Rules of Prof'l Conduct R. 8.4(c) (2010). In addition, "[a] lawyer shall not counsel a client to engage, or assist a client, in conduct that the lawyer knows is criminal or fraudulent." *Id*. R. 1.2. An attorney who is found to have engaged in fraudulent conduct is likely to be subject to serious disciplinary sanctions, because fraud is not a minor misstep, but a form of deliberate victimization.

b. The Elements of Deceit

Most cases refer to liability for "fraud," although some use the term "deceit." Whichever term is used, the civil cause of action is usually defined as having five elements. The plaintiff must show that: (1) the defendant made a material misrepresentation; (2) the defendant acted with "*scienter*" (meaning knowledge of the misrepresentation's falsity or reckless disregard for its truth); (3) the misrepresentation was intended or expected by the defendant to induce reliance; (4) the plaintiff justifiably relied upon the misrepresentation; and (5) damages resulted.

To impose liability, there must be evidence to establish each of the elements of fraud. In a recent case, a claim that lawyers committed fraud by submitting documents to a state court was dismissed because the plaintiff did not even allege that the lawyers knew the statements were false or otherwise acted with *scienter*. *See O'Neill v. Hernandez*, 2009 WL 860647, *8 (S.D.N.Y. 2009).

(1) Special Pleading Requirements

Under federal procedural rules, and similar provisions in most states, the circumstances constituting fraud must be pleaded with particularity. *See* Fed. R. Civ. Proc. R. 9(b) (2010). Some states say that the heightened pleading requirements do not apply to the damages element of a fraud action.

c. *Scienter*

"*Scienter*" is a highly blameworthy state of mind, entailing knowledge of falsity or reckless disregard for the truth. Thus, it is possible to establish the defendant's liability in either of two ways.

(1) Knowledge of Falsity

If the defendant is alleged to have made misrepresentations with knowledge of their falsity, the focus will be on what the defendant knew and when the defendant knew it. Suppose, for example, that a lawyer is alleged to have defrauded an opposing party into accepting an inadequate settlement by misrepresenting how much insurance coverage was available to the lawyer's client for purposes of covering the loss. One way that the plaintiff can prevail in an action for fraud is to show that the lawyer knew that the insurance policy had higher limits of liability when the lawyer made the statement.

Some kinds of evidence, if credited by the jury, leave little room for doubt about what a lawyer in fact knew. Such evidence might consist of e-mails, hard copy correspondence, or deposition testimony of another lawyer. In other cases, knowledge of falsity is proven by circumstantial evidence.

(2) Reckless Disregard for the Truth

The second way of proving *scienter* greatly expands the range of culpable conduct that may give rise to liability for fraud. Under this alternative, a plaintiff does not need to show that the defendant knew that a representation was false, but merely that the defendant acted with reckless disregard for the truth. To understand what this means, it is important to differentiate mere negligence from recklessness. Negligence is not sufficient to establish *scienter*.

Negligence is less culpable than recklessness, and involves nothing more than the failure to exercise reasonable care. Thus, the fact that a reasonably careful person would have detected the falsity of the statement uttered by the defendant does not prove that the defendant acted with *scienter*.

In contrast to negligence, recklessness is defined, in various areas of the law, either (a) objectively, as an extreme lack of care, or (b) subjectively, as conscious indifference to a known risk of serious harm.

Three examples illustrate *scienter* based on recklessness. First, a person acts with *scienter* if the person asserts something as a matter of fact, even though he or she does not know whether the assertion is true. In that case, the utterance is made with conscious disregard for whether the statement is true or false. The speaker *knows* that he or she *does not know* whether the statement is accurate. Suppose, for example, that a defendant represents that a corporation is making money, even though the defendant does not know whether it is running in the black or the red financially. The defendant will be liable for fraud if the assertion turns out to be false and foreseeably causes damages to a person who was expected to rely on the assertion.

Second, according to the *Restatement*, a person acts with *scienter* if the person lacks the factual basis that a statement implies. *See Restatement (Second) of Torts* § 526 (1977). For example, assume that a lawyer declines a case by telling a prospective client that there are no legal grounds for bringing suit. If the lawyer implies that the lawyer's decision was based on a careful review of the law, when that was not the case, and the prospective client is dissuaded from seeking other representation for what would have been a meritorious claim, the lawyer may be liable not just for negligence, but for fraud. (As to whether suing for fraud is preferable to suing for negligence, see Chapter 2 Part C (discussing the consequences of classifying a malpractice cause of action).)

Third, according to the *Restatement*, a person acts with *scienter* by making a misrepresentation in which the person lacks the confidence that is stated or implied. *See Restatement, Second, of Torts* § 526 (1977). Thus, an unequivocal assurance about the tax deductibility of certain expenditures may support a fraud action if the assertion proves erroneous and there is evidence that the lawyer had doubts about how taxing authorities would rule on the issue of deductibility.

Proof of *scienter* inevitably requires evidence of the defendant's state of mind regarding the truth or falsity of allegedly misrepresented matter. Suppose, for example, that a lawyer transmits a document containing a material misstatement of fact, but that the lawyer proves that he or she was unaware of the contents of the document and was merely acting as a courier. On these facts, the jury will be unable to conclude that the lawyer acted with *scienter*. It might be argued that the lawyer *should have known* about the contents of the document because a reasonable lawyer would have inquired, but that is only *negligence*, which is not sufficient to establish *scienter* and liability for fraud.

d. Materiality and Types of Misrepresentation

An action for fraud may be based on misleading words, conduct, or, in some cases, silence. These types of misrepresentation are discussed below.

To be actionable, a misrepresentation must be material. This simply means that the matter must be one to which a reasonable person would attach importance in making a decision, or one which the defendant knows is important to the particular plaintiff. *See Restatement (Second) of Torts* § 538 (1977).

(1) Words Written or Oral

A misrepresentation may, of course, consist of words, whether written or oral. Therefore, a real estate lawyer may be subject to liability for falsely telling a client that a contract has been signed and a deposit received. *See Stoecker v. Echevarria*, 408 N.J. Super. 597, 975 A.2d 975 (App. Div. 2009). Similarly, a lawyer may be liable for fraud based on backdating documents, if the misrepresented date is material.

In a recent case, a client sued its law firm after it settled an antitrust dispute with a rival G.P.S. company. The client alleged that the firm had misled it by incorrectly representing that the client did not have to worry about what fees it would incur in the dispute because it could recover all of its fees and costs if it prevailed on even one aspect of its antitrust claims. In refusing to dismiss the fraud claim, the court found that there was some evidence that the client relied on the assurance and, as a result, spent "lots and lots of money." *See* Kate Moser, "Quinn Emanuel Faces Trial in Dispute with Ex-Client Over \$15 Million Bill," www.law.com (Jun. 16, 2010).

On appropriate facts, ambiguous statements and half-truths will support an action for fraud. For example, a statement that a seller's title to property has been upheld by a particular court is a false representation if the speaker fails to disclose knowledge that an appeal from the decision is pending. *Cf. Restatement (Second) of Torts* § 529 cmt. a (1977).

(a) Words of Qualification

Words of qualification—such as "about," "more or less," or "roughly"—merely indicate a margin of error. They do not make a statement nonactionable. Consider the following examples involving similar, but different, statements.

If a lawyer says that the ranch being sold by a client has a thousand acres, when it only has 980 acres, there has been a misstatement of fact. If the other elements of fraud are established, the plaintiff can recover damages based on the reduced size of the property.

In contrast, if the lawyer says that the 980-acre ranch has "roughly a thousand acres," it is less clear that there has been a misrepresentation. The jury must determine if the size of the ranch was substantially as stated. If not, the representation is actionable to the extent of the deficiency.

(2) Conduct

A misrepresentation may also consist of conduct that communicates information. In an old case, a lawyer presented a release and demanded payment of a certain debt, which by prior agreement of the parties was to be paid only if the plaintiff's compensation carrier had agreed to waive its claim. The Wisconsin Supreme Court found that the lawyer, through his conduct, had fraudulently represented that the compensation carrier had been satisfied or had waived its claim. *See Scandrett v. Greenhouse*, 244 Wis. 108, 11 N.W.2d 510 (1943).

(3) Nondisclosure

In law, as in etiquette, the general rule is that silence is golden. Nondisclosure will support an action for fraud only if there is a duty to speak. There are at least five situations where such an obligation arises.

(a) Fiduciary Duty to Speak

First, the law of fiduciary duty may impose an obligation to speak. This means that it is often easier for a *client* to base a fraud action on silence, than for a *nonclient* to make the same argument. Lawyers, as fiduciaries, have broad obligations to keep clients informed of material information. (*See* Chapter 4 Part C). In contrast, nonclients stand on a very different footing. Lawyers typically do not owe fiduciary duties to nonclients.

Suppose that a lawyer involved with the management of a client's trust appoints as broker, developer, and manager of the trust's real estate holding a person who, unknown to the client, is a close friend of the lawyer. If the client suffers losses and the arrangement turns sour, it is easy to see how the client might allege that the lawyer is liable for fraudulent nondisclosure of material information.

In *Cummings v. Sea Lion Corp.*, 924 P.2d 1011 (Alaska 1996), the Supreme Court of Alaska held that a lawyer was liable for failing to reveal to the client corporation that the lawyer would only be paid if the transaction between the corporation and a previous client of the lawyer was successful.

In a recent case, a law firm promised to have a particular lawyer act as lead counsel. However, it later substituted another lawyer, whom it allegedly told the client was available "by a stroke of good fortune." In a subsequent suit against the law firm, alleging fraud and other theories of liability, the client claimed that it was not told that the second lawyer was brought in "because he had little or no other work." *See* Kate Moser, "Quinn Emanuel Faces Trial in Dispute with Ex-Client Over $15 Million Bill," law.com (Jun. 16, 2010).

(b) Half-Truths

The truth cannot be told in such a way as to leave a false impression. Thus, a lawyer cannot say that a property has been "sold" in an effort to trigger a person's promissory note repayment obligations, without also disclosing that the sale had no substance and was strictly *pro forma.*

A statement may be half-true because, although accurate when made, new developments have occurred. *See Restatement (Second) of Torts* § 551(2)(d) (1977). In this kind of situation, there is a duty to correct the earlier statement. The duty continues until it is no longer possible for the recipient of the original statement to avoid foreseeable reliance on the erroneous information. In *McMahan v. Greenwood*, 108 S.W.3d 467 (Tex. App. 2003), a Texas court recognized that a lawyer had a duty to correct misimpressions created by earlier statements to a nonclient.

(c) Facts Basic to the Transaction

There is a duty to disclose facts so "basic to a transaction" that nondisclosure amounts to "swindling." *Restatement (Second) of Torts* § 551 cmt. l (1977). In a recent case, lawyers who represented hedge funds allegedly failed to disclose that the person who headed the funds was a disbarred New York lawyer who had drained a client's escrow account. *See* Julie Kay, "Receiver in Alleged $347 Million Ponzi Scheme Sues Holland & Knight for Malpractice," law.com (Sept. 2, 2009). It could reasonably be argued that the duty to disclose basic facts applies to this sort of case.

In *Banco Popular North America v. Gandi*, 184 N.J. 161, 876 A.2d 253 (N.J. 2005), a lawyer's client provided a guarantee to a bank in connection with receiving a loan. In holding that the bank stated claims for fraud and negligent misrepresentation against the lawyer, who had negotiated the loan and who had written an opinion letter to facilitate the transaction, the court explained:

> [G]iven [lawyer] Freedman's knowledge of the worthlessness of the guaranty, he had a duty, in light of what he had done and what he knew, either to counsel Gandhi [the client] to tell the Bank the truth and see to it that he did so or to discontinue his representation ***. Freedman could *not* assist Gandhi in fraudulently securing further loans and, on the facts alleged, over-stepped his bounds in penning an opinion letter on Gandhi's behalf.

876 A.2d at 268.

(d) Facts Not Reasonably Discoverable

Many decisions hold that there is a duty to disclose material facts which are not reasonably discoverable. This exception reflects the limits of the rationale underlying the rule that silence is usually not actionable. The general rule creates an incentive for persons to exercise care to protect their own interests. They cannot stand by and expect others to do their work for them. They must conduct their own investigations, ask good questions, and draw reasonable conclusions. If they fail to do so, they risk incurring economic losses for which there will be no legal remedy.

However, if the relevant facts are not reasonably discoverable, no purpose would be furthered by a rule countenancing nondisclosure of material information.

The potential plaintiff would simply be relegated to making an uninformed decision. To avoid this result, disclosure of facts beyond the range of reasonable discovery is required. The cases recognizing this type of duty to disclose have generally involved the sale or leasing of real property. However, there is no reason that the same rational could not apply to the types of facts that give rise to legal malpractice actions.

(4) Misrepresentations by Lawyers About Credentials or Experience

Sometimes questions arise as to whether a lawyer misrepresented his or her credentials or experience. It is possible to analyze these kinds of statements or nondisclosures under the law of fraud. *See* Vincent R. Johnson & Shawn M. Lovorn, "Misrepresentation by Lawyers About Credentials or Experience," 57 *Okla. L. Rev.* 529, 536-61 (2004). Some misrepresentations about qualifications or prior work history are potentially actionable. For example, in *Nason v. Fisher*, 36 A.D.3d 486, 828 N.Y.S.2d 51, 52 (2007), a New York appellate court found that a client raised a triable issue of fact about whether a lawyer had committed constructive fraud by misrepresenting that he had experience in handling commercial partnership cases.

In a recent case, the plaintiff alleged that a law firm partner expressly stated that he had experience in corporate investigatory matters. However, the plaintiff later learned that, on the first day of the engagement, the partner directed the firm librarian to identify and copy articles discussing how internal corporate investigations should be conducted. This set the stage for the plaintiff to argue that there had been a fraudulent misrepresentation of the partner's experience.

Of course, it is important to remember that there are alternatives to suing for fraud. In some circumstances, those alternatives may be preferable. For example, nondisclosure may sometimes be characterized as negligent failure to obtain informed consent (*see* Chapter 3 Part B-7). Framing the claim as negligence, rather than fraud, may make it easier to impute the conduct to the defaulting lawyer's law firm and its principals (*see* Chapter 8), as well as more likely to fall within insurance coverage (*see* Chapter 11).

In *Aiken v. Hancock*, 115 S.W.3d 26, 28–29 (Tex. App. 2003), a Texas court held that a former client's allegations that his attorney falsely represented that he was prepared to try a case, and that an expert witness was prepared to testify, were actionable under a theory of "legal malpractice." Many states equate the term of "legal malpractice" with professional negligence.

e. Opinion v. Fact

Statements of *fact* are more readily actionable under the law of misrepresentation than statements of *opinion*. Thus, it is possible to sue a lawyer for falsely stating, "we have filed the appeal," but not for inaccurately predicting, "we probably will win on appeal."

Nevertheless, a complex matrix of rules makes clear that statements of opinion are sometimes actionable. Of particular relevance to issues of lawyer liability are the rules dealing with "puffing," implicit statements of fact, misrepresented intentions, and statements of "law." These topics are discussed in the following sections.

(1) "Puffing"

"Puffing" is sales talk, language which casts a warm glow over a transaction, but says nothing too specific. In general, puffing is treated as a non-actionable expression of opinion. A multinational law firm with many offices probably cannot be sued by a disappointed client based simply on the fact that the firm's website touted the availability of "world class" legal services.

However, once a lawyer (or other potential defendant) begins to assert specific facts, rather than conclusory opinions, the puffing rule affords little protection. A law firm cannot say that it has offices in three countries, if that is not true.

Lawyers can be expected to have a favorable opinion of themselves. There is usually nothing wrong with that. However, in some situations, statements about credentials or experience go far beyond puffing. Thus, in *Baker v. Dorfman*, 239 F.3d 415, 422-24 (2d Cir. 2000), a lawyer was found to have engaged in resume fraud to induce a client to hire him. The Second Circuit concluded that grossly false statements gave the impression that the lawyer was an experienced litigator, although this was not true. In *Baker*, an award of compensatory and punitive damages for fraud was affirmed.

(2) Implicit Statements of Fact

Every statement of opinion carries with it two implicit statements of fact. The first is that the maker of the statement has some factual basis for forming an opinion. The second is that the facts known to the speaker are not entirely inconsistent with the opinion expressed.

A lawyer cannot say that he or she is "good at corporate mergers and acquisitions" if the lawyer knows nothing about the subject. Nor can the lawyer make that claim if he or she has recently been held liable for malpractice based on incompetence in the M&A field.

(3) State of Mind

One's state of mind is a fact. A lawyer either does, or does not, intend to do what the lawyer states an intention of doing. It is sometimes difficult to prove that intentions were misrepresented. However, in the current Digital Age, e-mails, tweets, and postings on social networking sites may provide compelling evidence about the defendant's state of mind.

A knowingly false assertion of one's intent is actionable as fraud. For example, in *Graubard Mollen Dannett & Horowitz v. Moskovitz*, 86 N.Y.2d 112, 653 N.E.2d 1179, 1184, 629 N.Y.S.2d 1009 (N.Y. 1995), a partner in a law firm orally represented that he planned to "act to ensure the future of the firm." The New York Court of Appeals held that the law firm stated a claim for fraud by alleging the partner never intended to protect the firm's interests.

Similarly, in *Charnay v. Cobert*, 145 Cal. App. 4th 170, 51 Cal. Rptr. 3d 471 (2006), a California appellate court ruled that a client adequately pleaded claims for fraud and negligent misrepresentation by alleging that her lawyer falsely told her that she need not be concerned about escalating costs because she would recover those costs at the end of the litigation. The client argued, in part, that the lawyer made these representations knowing they were false because he did not believe them.

(4) Statements of Law

Statements about what the law is, or about what is or is not legal, are sometimes treated as statements of opinion which cannot form the basis for liability. In these cases, the conclusion that the statement is not actionable usually rests on one of two somewhat contradictory rationales. On the one hand, it is said that the law is so complex that any assertion about it is a mere opinion, which no one would be justified relying upon. On the other hand, it is said that everyone is presumed to know the law, so no one could be misled by a statement about what the law is or requires.

The "rule" that a statement of law is not a sufficient predicate for a tort action is subject to several exceptions. First, it is reasonable for clients to rely on what their lawyers tell them. Therefore, if the other elements of fraud are met, a lawyer will rarely escape liability to a client on the ground that a statement about the law was not a misrepresentation of fact.

Second, it is sometimes reasonable and appropriate for nonclients to rely upon a lawyer's statements. Thus, if a statement of law is uttered as an assertion of fact, it may be relied upon by the recipient, even though there is no attorney-client relationship.

For example, in *National Conversion Corp. v. Cedar Building Corp.*, 23 N.Y.2d 621, 246 N.E.2d 351, 298 N.Y.S.2d 499 (N.Y. 1969), a document contained a false representation that the leased premises were not subject to restrictions imposed by the zoning laws. Further, the lessor dissuaded the lessee from adjourning the negotiations to verify that fact by stating unequivocally, "[we] own the property, *** we know the area ***, we guarantee it." *Id*. at 354. The New York Court of Appeals held that it would be unfair not to allow reliance on that assurance.

Third, a statement of law may carry with it implicit statements of fact. If a lawyer for the seller asserts that a certain property complies with building code requirements, that may be regarded as a factual assurance that the building contains a certain type of electrical wiring or plumbing.

f. Justifiable Reliance

(1) Actual Reliance

A misrepresentation will form the basis of tort liability only if it causes damages. This means, among other things, that the plaintiff must have learned of the misrepresentation and relied upon it.

(a) Statements Known to Be False

A person who learns that a statement is false before incurring detrimental reliance cannot sue for fraud. Put differently, if the recipient knows a statement is false, his or her best and only remedy under tort law is self-help. The recipient must forbear reliance, rather than burden the courts with a request for redress.

(2) Danger Signals

If there are danger signals that would place a person on notice that a statement is untrustworthy, reliance on the statement is ordinarily not permitted. Rather than rely, the recipient of the statement must conduct whatever investigation is appropriate to protect his or her interests. Failure to do so, bars an action for fraud. Moreover, if a person makes an investigation of the facts, a potential fraud defendant is sure to argue (sometimes with success) that any harm that thereafter occurs was caused not by reliance on the initial misrepresentation, but by reliance on what was learned during the plaintiff's inquiry into the facts.

However, the presence of a danger signal is sometimes disregarded. First, if the plaintiff suffers from a mental disability, the law usually will not fault the plaintiff for having failed to make an investigation that a reasonable person would have made. Second, clients are expected to trust their lawyers. Therefore, a *client's* failure to investigate may be more easily excused than similar conduct by a *nonclient*. Third, if the results of a diligent investigation are inconclusive, a plaintiff may be allowed to argue that subsequent conduct, and resulting harm, was caused, at least in part, by justifiable reliance on the defendant's earlier statements.

(3) Failure to Doubt

In the absence of danger signals, there is no general duty to doubt the truthfulness of a person's affirmative statement. Thus, a positive utterance may be accepted at face value.

In *Media General, Inc. v. Tomlin*, 532 F.3d 854, 858-59 (D.C. Cir. 2008), there was evidence to support a jury finding that, when the purchaser of a business enquired about contingent liabilities, the sellers's law firm said that a suit by a terminated employee sought only $139,000 in damages, even though the seller had received a draft complaint in which the former employee asked for $6 million. The district court found that it was unreasonable for the purchaser to rely on the alleged misrepresentation of the magnitude of the claim because the purchaser, which was aware of a pending audit of the seller, could have asked to see the seller's letter to its auditor, which fully described the threatened litigation. Rejecting this line of analysis, the D.C. Circuit found that the purchaser was not required to make such a request to see if the seller was lying.

(4) Contractual Disclaimers of Reliance

Contracts sometimes contain language stating that one party has not relied on any statements by the other. This type of provision may preclude proof of detrimental reliance in a fraud action. However, many courts take the position that a contractual disclaimer of reliance is only one factor to consider in determining whether justifiable reliance occurred. *See generally* Robert K. Wise *et al.*, "Of Lies and Disclaimers—Contracting Around Fraud," 41 *St. Mary's L.J.* 119 (2009).

g. Intent to Induce Reliance or Expectation of Reliance

A misrepresentation is actionable only if it is meant to be known by the plaintiff and to induce reliance, or if there is negligence in these respects. For example, in *Banco Popular North America v. Gandi*, 184 N.J. 161, 876 A.2d 253, 266 (N.J. 2005), the Supreme Court of New Jersey found that a lawyer was not liable for assisting a client with a transaction because the transaction was intended to be carried out without the plaintiff's knowledge, the lawyer did not expect reliance, and no reliance, in fact, ensued.

h. Resulting Damages

In the typical fraud case, an award of compensatory damages is mainly concerned with economic losses, which may be measured in either of two ways. Under the "contract rule," also known as the "benefit of the bargain rule," the plaintiff may recover the difference between the value of what the plaintiff was promised and the value of what was received. Under the "tort" or "out of pocket rule," the plaintiff recovers the difference between what the plaintiff paid and the value of what the plaintiff received.

For example, suppose that a piece of property would have been worth $200,000 if the plaintiff received what was bargained for. However, because the facts were misrepresented, the property was worth only $100,000. If the plaintiff paid $130,000 for the property, the plaintiff could recover $100,000 under the "benefit of the bargain" rule, but only $30,000 under the "out of pocket rule.

Courts typically have discretion to determine which measure of damages—"benefit of the bargain" or "out of pocket"—applies to a particular case. The "contract" measure of damages is available in a fraud action only if there was a bargain between the parties, and only if the plaintiff can prove with reasonable certainty the value of the bargain.

Many misrepresentations relate to real property. Sometimes there are conflicting estimates as to what property would have been worth absent a misrepresentation, but clear evidence as to both what the plaintiff paid and what the plaintiff received when the property was resold. In that case, it may be easier to prove "out of pocket" losses with reasonable certainty, than to prove the value of the lost bargain.

2. Liability for Aiding and Abetting Fraud

Lawyers may be liable not only for committing fraud, but for aiding and abetting the fraudulent conduct of others. For example, in *Oster v. Kirschner,* 2010 WL 2650532 (N.Y. App. Div.), a law firm drafted the private placement memorandum whereby its client was able to perpetrate a $22 million fraud on investors. In an action against the law firm, a New York appellate court concluded that "[a] plaintiff alleging an aiding-and-abetting fraud claim must allege the existence of the underlying fraud, actual knowledge, and substantial assistance." *Id.* at *3. On the facts of the case, the court found that these elements were adequately pleaded based on circumstantial evidence.

C. NEGLIGENT MISREPRESENTATION

Numerous states recognize a cause of action for negligent misrepresentation. This theory of liability is a well-established exception to the "economic loss rule," which holds that, in some circumstances, negligence that causes purely economic losses is not actionable under tort law. *See Van Sickle Const. Co. v. Wachovia Commercial Mortg., Inc.*, 783 N.W.2d 684, 691-94 (Iowa 2010).

Negligent misrepresentation shares many of the doctrinal features of the law of fraud. For example, the principles that govern the actionability of half-truths and statements of opinion in suits for fraud also generally apply to claims alleging negligent misrepresentation.

Similarly, a plaintiff suing for negligent misrepresentation must prove justifiable reliance. For example, in *Breen v. Law Office of Bruce A. Barket, P.C.*, 52 A.D.3d 635, 862 N.Y.S.2d 50, 53 (2008), a deed was incorrectly drawn by a husband's attorney in a divorce action. A New York appellate court concluded that the husband's wife could not state a claim for negligent misrepresentation because she could not prove justifiable reliance. The facts established that the wife discovered the error, brought it to her lawyer's attention, and was advised by her lawyer to nevertheless sign the incorrect deed.

However, negligent misrepresentation differs from fraud in two key respects. First, negligent misrepresentation permits recovery of damages based on a less demanding showing of culpability than is required in fraud actions. What is needed is negligence as to the falsity of the misleading statement, rather than knowledge of falsity or reckless disregard for its truth. Second, negligent misrepresentation typically restricts the scope of liability more tightly than the law of fraud.

Note also that some (but not all) courts hold that a negligent misrepresentation action cannot be based on silence, and requires proof of an affirmative misstatement. Further, a claim for negligent misrepresentation, unlike fraud, is subject to defenses based on the plaintiff's failure to exercise care (*i.e.*, contributory negligence, comparative negligence, or comparative fault, depending on the law of the state). These various topics are discussed below.

The absence of a lawyer-client relationship is generally not an obstacle to a suit for negligent misrepresentation. *See Restatement (Third) of the Law Governing Lawyers* § 51(2) (2000). Therefore, this cause of action is an important weapon in the litigation arsenal of nonclients.

1. Restatement (Second) of Torts § 552

The most common point of reference in the law of negligent misrepresentation is § 552 of the *Restatement (Second) of Torts*. This section has been so widely endorsed and influential that, unlike most *Restatement* provisions, it is commonly referred to by number. Section 552 provides:

> One who, in the course of his business, profession or employment, or in any other transaction in which he has a pecuniary interest, supplies false information for the guidance of others in their business transactions, is subject to liability for pecuniary loss caused to them by their justifiable reliance upon the information, if he fails to exercise reasonable care or competence in obtaining or communicating the information.

Restatement (Second) of Torts § 552(1) (1977).

In *Banco Popular North America v. Gandi*, 184 N.J. 161, 876 A.2d 253 (N.J. 2005), a lawyer made false statements while negotiating the terms of a loan guarantee on behalf of a client, and in issuing a related opinion letter to a bank. In holding that the bank properly alleged claims against the lawyer for fraud and negligent misrepresentation, the Supreme Court of New Jersey explained:

> Freedman [the lawyer] knew of the true state of *** [the financial affairs of his client because he was the architect of his client's divestiture of assets]; and Freedman nevertheless negotiated the terms of the loan and rendered an opinion letter that falsely stated in paragraph ten, "After

due investigation, we are unaware of any material matters contrary to the representations and warranties of the Borrower or the Guarantor contained in the Loan Documents." That Freedman intended the Bank to rely on that misrepresentation cannot be disputed: Freedman's opinion letter is addressed to the Bank ***. [T]he assertion that Freedman was "unaware of any material matters contrary to the representations and warranties ***" provided the basis for a direct misrepresentation claim against Freedman, which may be characterized as negligent or intentional.

876 A.2d at 267-68.

2. Limits on the Scope of Liability

The scope of potential liability to nonclients is more tightly circumscribed for negligent misrepresentation than for fraud. This is true because when culpability is slight (*i.e.*, when falsity is negligent, rather than intentional or reckless), imposition of broad exposure to damages would more easily offend the principle that liability should be proportional to fault. Proportionality is a fundamental policy in modern tort law.

The rules which courts have endorsed for limiting the scope of liability for fraud differ from those which apply to negligent misrepresentation actions. The applicable legal principles are discussed below.

a. Scope of Liability for Fraud

It is said that to be liable for fraud the defendant must intend to induce reliance by the plaintiff. However, in some cases, expectation of reliance will suffice as a basis for liability, even if the defendant does not intend to induce reliance. Thus, the *Restatement* says that liability for fraud extends to persons whom the defendant "intends or has reason to expect to act or to refrain from action in reliance upon the misrepresentation." *Restatement (Second) of Torts* § 531 (1977). In thinking about what this rule means, it is useful to differentiate directly transmitted fraudulent representations from those which indirectly reach the plaintiff.

(1) Direct Dissemination of a Fraudulent Representation

If the defendant directly transmitted the misstatement to the plaintiff, it is highly likely that the plaintiff's losses fall within the scope of liability. Absent facts proving otherwise, the parties' conduct shows that reliance was expected or desired by the defendant.

However, if the defendant did not deal directly with the plaintiff, but merely knew that the recipient of the statement intended to convey that information to the plaintiff or other persons, or that there was a possibility that the recipient might do so, the analysis must be more complex. It may still be possible to show that reliance by the plaintiff was intended or expected. However, a more detailed examination of the facts and applicable law is required.

(2) Indirect Dissemination of a Fraudulent Representation

To address liability issues related to indirectly disseminated fraudulent statements, the *Restatement* articulates two special rules related to commercial documents and public filings, as well as a general rule which purports to require something more than foreseeability of reliance. The following sections explore these topics.

(a) Commercial Documents

The *Restatement (Second) of Torts* contains a provision dealing with written misrepresentations incorporated into commercial documents. Section 532 provides:

> One who embodies a fraudulent misrepresentation in an article of commerce, a muniment of title, a negotiable instrument or a similar commercial document, is subject to liability for pecuniary loss caused to another who deals with him or with a third person regarding the article or document in justifiable reliance upon the truth of the representation.

Restatement (Second) of Torts § 532 (1977). However, the *Restatement* rule is:

> limited to those documents or chattels that are in themselves articles of commerce. It does not apply to an ordinary letter misrepresenting the title to land or to a report furnished by an accountant to a corporation concerning its finances, because these documents are not to be expected to have

commercial circulation.

Id. at § 532. An "article of commerce" is something that is offered for sale and which has a value and existence independent of the parties. Examples in the *Restatement* include deeds, bonds, promissory notes, and merchandise containers.

The Maryland Court of Appeals followed the *Restatement* rule in *Diamond Point Plaza Ltd. Partnership v. Wells Fargo Bank, N.A.*, 929 A.2d 932 (Md. 2007), a case involving loan documents. There, the assignee of a mortgage sued for fraud. The court wrote:

> Diamond Point *** made a fraudulent misrepresentation in a commercial document, for the purpose of inducing Pinnacle and PaineWebber to extend a loan, aware that PaineWebber likely would sell that loan in the secondary market. Diamond Point would thus have reason to expect that the loan documents, including its borrower's certificates, would be presented to, would be considered by, and would influence the decision of prospective buyers in the secondary market ***. Liability is not defeated by the fact that Diamond Point's representations were not made directly to Wells Fargo.

929 A.2d at 946.

(b) Public Filings

An action for fraud may sometimes be based on false statements in a public filing, if the plaintiff is a member of the class the information is intended to protect. *Restatement (Second) of Torts* § 536 (1977).

Thus, reports made by corporations required to publicly disclose their financial positions may usually be relied upon by persons making deposits or investments, as well as by those lending money to the entities in question. *Id.* at § 536 cmt. e.

In some states, oil and gas well operators are required to report information to a state commission, which is then available to others doing business in the field. If such filings contain fraudulent statements, they may be actionable by persons who suffer harm in reliance on those misrepresentations. *Cf. NationsBank of Texas, N.A. v. Akin, Gump, Hauer & Feld, L.L.P.*, 979 S.W.2d 385, 389-90 (Tex. App.1998).

(c) Special Reason to Expect Reliance

The official commentary to the *Restatement's* basic rule on "expectation of influencing conduct" states that a general risk of reliance—the type of risk that is inherent in virtually every misrepresentation—is an insufficient predicate for liability. Thus:

> The maker of the misrepresentation must have information that would lead a reasonable man to conclude that there is an especial likelihood that it will reach those persons and will influence their conduct ***.

Id. at § 531 cmt. d. Some courts have gone to great lengths to indicate that merely foreseeable reliance is an insufficient basis for a fraud action. These authorities hold that a special reason to expect reliance is necessary even in cases involving misrepresentations in documents intended for commercial circulation or in publicly filed reports.

For example, after the Enron corporation collapsed, investors sued the investment professionals who had deliberately disseminated false information to the public for the purpose of hiding the deteriorating financial condition of the company. A federal court in Texas held that those widely disseminated fraudulent statements were not actionable. As the court explained:

> [T]o establish fraudulent intent, Plaintiffs must allege and show more than that information was available in the investment community, pursuant to industry custom, and that it was foreseeable that it would reach them; Plaintiffs must show that Plaintiffs' "reliance must be 'especially likely' and justifiable, and that the transaction sued upon must be the type the defendant contemplated."

In re Enron Corporation Securities, Derivative & "ERISA" Litigation, 490 F. Supp. 2d 784, 824 (S.D. Tex. 2007) (*"Enron"*). The court found that these standards were not satisfied even though the principal defendant, Merrill Lynch, had allegedly "cooked the books" by devising fraudulent transactions to mislead investors and rating agencies and had "issued through its analysts, even as Enron was descending into bankruptcy ***, 'buy' or 'strong buy' recommendations for Enron securities, which Merrill Lynch knew would be 'widely disseminated in the financial news media.'" 490 F. Supp. 2d at 787.

The wisdom of decisions like *Enron* is open to question. Why should professionals who deliberately deceive large groups of potential investors not be held liable for the losses suffered by those who are misled?

What good purpose is served by insulating such malefactors from liability just because they were not certain which persons would successfully be deceived? Not surprisingly, there have been calls to abandon such harsh applications of the "special reason to expect reliance" rule. *See* Andrew R. Simank, Comment, "Deliberately Defrauding Investors: The Scope of Liability," 42 *St. Mary's L.J.* (2010). Of course, even if the "special reason to expect reliance" obstacle can be surmounted, a fraud claim related to securities can still be very difficult to litigate. *See* Robert W. Taylor, Comment, "Reevaluating Holder Actions: Giving Defrauded Securities Holders a Fighting Chance," 86 *Notre Dame L. Rev.* (2010-11).

b. Scope of Liability for Negligent Misrepresentation

In contrast to the rules governing liability for fraud (discussed above), states adhere to one of three positions regarding the scope of liability for negligent misrepresentation. These limits on liability are often referred to as: (1) the "foreseeability" view; (2) the "near privity" view; and (3) the "limited group" view.

These three views are important in the law of legal malpractice only with respect to claims by nonclients. Clients are owed duties of care by their lawyers under generally applicable principles of negligence law. Therefore, clients can sue their lawyers for harm caused by negligently false statements, as well as for losses caused by other forms of negligence. Lack of privity is not a problem.

In contrast, lawyers have no general obligation to exercise care to protect nonclients from harm. Liability to nonclients for negligent misrepresentation is therefore a special rule which imposes a limited duty on lawyers to exercise care to protect the pecuniary interests of nonclients. The three views, mentioned above, determine how far that limited duty of care extends. Some nonclients are beyond the scope of the obligations imposed by the law of negligent misrepresentation even if they rely on negligently false information and suffer damages. Depending on applicable state law, they are denied recovery for harm caused by a lawyer's negligently false statements because (1) their harm was unforeseeable, (2) they did not stand in a relationship of "near privity, or (3) they were not members of a special limited group.

(1) The "Foreseeability" View

The "foreseeability" view essentially treats purely economic losses—the type of damages characteristic of misrepresentations related to business affairs—as no different from losses arising from physical harm (personal injuries or property damage). In either case, the fairness of holding the defendant accountable is determined by principles of foreseeability. Thus, the question is simply whether it was reasonably foreseeable that the plaintiff would rely and suffer damages as a result of the lawyer's negligently false statement. In states adhering to the "foreseeability" view, liability for negligent misrepresentation *is not* more tightly circumscribed than it is for fraud.

In *Touche Ross & Co. v. Commercial Union Insurance Co.*, 514 So. 2d 315 (Miss. 1987), the Mississippi Supreme Court explained its variety of the "foreseeability" view in the context of a dispute involving auditors:

> [A]n independent auditor is liable to reasonably foreseeable users of the audit, who request and receive a financial statement from the audited entity for a proper business purpose, and who then detrimentally rely on the financial statement, suffering a loss, proximately caused by the auditor's negligence. Such a rule protects third parties, who request, receive and rely on a financial statement, while it also protects the auditor from an unlimited number of potential users, who may otherwise read the financial statement, once published. Of course, the auditor remains free to limit the dissemination of his opinion through a separate agreement with the audited entity.

514 So. 2d at 322-23.

Very few jurisdictions adhere to the foreseeability view on liability for negligent misrepresentation. This is because the foreseeability view, unless narrowly interpreted, may impose an unwarrantedly broad range of liability as a result of mere negligence. States rejecting the foreseeability view may also be concerned that the rule discourages potential defendants (*e.g.*, lawyers and accountants) from undertaking to provide professional services important to a market economy.

(2) The "Near Privity" View

New York and a number of other states adhere to the "near privity" view on liability to persons not party to a contract with the negligent misrepresentation defendant. This view greatly limits the liability of lawyers and other professionals to persons who have not employed them. Under this type of rule, a person who has never dealt with a lawyer generally cannot sue for negligent misrepresentation, regardless of whether reliance was foreseeable.

In *Credit Alliance Corp. v. Arthur Andersen & Co.*, 65 N.Y.2d 536, 483 N.E.2d 110, 493 N.Y.S.2d 435 (N.Y. 1985), the New York Court of Appeals explained its variation of the "near privity" view. *Credit Alliance* involved the appeal of two cases against auditors. In one case, audited financial statements had been passed indirectly to the plaintiff by the audited party. The court held there was no liability. In the other case, the auditors had frequently been in direct communication with the plaintiff. On those facts, the court held that the plaintiff could sue for negligent misrepresentation. According to the court, auditors are liable for negligent preparation of financial reports only to persons who are in privity of contract with them, or to persons whose relationship with the auditors is "so close as to approach that of privity." 483 N.E.2d at 115. As Judge Matthew Jasen explained:

> Before accountants may be held liable in negligence to noncontractual parties who rely to their detriment on inaccurate financial reports, certain prerequisites must be satisfied: (1) the accountants must have been aware that the financial reports were to be used for a particular purpose or purposes; (2) in the furtherance of which a known party or parties was intended to rely; and (3)

there must have been some conduct on the part of the accountants linking them to that party or parties, which evinces the accountants' understanding of that party or parties' reliance."

483 N.E.2d at 118. The third requirement stated above was satisfied in the second appeal because the negligently false statement was directly transmitted by the defendant to the plaintiff.

In the legal malpractice context, suppose that a corporation hires a lawyer to draft an opinion letter about the tax treatment of an investment the corporation is offering to investors. If the letter is distributed by the corporation to unknown persons, who rely upon its statements, those persons cannot sue the lawyer for negligent misrepresentation even if the statements were negligently false.

(3) The "Limited Group" View

The remaining states follow the *Restatement* view on liability to third persons for negligent misrepresentation causing purely economic losses. That view is more restrictive than the "foreseeability" approach, but less demanding than the "near privity" approach. According to the *Restatement*, liability for negligent misrepresentation extends only to:

the person or one of a limited group of persons for whose benefit and guidance *** [the defendant] intends to supply the information or knows that the recipient intends to supply it***.

Restatement (Second) of Torts § 552 (1977). Moreover, there is liability only where the reliance takes place in a transaction substantially similar to the one the defendant intended to influence or knew the recipient intended to influence.

While it is not essential that the maker of the statement know the identity of the person for whose guidance the information is supplied, it "may be vitally important" that he be aware of the "number and character of the persons to be reached and influenced, and the nature and extent of the transaction for which guidance is furnished," because those factors define the "risk of liability to which the supplier subjects himself by undertaking to give the information." *Id.* § 552 cmt. h. This requirement ensures that liability is not only based on fault, but limited in proportion to fault. Unless the defendant has access to the facts which indicate the magnitude of the harm that might result from mere negligence, and thus has the opportunity and incentive to exercise an appropriate degree of care, it is unfair to impose liability for resulting losses.

(4) Summary

In many cases, it makes a great difference to plaintiffs and defendants which view a jurisdiction follows with respect to the scope of liability for negligent misrepresentation. Unless there has been direct communication between a lawyer and a nonclient, or other conduct which evinces the lawyer's understanding of the nonclient's reliance, there is no liability for negligent misrepresentation under the "near privity" view. And, unless the nonclient was a member of a limited group who was intended to be benefitted by the representation, and unless the reliance occurred in the type and magnitude of transaction of which the defendant had been apprised, there is no liability under the *Restatement* view.

It must be emphasized that the limitations applicable to negligent misrepresentation do not apply to an action for fraud. As discussed earlier, fraud has its own demanding requirements. (*See* B of this Chapter). Nevertheless, in general, it is much easier for a nonclient to recover for fraud than for negligent misrepresentation. Consequently, whether the plaintiff can obtain compensation for purely economic losses often depends upon whether the plaintiff can prove that the defendant acted with *scienter* (knowledge of falsity or reckless disregard for the truth; *see* Part B-1-c of this Chapter) and was not simply negligent. Even if the plaintiff proves that the defendant acted with careless falsity, an action for negligent misrepresentation may fail because the plaintiff was not within the scope of liability.

3.   Negligent Misrepresentation Based on Silence

There is an issue, not definitively resolved, as to whether an action for misrepresentation requires proof of an affirmative misstatement, as opposed to misleading silence. Some cases have held that silence is not a sufficient predicate for a negligent misrepresentation action. *See Eberts v. Goderstad*, 569 F.3d 757, 765-66 (7th Cir. 2009). Others hold that silence is actionable under the law of negligent misrepresentation if there is a duty to speak. Thus, in *In re Agrobiotech, Inc.*, 291 F. Supp. 2d 1186, 1192 (D. Nev. 2003), a federal court in Nevada found that "silence about material facts basic to the transaction, when combined with a duty to speak, is the functional equivalent of a [negligent] misrepresentation ***."

In thinking about this issue, it is useful to draw a distinction based on whether the plaintiff is a client or a nonclient. In some cases, whether there is a duty to disclose may depend upon the fact that the plaintiff is a client to whom fiduciary duties are owed (*see* B-1-d-(3) of this Chapter). In contrast, those same obligations are not owed to a nonclient. In such situations, it is not surprising that silence will not support a suit for negligent misrepresentation, because in the absence of some other duty to disclose, even a fraud claim by the nonclient would fail. Of course, some rules imposing a duty to speak are not rooted in fiduciary obligations. If the facts of the case fall within those rules, it is harder to argue that a negligent nondisclosure, even to a nonclient, is outside the range of legal liability.

4. Comparative Negligence Defense

Because negligent misrepresentation is merely a special kind of negligence, defenses that can be raised in any negligence action may be pleaded and proved by the defendant. Carelessness on the part of the plaintiff which contributes to the harm for which recovery is sought is a total or partial defense, depending on whether the state adheres to principles of traditional contributory negligence, comparative negligence, or comparative fault. (*See* Chapter 7 Part A).

In a case not involving legal malpractice, *Staggs v. Sells*, 86 S.W.3d 219 (Tenn. Ct. App. 2001), the defendants' agent had incorrectly represented that residential property was not prone to flooding. The court allowed the buyers to recover for negligent misrepresentation, but reduced the damages by 40% because the buyers had neglected to follow their appraiser's advice to have the property surveyed for the risk of this type of damage.

D. DECEPTIVE TRADE PRACTICES ACTS

Every state has adopted a deceptive trade practices act (DTPA). These laws supplement the common law remedies afforded by the actions for fraud and negligent misrepresentation. In many cases, the terms of the state DTPA provides an easier or better path to recovery by relaxing or dispensing with requirements of the parallel tort actions or offering more generous compensation.

However, any statutory action for damages has limits. This is particularly true of DTPA laws because "reformers" in many states have lobbied successfully to restrict DTPA remedies. Consequently, the common law actions for fraud and negligent misrepresentation remain useful. Indeed, victims of deception in the field of legal services frequently allege claims for fraud, negligent misrepresentation, and violation of the DTPA as separate counts in a single malpractice action.

A detailed exploration of professional liability under state DTPA laws must be left to another occasion. However, the following sections sketch some of the important features of this area of legal malpractice law.

1. Applicability to Lawyers

Some states make it difficult or impossible to sue lawyers under DTPA laws. For example, in Texas, it is hard for corporate plaintiffs to state a DTPA claim in cases involving large potential damages. The state's DTPA law does not "apply to a cause of action arising from a transaction, a project, or a set of transactions relating to the same project, involving total consideration by the consumer of more than $500,000 ***." Tex. Bus. & Com. Code § 17.49(g) (Westlaw 2010).

In addition, the Texas DTPA does not apply to "a claim for damages based on the rendering of a professional service, the essence of which is the providing of advice, judgment, opinion, or similar professional skill," unless there was "an express misrepresentation of a material fact" that cannot be characterized as advice, judgment, or opinion; a failure to disclose certain types of information intended to induce a consumer to participate in a transaction; an "unconscionable action or course of action that cannot be characterized as advice, judgment, or opinion"; or a "breach of an express warranty that cannot be characterized as advice, judgment, or opinion." *Id.* at § 17.49(c).

In *United Genesis Corp. v. Brown*, 2007 WL 1341358 (Tex. App. 2007), a lawyer prepared closing documents and conducted a lien search using a name for the seller of a restaurant that was provided to the lawyer by a real estate agent. The name was wrong, and therefore the search failed to reveal outstanding liens against the restaurant's equipment. The court held that the buyer could not state a claim against the lawyer under the Texas Deceptive Trade Practices Act. The lawyer's conduct consisted of omissions (*e.g.*, the failure to independently ensure the identity of the seller and that the seller owned the property), not express misrepresentations. Moreover, the court found that the misrepresentation of fact with regard to the ownership of the business was a misrepresentation by the real estate agency, not by the lawyer.

Garden-variety malpractice is not actionable under the Connecticut Unfair Trade Practices Act. "CUTPA covers only the entrepreneurial or commercial aspects of the profession of law." *Haynes v. Yale-New Haven Hosp.*, 243 Conn. 17, 699 A.2d 964, 973 (Conn. 1997). Thus, a claim that a law firm failed to supervise a lawyer who misappropriated client funds was not actionable under the Connecticut statute because it did not involve the entrepreneurial or business aspects of the provision of legal services. *See Vanacore v. Kennedy*, 86 F. Supp. 2d 42, 52 (D. Conn. 1998), *aff'd* 208 F.3d 204 (2d Cir. 2000).

2. Advantages Over Common Law

DTPA laws typically require a showing of deception based on fault. However, the level of culpability that is required may be less demanding than what would be needed in a parallel tort action. Whether that is knowledge of falsity, reckless disregard for the truth, or negligence as to falsity depends on the statute in question.

A DTPA action is sometimes subject to a relaxed causation requirement which obviates the need for a "trial within a trial," and may permit recovery of emotional distress damages that would not normally be recoverable under some common law theories of liability. *See Latham v. Castillo*, 972 S.W.2d 66 (Tex. 1998).

Of great importance, DTPA laws often allow recovery of multiple damages (*e.g.*, treble damages to deter unconscionable conduct) and attorneys fees.

3. DTPA Suits by Nonclients

It is often difficult or impossible for a nonclient to state a DTPA claim because such laws typically require a plaintiff to prove that he or she was a "consumer" of legal services. However, occasional decisions have allowed recovery by persons for whom legal services were purchased by someone else. *Cf. Perez v. Kirk & Carrigan*, 822 S.W.2d 261, 268 (Tex. App. 1991).

E.   CLAIMS BASED ON REPRESENTATION OF FIDUCIARIES

According to the *Restatement*, a lawyer is liable to a nonclient for negligence if:

(a) the lawyer's client is a trustee, guardian, executor, or fiduciary acting primarily to perform similar functions for the nonclient;

(b) the lawyer knows that appropriate action by the lawyer is necessary with respect to a matter within the scope of the representation to prevent or rectify the breach of a fiduciary duty owed by the client to the nonclient, where (i) the breach is a crime or fraud or (ii) the lawyer has assisted or is assisting the breach;

(c) the nonclient is not reasonably able to protect its rights; and

(d) such a duty would not significantly impair the performance of the lawyer's obligations to the client.

In re Food Management Group, LLC, 380 B.R. 677, 708 (Bkrtcy. S.D.N.Y. 2008) (quoting *Restatement (Third) of the Law Governing Lawyers* § 51(4) (2000)).

Thus, if a lawyer is representing a trustee and knows that the trustee intends to embezzle trust assets, the lawyer has a duty to the beneficiary to take reasonable steps to prevent that harm from occurring. *See Restatement (Third) of the Law Governing Lawyers* § 51 illus. 5 (2000).

F.   FUNDS AND PROPERTY OF NONCLIENTS

There is a well-known rule of professional conduct which recognizes that lawyers have *ethical* obligations to nonclients with respect to the handling or disbursement of funds or property in which nonclients have an interest. For example, Rule 1.15 of the Indiana Rules of Professional Conduct, which is identical in relevant part to Rule 1.15 in the American Bar Association's Model Rules of Professional Conduct (2010), states that:

(d) Upon receiving funds or other property in which a client or third person has an interest, a lawyer shall promptly notify the client or third person. Except as stated in this rule or otherwise permitted by law or by agreement with the client, a lawyer shall promptly deliver to the client or third person any funds or other property that the client or third person is entitled to receive and, upon request by the client or third person, shall promptly render a full accounting regarding such property.

(e) When in the course of representation a lawyer is in possession of property in which two or more persons (one of whom may be the lawyer) claim interests, the property shall be kept separate by the lawyer until the dispute is resolved. The lawyer shall promptly distribute all portions of the property as to which the interests are not in dispute.

Ind. Code Ann. Tit. 34 App. Court Rules (Civil) (Westlaw 2010). These types of state rules are enforceable in disciplinary proceedings. A violation may give rise to sanctions such as reprimand, suspension, or disbarment.

However, it is not surprising that nonclients have argued, sometimes with success, that the same professional obligations are *legally* enforceable, on some theory, in a civil action for damages.

In *Hsu v. Parker*, 116 Ohio App.3d 629, 688 N.E.2d 1099 (Ohio Ct. App. 1996), a client who was injured in an auto accident, executed a document entitled "Security Agreement for Medical Services," which granted a doctor "a security interest" in any and all proceeds from the client's pending personal injury action. The agreement authorized the client's lawyer, who had not prepared the assignment, "to withhold sufficient funds from any settlement, judgment, or verdict" that were due to the doctor and to pay such funds to the doctor. When the case was settled, the client instructed her lawyer to transfer all of the settlement proceeds to her and not to pay the doctor's medical fees. The Ohio Court of Appeals held that the lawyer acted improperly in following those instructions and ordered the lawyer to reimburse the doctor. However, the court did not specify the legal theory on which the lawyer was held responsible, other than to emphasize that the lawyer had knowledge of the assignment.

An attorney may be liable to a nonclient for the tort of conversion based on nonpayment of funds to which the nonclient is entitled. For example, in *Ellis v. City of Dallas*, 111 S.W.3d 161 (Tex. App. 2003), a lawyer, Ellis, represented an injured firefighter in a worker's compensation claim against the City and in a lawsuit against a third-party tortfeasor. The settlement check in the lawsuit was made payable to Ellis and his client, and Ellis knew that the City had a subrogation interest in those funds. There was some dispute about the amount to which the City was entitled, and whether the City had agreed to accept a lesser amount. However, the jury resolved those factual issues against the lawyer, and the Texas Court of Appeals affirmed a judgment holding Ellis liable for conversion based on the fact that he paid the City less than the value of its subrogation claim.

In *Smith v. Patout*, 956 So.2d 689 (La. Ct. App. 2007), a Louisiana appellate court concluded that a lawyer had a duty to provide an accounting to the plaintiff regarding funds in which the plaintiff had an interest. This was true even if the plaintiff was not a client. Because there was a factual dispute as to whether such an accounting had occurred, the court concluded that summary judgment could not be granted to the defendant lawyer.

G. INTENDED BENEFICIARIES

Nonclients can sometimes prevail in a malpractice action because they were intended third-party beneficiaries of a lawyer-client contract. The general rule is that a lawyer owes a duty of care to a nonclient when and to the extent that:

(a) the lawyer knows that a client intends as one of the primary objectives of the representation that the lawyer's services benefit the nonclient;

(b) such a duty would not significantly impair the lawyer's performance of obligations to the client; and

(c) the absence of such a duty would make enforcement of those obligations to the client unlikely ***.

Petrine v. Sinchak-Higby, 2009 WL 1530727, *3 (Ariz. Ct. App.) (quoting *Restatement (Third) of the Law Governing Lawyers* § 51(3) (2000)).

1. Invalid Wills

A majority of courts allow the intended beneficiaries of a will to sue for negligence suffered as a result of the negligent preparation of a will or otherwise deficient estate planning. For example, in *Young v. Williams*, 285 Ga. App. 208, 645 S.E.2d 624 (2007), a lawyer neglected to include provisions in a husband's will for distribution of real property. As a result, after the husband died, the real property was disbursed under the rules of intestate succession, and the surviving wife received only one-third of the real property, rather than all of it as the decedent had intended. Addressing applicable law, the Court of Appeals of Georgia wrote:

> [A]n attorney may owe a duty to a party who is not his client, but who is a third-party beneficiary to an agreement between the attorney and his client. For a third party to claim such a duty exists, it must clearly appear from the contract that it was intended for her benefit. The mere fact that the third party would benefit from performance of the agreement is not alone sufficient.

645 S.E.2d at 625. Finding that it was clear that the decedent had hired the defendant lawyer so that certain persons would inherit particular property upon his death, the court affirmed a judgment against the lawyer in favor of the surviving wife.

a. Minority View

On the facts of the case, the issue before the court in *Young* (discussed above) was not difficult. The defendant lawyer admitted that the deceased husband had intended for the will to benefit the husband's wife in the amount that she claimed. The lawyer merely asserted (unsuccessfully) that the surviving wife could not sue him because there was no privity of contract between the wife and the lawyer. However, in many cases, the facts are less clear as to what the decedent intended. These types of uncertainties have caused a minority of courts to reject malpractice claims by estate beneficiaries.

For example, in *Barcelo v. Elliott*, 923 S.W.2d 575 (Tex. 1996), the Texas Supreme Court explained:

In most cases where a defect renders a will or trust invalid, *** there are concomitant questions as to the true intentions of the testator. Suppose, for example, that a properly drafted will is simply not executed at the time of the testator's death. The document may express the testator's true intentions, lacking signatures solely because of the attorney's negligent delay. On the other hand, the testator may have postponed execution because of second thoughts regarding the distribution scheme. ***.

*** [Here, plaintiffs] contend that Elliott was negligent in failing to fund the trust during Barcelo's lifetime, and in failing to obtain a signature from the trustee. These alleged deficiencies, however, could have existed pursuant to Barcelo's instructions, which may have been based on advice from her attorneys attempting to represent her best interests. An attorney's ability to render such advice would be severely compromised if the advice could be second-guessed by persons named as beneficiaries under the unconsummated trust.

923 S.W.2d at 578. Finding it impossible to "craft a bright-line rule that allows a lawsuit to proceed where alleged malpractice causes a will or trust to fail in a manner that casts no real doubt on the testator's intentions, while prohibiting actions in other situations," the Texas Supreme Court concluded that the greater good would be served by denying a cause of action to all beneficiaries whom the attorney did not represent. *Id.*

2. Insurers

An insurer who hires a lawyer to defend an insured, and who suffers losses as a result of the lawyer's negligence, is sometimes permitted to sue for malpractice on the ground that the insurer was an intended beneficiary of the contract. As a federal court in West Virginia explained:

> Recognizing that the lawyer owes a duty to the insurer promotes enforcement of the lawyer's obligations to the insured. However, such a duty does not arise when it would significantly impair *** the lawyer's performance of obligations to the insured. For example, if the lawyer recommends acceptance of a settlement offer just below the policy limits and the insurer accepts the offer, the insurer may not later seek to recover from the lawyer on a claim that a competent lawyer in the circumstances would have advised that the offer be rejected. ***.

State and County Mut. Fire Ins. Co. v. Young, 490 F. Supp. 2d 741, 744 (N.D. W. Va. 2007) (quoting *Re-*

statement (Third) of the Law Governing Lawyers § 51 cmt. g (2000)).

However, not all states agree that an insurer should be treated as an intended beneficiary of the lawyer-client contract. According to a federal court in Virginia:

> [While the] *** courts of other jurisdictions generally recognize such a cause of action, they differ markedly on the theory of liability under which such a claim may be brought. In most jurisdictions, the retaining insurer may sue the law firm directly as its client. *** [Some cases] reflect the view that a "tripartite relationship" exists among insurer, insured, and counsel, with both insurer and insured as co-clients of the firm in the absence of a conflict of interest. ***. Some courts and the *Restatement* recognize an additional or substitute cause of action by the insurer as a non-client beneficiary of the firm's legal services. Both theories of liability, of course, depend on the existence of a duty of care running from the firm to the retaining insurer, and acknowledge that such a duty disappears when a conflict of interest threatens the firm's ability to represent the insured. Some jurisdictions go one step further, however, and reject outright the idea of a duty owed by the firm to the insurer, contending that such a duty would compromise the law firm's loyalty to the insured. Although these rejecting jurisdictions thus preclude any direct legal malpractice liability from the firm to the insurer, they nevertheless permit the insurer to be subrogated to the insured and thus to sue the firm standing

in the insured's shoes. Accordingly, despite sharp doctrinal differences regarding the relationship between the insurer and the firm it retains, nearly all jurisdictions in the United States permit some form of legal malpractice action by an insurer against the firm it retains to defend an insured.

General Sec. Ins. Co. v. Jordan, Coyne & Savits, LLP, 357 F. Supp. 2d 951, 956-57 (E.D. Va. 2005).

In *State and County Mut. Fire Ins. Co. v. Young*, 490 F. Supp. 2d 741 (N.D. W.Va. 2007), a lawyer hired to defend an insured failed to respond to discovery and dispositive motions. As result, the insurer alleged that it was forced to settle the underlying claims for amounts in excess of their true value. The court held that since the insurer hired the lawyer, it could sue to recover its losses without any need to show additional evidence of a duty.

3. Other Intended Beneficiaries

Lawyers are often asked by clients to furnish opinion letters assuring nonclients about legal aspects of proposed transactions, such as tax consequences or the presence of liens. The recipients of such letters qualify as intended beneficiaries of the lawyer-client relationship and may therefore sue the authoring lawyer for harm caused by the failure to exercise care. *See Restatement (Third) of the Law Governing Lawyers* §§ 51(2) & 52 illus. 2 (2000).

Cases occasionally focus more on whether reliance was expected than on whether it was intended. For example, in *Estate of Spencer v. Gavin*, 400 N.J.

Super. 220, 946 A.2d 1051 (N.J. Super. Ct. App. Div. 2008), a lawyer represented three interrelated estates of a mother and her two daughters. A second lawyer, who was enlisted by the first lawyer, did a small amount of work related to one of the estates, but no work at all for the other two estates. A New Jersey appellate court held that if the second lawyer learned that the first lawyer was misappropriating funds from the three estates, he could be liable to all three estates for harm caused by not disclosing that information. The estate for which the second lawyer did legal work was a client, so there were clear grounds for liability based on failure to reveal material information (such as, presumably, actions for negligence, breach of fiduciary, fraud, and negligent misrepresentation). Although the other two estates were nonclients, the court found that they too could state a claim for damages. As the court explained, "an attorney may be liable to a nonclient in certain situations where the attorney knows, or should know, that the nonclient will rely on the attorney." Because the estates of the three close family members were interrelated in terms of their disposition of assets, such reliance was to be expected.

Nevertheless, it must be emphasized that, in many cases, it is difficult for a nonclient to establish the right to sue as an intended third-party beneficiary. For example, in *Breen v. Law Office of Bruce A. Barket, P.C.*, 52 A.D.3d 635, 862 N.Y.S.2d 50, 52-53 (2008), a New York court concluded, in the context of a divorce action, that a wife, who was represented by her own lawyer, was at most an incidental beneficiary of the retainer agreement between her husband and his lawyer.

In *Sutton v. Llewellyn*, 2006 WL 3371623 (N.D. Cal. 2006), a lawyer was appointed as counsel to an elderly woman in her conservatorship proceedings. After the woman passed away, her surviving family members sued the lawyer for legal malpractice and other wrongful conduct. They alleged that the lawyer had bankrupted the estate and kept the elderly woman away from her home and family, even though the woman had allegedly wanted to move to New York to be with them. In granting judgment on the pleadings for the lawyer on the professional negligence claim, a federal court in California wrote:

> In determining whether a legal duty exists, the main inquiry is "whether the principal purpose of the attorney's retention [was] to provide legal services for the benefit of the plaintiff." ***. Try as they might to characterize them otherwise, plaintiffs' allegations arise entirely from [lawyer] Nicora's performance of professional services as *counsel for Rose* [the elderly woman] in her conservatorship proceeding. Nicora performed these legal services to benefit Rose, not plaintiffs.
>
> Plaintiffs claim, however, "[t]he minute that *** [Rose] requested the right to live with her children, plaintiffs became third party beneficiaries of the attorney-client relationship to provide legal services." ***. This argument, while creative, is without support in case law. ***. Finding a duty outside of the estate planning context is rare. ***.

Plaintiffs' allegations are insufficient to establish that they were the intended beneficiaries of Nicora's services. First, Rose's will is not before the court and there is no trust at issue. Moreover, Nicora was appointed counsel for Rose in her conservatorship ***, and "[t]he purpose of a conservatorship is to enable a competent person to assist the *conservatee* in the management of [her] property." ***. Hence, the only intended beneficiary of Nicora's legal services was Rose.

Id. at *3.

H. DUTIES TO CO-COUNSEL

1. In General

One particular category of nonclients is the other lawyers with whom one works. This includes partners or associates in one's firm, as well as lawyers outside the firm who serve as co-counsel on cases.

To a limited extent, legally enforceable obligations are owed to other lawyers. As noted in Chapter 4 (Part F), a lawyer may be liable to other members of the lawyer's firm for breach of fiduciary duties. And, as will be discussed in Chapter 7 (Part E), lawyers who are subject to liability for malpractice may sometimes assert reimbursement claims against other lawyers seeking indemnity or contribution.

However, legal duties to other lawyers must not conflict with the duties to clients. As discussed below, this may mean that one lawyer has no duty to protect the interest of another lawyer in earning a contingent fee.

2. Protecting Fee Interests

Several recent cases suggest that lawyers do not have an obligation to protect the fee interests of co-counsel. Thus, in *Mazon v. Krafchick*, 158 Wash. 2d 440, 144 P.3d 1168 (2006), the Supreme Court of Washington held that there are no duties between co-counsel that will allow recovery for lost or reduced prospective fees. As the court explained, "decisions about how to pursue a case must be based on the client's best interests, not the attorneys'." 144 P.3d at 1172. According to the court, the "undivided duty of loyalty means that each attorney owes a duty to pursue the case in the client's best interests, even if that means not completing the case and forgoing a potential contingency fee." *Id*.

Of course, there are limits to any no-duty rule. Recall from the preceding chapter that a lawyer in a firm may be liable for a firm's loss of fees due to surreptitious diversion and usurpage of a potential engagement. (*See* Chapter 4 Part F.)

It might be argued that no harm would be done by recognizing a claim by co-counsel for lost fees if that claim is entirely consistent with the interests of the client. However, thus far, courts have generally not focused on whether lost-fee claims are consistent with, or adverse to, the interests of the client. Rather, they have tended to adopt black-and-white no-duty rules.

In *Beck v. Wecht*, 28 Cal. 4th 289, 48 P.3d 417, 121 Cal. Rptr. 384 (2002), three lawyers, *B*, *M*, and *W*, served as co-counsel to clients in a personal injury case. The night before closing arguments at trial, with a $6 million settlement offer from the defendants on the table, the clients decided to settle. At a meeting with *M* and *W*, they instructed *M* to contact the defendant to arrange a settlement. However, *M* never followed those instructions. Then, at trial, the jury ruled for the defense.

Subsequently, the clients sued *M* and *W* for malpractice, and *B* sued *W* to recover the share of the contingent fee that he would have received if the case had been settled for $6 million. (*M* had already paid *B* a settlement.)

The California Supreme Court rejected *B's* claim for lost-fees. Adopting a bright-line rule, the court held that it "would be contrary to public policy to countenance actions based on the theory that co-counsel have a fiduciary duty to protect one another's prospective interests in a contingency fee."

It is difficult to see how recognizing *B's* claim would have interfered with the representation of the client. *M* and *W* (because *W* was vicariously liable for *M's* conduct under joint venture principles) had a duty to follow their clients' instructions to settle the case. That was precisely the same argument that *B* was making.

I. LIABILITY TO ADVERSE PARTIES

1. General Rule: No Duty

A lawyer's duties run mainly to clients, not to opposing parties. Therefore, a lawyer representing a person on one side of a transaction or litigation rarely has an obligation to protect the interests of a person on the other side. Because there is usually no duty to exercise care, there is no liability. As a practical matter, this makes good sense. The undivided loyalty that a lawyer owes to a client would be greatly impaired by the easy recognition of obligations to protect a client's adversaries.

The fact that liability to adverse clients is rarely imposed does not mean such claims are not filed. In *DeFelice v. Costagliola*, 25 Misc. 3d 278, 882 N.Y.S.2d 882 (N.Y. City Civ. Ct. 2009), the buyer of a premises who later encountered furnace problems sued the seller's lawyer—apparently because the seller was unavailable to be sued, having moved from the jurisdiction. In concluding that the claim was "completely baseless," a New York court wrote:

> Claimant admitted that he had no contractual relationship with the defendant; that the defendant was not his attorney; that the defendant made no representations as to the working order of any systems in the house ***. This is another case of what appears to be a disturbing trend of litigation being brought by persons suing attorneys who did not represent them for that attorney's proper representation of his or her client. The theory behind bringing these baseless legal actions being that owing to the small amount of money involved, the lawyer would pay the claim rather than engage in the cost of litigation.

Id. at 884. The court rejected the plaintiff's claim and granted the defendant lawyer's counterclaim for damages resulting from frivolous litigation.

2. Malicious Prosecution and Malicious Use of Process

Although many claims by adverse clients fail because of lack of duty or privilege (*see* Chapter 7 Part G), some claims do succeed. As noted earlier in this chapter, a lawyer may be liable to an adverse party for fraud (*see* Part B) or for negligent misrepresentation (*see* Part C). Those causes of action are very significant exceptions to the general rule of no liability. Less important, because it usually fails, is the cause of action for malicious use of process (or what is sometimes called malicious prosecution). This cause of action can be brought by nonclient against a lawyer who unsuccessfully represented a client in a lawsuit (as well as against the client personally).

a. Elements

To recover for malicious misuse of process, a plaintiff must generally prove that (1) an underlying action was commenced by the defendant, (2) with malice, and (3) without probable cause, and that the action (4) was terminated on the merits in favor of the plaintiff and (5) caused damages. It is normally very difficult to establish all of these elements. Actions against lawyers rarely succeed because the plaintiff must prove that the lawyer knew the underlying action was baseless and that the lawyer, personally, had an improper purpose.

Spite, ill-will, or vindictiveness will generally satisfy the malice requirement. In addition, acting for an improper purpose (such as to coerce an adversary to settle a dispute or sell a piece of land) will also suffice. However, a lawyer is not liable for malicious misuse of process if the lawyer acts primarily to help the client obtain a proper adjudication of the client's claim. *See Restatement (Third) of the Law Governing Lawyers* § 57(2) (2000).

Lack of probable cause means that there was no reasonable basis, in law and in fact, for the defendant to believe that the claim could succeed. According to the American Law Institute, a "decision by a competent tribunal upholding the client's claim on the merits is ordinarily conclusive evidence of probable cause, even if it is reversed on appeal ***." *Restatement (Third) of the Law Governing Lawyers* § 57 cmt. d (2000).

With respect to damages, some courts say that, if the underlying action was civil, the plaintiff must allege a "special grievance." Thus, the New Jersey Supreme Court explained:

> the special grievance is designed to take the place of the injurious effects, including arrest, restraint, or the attendant humiliation of being held on bail, finger-printed, and photographed, that ordinarily flow from a wrongfully instituted criminal charge.

LoBiondo v. Schwartz, 199 N.J. 62, 970 A.2d 1007, 1023 (N.J. 2009). Interference with the constitutional rights of speech, press, and petition, are among the things which establish "special grievance." *Id.* at 1012. However, other courts do not require proof of a special grievance and permit recovery for harm to reputation, emotional distress, expenses incurred, and interference with legally protected interests. *See Restatement (Second) of Torts* § 681 (1977).

b. Terminology

In some jurisdictions, a distinction is carefully drawn based on the criminal or civil nature of the underlying action. Misuse of *criminal* processes can give rise to an action for malicious prosecution. *Cf. Restatement (Second) of Torts* §§ 653-71 (1977). In contrast, misuse of *civil* litigation is actionable as malicious use of process. *Cf. id.* §§ 674-681B. In other places, authorities use the term "malicious prosecution" to encompass misuse of civil proceedings. *See Franklin Mint Co. v. Manatt, Phelps & Phillips, LLP*, 184 Cal. App. 4th 313, 109 Cal. Rptr. 3d 143 (2010).

There are other terminological complexities. The *Restatement* differentiates between "wrongful *use* of civil proceedings" and "*abuse* of process." *Restatement (Second) of Torts* §§ 674-82 (1977) (emphasis added). Consequently, particular care must be exercised in reviewing precedent in this area of the law.

c. Advice of Counsel Defense and Related Claims Against Lawyers

In *LoBiondo v. Schwartz*, 199 N.J. 62, 970 A.2d 1007 (N.J. 2009), malicious use of process claims were filed against both a client who had sued a neighbor for defamation and the client's lawyers. The defamation claim, which was ultimately found to be without merit, was based on the neighbor's opposition to the client's proposed business expansion and related requests for governmental approval. As a defense to the malicious use of process charge, the client argued that it was immune from suit because it had acted on advice of counsel. The Supreme Court of New Jersey acknowledged that advice of counsel is a long-recognized complete defense, but took care to articulate its requirements. As the court explained:

> The advice-of-counsel defense *** has its own set of proof requirements. To claim its benefit, the original plaintiff must prove that he or she relied on counsel's advice and that the advice was given after a full and fair presentation to counsel of all of the relevant facts. ***. "Full and fair" means disclosure to counsel of all information known to the original plaintiff that could justify or militate against the filing of the proposed cause of action. ***. In this context, if any of the facts so reported to counsel were known to the original plaintiff to be false, the advice-of-counsel defense will not operate as a shield against the claim.

970 A.2d at 1025. Satisfactory proof that the client acted on advice of counsel defeats a malicious use of process action because it proves that the client acted with probable cause in the underlying litigation.

The *LoBiondo* court further held that if, and only if, a client sued for malicious use of process raises an advice of counsel defense, the client's lawyer can be sued on the same grounds. After reviewing precedent establishing that lawyers are subject to ethical rules and penalties for frivolous litigation, and rarely have a legal duty to nonclients, the court wrote:

> Our decision to permit the nonclient to proceed against the attorney [for malicious use of process] is a limited one ***. [W]e limit the cause of action to the circumstance in which the client has first raised the defense of advice of counsel in order to prevent the claim from being used for purposes of

creating an adverse relationship between counsel and client. Because we recognize that the attorney's first duty is to zealously represent the client, and because an attorney faced with a claim of malicious use of process may as a practical matter be unable to mount a defense by reason of the bounds of confidentiality or privilege, we limit the grounds for the claim to those in which the client has already called the attorney's advice into issue. Fairness demands no less.

970 A.2d at 1031. *LoBiondo* demonstrates that in some jurisdictions, a malicious use of process claim cannot be asserted against a lawyer, unless the client has also been sued and has raised an advice of counsel defense.

In *LoBiondo*, the underlying defamation action was a SLAPP suit (a Strategic Lawsuit Against Public Participation), which under the law of many states is subject to early dismissal because of the protections afforded to speech on public issues by the First Amendment. The subsequent claim for malicious use of process was referred to by the New Jersey Supreme Court as a SLAPP-back suit. Consequently, there is reason to think that cases which successfully invoke SLAPP laws to protect speech on public issues are the type of cases which may give rise to malicious use of process claims against lawyers.

J. SECURITIES LAW VIOLATIONS

Lawyers are sometimes liable to nonclients under state or federal securities laws. Under federal Rule 10b-5, it is unlawful to make "any untrue statement of a material fact or to omit to state a material fact necessary in order to make the statements made, in light of the circumstances under which they were made, not misleading *** in connection with the purchase or sale of any security." 17 C.F.R. § 240.10b-5 (Westlaw 2010); *see also* 15 U.S.C. § 78j(b) (Westlaw 2010).

It is difficult for a nonclient to maintain an action against a lawyer based on violation of federal securities laws. Nevertheless, some claims succeed. In *Media General, Inc. v. Tomlin*, 532 F.3d 854 (D.C. Cir. 2008), the D.C. Circuit found that a law firm which had been actively involved with concealing a contingent liability in connection with the sale of a business was subject to liability for both common law fraud and securities fraud.

1. "Aiding and Abetting" and "Scheme" Liability

In *Central Bank of Denver, N.A. v. First Interstate Bank of Denver, N. A.*, 511 U.S. 164, 191, 114 S. Ct. 1439, 128 L. Ed. 2d 119 (1994), the Supreme Court ruled that there is no liability for merely aiding and abetting a violation of the federal securities laws. However, the court acknowledged that "[a]ny person or entity, including a lawyer, *** who employs a manipulative device or makes a material misstatement (or omission) on which a purchaser or seller of securities relies may be liable as a primary violator under 10b-5, assuming *all* of the requirements for primary liability under Rule 10b-5 are met."

More recently, the Supreme Court has emphasized that, in order to be recoverable, economic losses must be directly linked to a defendant's misrepresentations. In *Stoneridge Investment Partners, LLC v. Scientific Atlanta, Inc.* 552 U.S. 148, 128 S. Ct. 761, 169 L. Ed. 2d 627 (2008), an action by investors against a corporation, its executives, an independent auditor, and the corporation's vendors and customers, the Supreme Court ruled that the investors had failed to show that they had relied upon deceptive behind-the-scenes behavior when purchasing stock. Thus, the court greatly limited what some authorities had called "scheme liability." The court wrote:

["Scheme liability"] does not answer the objection that petitioner did not in fact rely upon respondents' own deceptive conduct.

Liability is appropriate, petitioner contends, because respondents engaged in conduct with the purpose and effect of creating a false appearance of material fact to further a scheme to misrepresent Charter's revenue. The argument is that the financial statement Charter released to the public was a natural and expected consequence of respondents' deceptive acts; had respondents not assisted Charter, Charter's auditor would not have been fooled, and the financial statement would have been a more accurate reflection of Charter's financial condition. ****

In effect petitioner contends that in an efficient market investors rely not only upon the public statements relating to a security but also upon the transactions those statements reflect. Were this concept of reliance to be adopted, the implied cause of action would reach the whole marketplace in which the issuing company does business; and there is no authority for this rule.

*** [W]e conclude respondents' deceptive acts, which were not disclosed to the investing public, are too remote to satisfy the requirement of reliance. It was Charter, not respondents, that misled its auditor and filed fraudulent financial statements; nothing respondents did made it necessary or inevitable for Charter to record the transactions as it did.

552 U.S. at 160-61.

K. FAIR DEBT COLLECTION PRACTICES

The federal Fair Debt Collection Practices Act (FDCPA) proscribes a wide range of abusive conduct related to debt collection. *See* 15 U.S.C. §§ 1692A–1692K (Westlaw 2010) (FDCPA). Persons injured by an intentional violation of its terms may maintain a civil cause of action against an offending debt collector for actual damages (including emotional distress), costs, attorney fees, and, in the case of an individual plaintiff, additional damages not exceeding $1000.

The FDCPA restricts communications by debt collectors with debtors and third persons, and compels certain written disclosures. Section 1692c provides in part:

[A] debt collector may not communicate with a consumer in connection with the collection of any debt—(1) at any unusual time or place or a time or place known or which should be known to be inconvenient to the consumer *** [or] (3) at the consumer's place of employment if the debt collector knows or has reason to know that the consumer's employer prohibits the consumer from receiving such communication.

In addition, section 1692d provides:

A debt collector may not engage in any conduct the natural consequence of which is to harass, oppress, or abuse any person in connection with the collection of a debt. Without limiting the general application of the foregoing, the following conduct is a violation of this section:

(1) The use or threat of use of violence or other criminal means to harm the physical person, reputation, or property of any person.

(2) The use of obscene or profane language or language the natural consequence of which is to abuse the hearer or reader.

(3) The publication of a list of consumers who allegedly refuse to pay debts, except to a consumer reporting agency or to persons ***[who lawfully may receive reports from such agencies].

(4) The advertisement for sale of any debt to coerce payment of the debt.

(5) Causing a telephone to ring or engaging any person in telephone conversation repeatedly or continuously with intent to annoy, abuse, or harass any person at the called number.

(6) Except as provided in section 1692b of this title [which imposes limitations on collection of information about the location of a consumer], the placement of telephone calls without meaningful disclosure of the caller's identity.

The requirements of the Fair Debt Collection Practices Act apply to a lawyer or law firm that "regularly" collects debts on behalf of third parties. *See Heintz v. Jenkins*, 514 U.S. 291, 115 S. Ct. 1489, 131 L. Ed. 2d 395 (1995). Thus, a lawyer may be liable for the misleading nature of debt collection letters sent on creditor's behalf. In *Lesher v. Law Office of Mitchell N. Kay, P.C.*, 2009 WL 3487795 (M.D. Pa. 2009), a federal court in Pennsylvania held that a lawyer's letter advising a debtor that payments were due was misleading in that it gave the debtor the impression that legal action would be taken if the debt was not settled. In fact, as language buried in the body of the letter pointed out, no lawyer with the firm had reviewed the circumstances of the account at the time the letter was mailed.

Some states have also enacted statutes which impose additional limitations on debt collection practices.

CHAPTER SIX

REMEDIES FOR LEGAL MALPRACTICE

A. COMPENSATORY DAMAGES

1. Basic Rules

No matter how serious a lawyer's error, a malpractice plaintiff may recover damages only if the error caused harm. Thus, even if a lawyer fails to adequately investigate the facts of a case, there is no liability if the settlement the lawyer recommended was a good one. *See Restatement (Third) of the Law Governing Lawyers* § 52 cmt. c (2000).

a. No Speculation

Malpractice damages must always be proved with reasonable certainty. This means that a jury must be provided with evidence that will support a finding, without speculation, of what losses the plaintiff sustained. While this basic rule is simple, there are many ways in which plaintiffs come up short of its requirements.

In some cases, the plaintiff simply fails to introduce evidence of harm. For example, in *United Genesis Corp. v. Brown*, 2007 WL 1341358, *2 (Tex. App.), the Texas Court of Appeals held that a conclusory assertion, unsupported by evidence, that alleged malpractice caused $75,000 in damages was insufficient to raise a fact issue to defeat the defendant's motion for summary judgment.

In other cases, the plaintiff errs by failing to link evidence of harm to the alleged malpractice. Thus, in *Talmage v. Harris*, 486 F.3d 968 (7th Cir. 2007), a lawyer's negligence meant that the plaintiff was unable to pursue a bad faith claim against an insurance company (United Fire) related to the destruction of a shop. In a subsequent malpractice action, the plaintiff sought to recover damages for the interest he had been charged. As the Seventh Circuit explained:

> Talmage's theory was that United Fire's delays and under-payments required him to carry large balances on his credit cards, for which he paid a substantial amount of interest. The only evidence Talmage offered on this point was a report from his accounting expert *** [which] displayed and quantified the interest charges that he paid during the period after the shop was destroyed. It does not, however, segregate charges related to the reconstruction from other charges he may have incurred during that period. This evidence fell so far short of anything revealing a causal link between the interest paid and United Fire's alleged bad faith that the district court properly kept it from the jury.

486 F.3d at 975.

In some cases, there are too many unconvincing links in the causation chain to make ascertainment of damages reasonably certain. For example, in *GUS Consulting GMBH v. Chadbourne & Parke LLP*, 74 A.D.3d 677, 905 N.Y.S.2d 158 (2010), Austrian clients alleged that an American law firm had failed to properly advise it that the use of a certain business structure would expose them to criminal investigation and possible prosecution in the Russian Federation, where they were investing in natural gas operations. In rejecting the $500 million suit, a New York appellate court concluded that the plaintiffs' contention that they would have changed or ceased their use of the business structure, and would have been able to maintain and grow their business in Russia over the next six years while the Russian economy rebounded, was too speculative to support a legal malpractice claim.

Finally, in some cases, proof of damages fails because there is no way of knowing what someone would have done. For example, *Rudolf v. Shayne, Dachs, Staniscl, Corker & Sauer*, 8 N.Y.3d 438, 867 N.E.2d 385, 835 N.Y.S.2d 534 (2007), was a malpractice action that arose from the mishandling of an auto accident claim. At the first trial, the jury was erroneously instructed on the duties of pedestrians. The result was a jury verdict for $255,000, which was reduced by 50% based on the plaintiff's comparative negligence. At a second trial intended to cure the erroneous charge, the jury was properly instructed. However, before a verdict was returned, the parties settled the case for $750,000. In the subsequent malpractice action based on the original lawyer's failure to object to the erroneous instruction, the New York Court of Appeals denied the plaintiff's request for compensatory damages for interest that could have been earned from investment of the judgment if $750,000 had been awarded at the first trial. The court reasoned that the "plaintiff's assertion that, had the proper instruction been charged, the first jury would have awarded $750,000—instead of the $255,000 it actually awarded—is pure speculation." 867 N.E.2d at 388.

b. Proximately Caused Losses

Legal malpractice tort actions are subject to the usual principles of causation. In order to be recoverable, damages must have been factually and proximately caused by the defendant's tortious conduct. (*See* Chapter 3 Part C.)

The particular components of compensatory damages vary from case to case, depending on what the plaintiff lost. With proper factual support, an award might include amounts for:

- the loss of a transaction's intended tax advantages (*see, e.g., Williams v. Lakin*, 2007 WL 1170597, *3 (N.D. Okla.));

- loss of "control" of a corporation (*cf. Price v. Ragland*, 966 So.2d 246 (Ala. 2007)); and

- prejudgment interest on amounts that should have been received earlier (*see* Part A-1-f of this Chapter).

c. Emotional Distress Damages

Compensation for emotional distress is generally not available in a legal malpractice action based on *negligence.* Thus, if a lawyer provides negligently incorrect advice about a child visitation order, a client ordinarily cannot recover compensation for mental anguish, even if emotional distress in fact results. *See Long-Russell v. Hampe*, 2002 Wy. 16, 39 P.3d 1015, 1019-20 (2002). This is not surprising for, in the law of torts generally, negligent infliction of emotional distress is actionable only in a narrow range of cases.

However, there are exceptions to the rule. For example, if emotional distress arising from a lawyer's lack of care is not just a possibility, but a special probability, compensation for emotional harm may be recoverable as an aspect of compensatory damages. This may be true, for example, if a lawyer's negligence results in a client's imprisonment. *See Restatement (Third) of the Law Governing Lawyers* § 53 cmt. g (2000).

Emotional distress resulting from *intentionally* tortious conduct is more readily compensable than similar harm based on *negligence.* This is true because deliberate victimization of a potential plaintiff not only makes such harm more likely to result, but warrants deterrence through imposition of liability for emotional distress damages.

Malpractice claims for *breach of contract* seldom support an award of emotional distress damages. Such losses do not qualify as consequential damages under principles of contract law and are actionable only if there is an independent tort.

d. Harm to Reputation

Damages for harm to the plaintiff's reputation are not often available in legal malpractice actions. The critical question is whether such losses were a foreseeable and probable consequence of the defendant's conduct. This standard is more easily satisfied if the defendant *intended* to cause such harm, than if the defendant was merely careless. However, occasional cases permit recovery of reputation damages in actions for *negligent* malpractice. Thus, if it can be said that, but for a lawyer's negligence, a doctor would not have been found liable for medical malpractice, the doctor may be permitted to garner compensation for harm to his or her professional reputation.

e. Attorney's Fees as Compensatory Damages

Whether a malpractice plaintiff can recover attorney's fees depends on the reason they were incurred. In this regard, it is possible to distinguish at least four categories: (1) fees paid in the legal malpractice action itself; (2) fees paid in the earlier representation giving rise to the malpractice claim; (3) fees that would have been recovered in earlier litigation but for the malpractice; and (4) fees paid to remedy or mitigate the consequences of the defendant lawyer's malpractice. Attorney's fees falling within the first category are generally not recoverable as compensatory damages. The contrary is true regarding attorney's fees falling within the last two categories, provided that the fees are reasonable. The recoverability of attorney's fees falling into the second category depends on whether the lawyer properly rendered the services that were due. These issues are discussed below.

(1) Attorney's Fees Incurred in the Malpractice Action

Addressing category one, the *Restatement* notes that there are exceptions to the general rule against recovery of malpractice action attorney's fees. Thus, "many jurisdictions allow recovery of attorney's fees against a plaintiff or defendant that litigates in bad faith ***." *Restatement (Third) of the Law Governing Lawyers* § 53 cmt. f (2000). Under Mississippi law, if a malpractice award against a lawyer includes punitive damages, attorney's fees are also recoverable. *See Duggins v. Guardianship of Washington*, 632 So. 2d 420, 431 (Miss. 1993). As noted in Chapter 5 (Part D), malpractice that amounts to a deceptive trade practice frequently entitles a plaintiff to an award of attorney's fees, in addition to compensatory damages.

(2) Attorney's Fees Incurred in Earlier Representation

As to attorney's fees paid in the underlying representation, courts have often denied recovery. *See Jones v. Link*, 493 F. Supp. 2d 765, 771 (E.D. Va. 2007). That would seem to be the appropriate result if the underlying work was properly performed. However, some cases apply the general rule barring recovery even if the lawyer's work was clearly infirm.

For example, in *Jones*, the defendant lawyer had failed to object to a five-level enhancement of punishment. As a result, his client was sentenced to 36-extra months of imprisonment. The sentencing error was later corrected through post-conviction proceedings, which established that the client had received ineffective assistance of counsel. Nevertheless, the client was not permitted to recover, in a malpractice action, the attorney's fees he had paid his lawyer for the initial representation.

In many instances, the reason the lawyer is being sued for malpractice is that services were not performed or were performed badly. In those kinds of cases, in some states, the fees paid by the client may be recoverable as compensatory damages. Arguably, they should be.

(3) Attorney's Fees Not Recovered in Earlier Litigation

Some types of claims entitle a plaintiff to recover attorney's fees in addition to other damages. Thus, if as a result of malpractice a claim is lost, one of the consequences of the lawyer's misconduct is the loss of the attorney's fees that would have been reimbursed if the claim had been successful. In these kinds of cases, the lost attorney's fees are generally compensable.

For example in *Cadle Co. v. Sweet & Brosseau, P.C.*, 2007 WL 1958915 (N.D. Tex.), a federal court in Texas permitted recovery not only of the damages that the plaintiff should have recovered in a suit on a promissory note, but also the amount of attorney's fees that it paid the defendants. The court reasoned that both amounts would have been recovered in the underlying action but for the defendants' negligence.

(4) Attorney's Fees Incurred to Remedy or Mitigate Malpractice

Fees incurred in an effort to remedy or mitigate the consequences of a lawyer's malpractice are generally recoverable. For example, suppose that a document drafted by the lawyer is invalid and unenforceable, and that legal proceedings must be commenced to reform the document by correcting the lawyer's errors. The attorney's fees paid by the plaintiff related to the reformation will be treated as an element of consequential damages, and will be recoverable, provided they are reasonable in amount.

In *Rudolf v. Shayne, Dachs, Staniscl, Corker & Sauer*, 8 N.Y.3d 438, 867 N.E.2d 385, 835 N.Y.S.2d 534 (2007), a lawyer failed to object at trial to an erroneous instruction to the jury. "The erroneous charge forced the plaintiff to hire new counsel to move to set aside the verdict ***, pursue an appeal *** and retain expert witnesses to testify at the second trial." 867 N.E.2d at 388. Finding that these steps would not have been necessary but for the original lawyer's negligence, the New York Court of Appeals permitted recovery of these fees and expenses in the subsequent malpractice action.

However, it is important to be precise as to whether a client was forced to incur attorney's fees as a result of malpractice, as opposed to other factors. For example, in *Akin, Gump, Strauss, Hauer & Feld, L.L.P. v. National Development and Research*, 299

S.W.3d 106, 122 (Tex. 2009) (*NDR*), a law firm's failure to request inclusion of necessary questions in a jury charge preceded an appeal. In a subsequent malpractice action, the plaintiff sought to recover as damages the costs of appealing an adverse judgment, including the expenses of hiring law professors as consultants to focus on the jury charge. The Texas Supreme Court refused to allow recovery of attorney's fees and expenses related to the appeal generally because, even if the charge had been correct and the malpractice plaintiff had prevailed in the underlying action, the plaintiff might have been required to defend its judgment on appeal. It could not be said that but for the law firm's negligence, there would not have been an appeal. However, the court further ruled that, if properly supported by relevant evidence, the costs related to the retention of the law professors were recoverable. But for the errors in the jury charge, it would not have been necessary to hire experts to focus on the charge.

f. Adjustments to Damages

(1) Reduction to Present Value

Legal malpractice damages are sometimes intended to compensate the plaintiff for losses that will not occur until various points in the future. This would be true, for example, if a lawyer's negligence causes the loss of periodic payments under an annuity.

As in other types of tort cases, compensation for future losses is reduced to present value. Thus, a plaintiff may not recover now the total value of future losses, but only a reduced amount which, if safely invested, would generate sufficient compensation to fully pay future losses at the date those losses would accrue.

(2) Prejudgment Interest

Damages in a legal malpractice action may be intended to reimburse the plaintiff for losses that accrued long before a judgment was entered. The delay in the receipt of those amounts has deprived the plaintiff of the time value of money. To remedy this loss, prejudgment interest may be awarded in addition to the usual amounts of compensatory damages. *See Cadle Co. v. Sweet & Brosseau, P.C.*, 2007 WL 1958915 (N.D. Tex.).

In most states, the calculation of prejudgment interest is regulated by statute. Often, such awards are not a matter of entitlement, but of judicial discretion. This allows a court to take into account which party bears responsibility for delays in the litigation process.

g. Collectibility

(1) Treated as the Plaintiff's Burden

In some states, a plaintiff suing with respect to malpractice committed in earlier litigation must prove that damages related to an underlying action would have been collectible. *See, e.g., Williams v. Kublick*, 41 A.D.3d 1193, 837 N.Y.S.2d 803 (2007). Obviously, it may be hugely important to a malpractice plaintiff whether a state subscribes to this rule, and, if so, what specifically the rule requires.

Cases sometimes address the plaintiff's burden of proving collectibility in detail. Thus, in *Akin, Gump, Strauss, Hauer & Feld, L.L.P. v. National Development and Research*, 299 S.W.3d 106 (Tex. 2009), the Texas Supreme Court specified that "(1) the amount of damages that would have been collectible in the prior suit is the greater of the amount of a judgment for damages that would have been either paid or collected from the underlying defendant's net assets; and (2) the time at which collectibility is determined is as of or after the time a judgment was first signed in the underlying case." 299 S.W.3d at 109. Further, the court explained, "[g]enerally, *** the amount that would have been collectible in regard to an underlying judgment *** will be the greater of either (1) the fair market value of the underlying defendant's net assets that would have been subject to legal process for satisfaction of the judgment as of the date the first judgment was signed or at some point thereafter, or (2) the amount that would have been paid on the judgment by the defendant or another, such as a guarantor or insurer." 299 S.W.2d at 114.

(2) Treated as an Affirmative Defense

Not all jurisdictions subscribe to the rule requiring the plaintiff to prove collectibility of malpractice damages. Some states treat uncollectibility of damages as an affirmative defense to be pleaded and proved by the defendant.

B. PUNITIVE DAMAGES

It is very hard to obtain and sustain through appellate review a substantial award of punitive damages. Nevertheless, some types of lawyer malpractice may justify such an award.

The terms "punitive damages" and "exemplary damages" are often used interchangeably. The purpose of such an assessment is to punish and make an example of the defendant.

1. State Law Limitations

a. Highly Culpable Conduct Clearly Established

Punitive damages (also called exemplary damages) are available only in cases of highly culpable conduct. Proof of mere negligence in a legal malpractice action will never support a punitive award. *See Call v. Czaplicki*, 2010 WL 3001395, *8 (D.N.J. 2010)

In some states, the standard for recovery of punitive damages is exceedingly demanding. For example, a Texas statute provides:

(a) *** [E]xemplary damages may be awarded only if the claimant proves by clear and convincing evidence that the harm with respect to which the claimant seeks recovery of exemplary damages results from: (1) fraud; (2) malice; or (3) gross negligence. ***

(d) Exemplary damages may be awarded only if the jury was unanimous in regard to finding liability for and the amount of exemplary damages.

Tex. Civ. Prac. & Rem. Code § 41.003 (Westlaw 2010). Discussing the "malice" provision in this statute, the Texas Supreme Court explained in a legal malpractice case:

Malice has both an objective and a subjective prong; proof of malice involves an objective determination that the defendant's conduct involves an extreme risk of harm, and a subjective determination that the defendant had actual awareness of the extreme risk created by his conduct.

Smith v. O'Donnell, 288 S.W.3d 417, 423 (Tex. 2009). Addressing the claim before it, which involved allegedly defective advice to an estate executor, the *Smith* court found no evidence that the defendant law firm intended to cause injury or acted with actual awareness of an extreme risk of harm. Consequently, there was no basis for an award of exemplary damages under Texas law. Of course, other states frame the requirements for an award of punitive damages in different terms.

To justify an award of punitive damages, conduct must be not only highly culpable, but clearly established. A majority of states now require clear and convincing evidence of entitlement to a punitive award.

b. Caps and Bans on Punitive Damages

Many jurisdictions have capped the amount of punitive damages that may be recovered from a defendant, either in tort actions generally or in legal malpractice suits in particular. However, these restrictions vary greatly.

For example, Alaska generally restricts a punitive award to the greater of three times compensatory damages or $500,000. *See* Alaska Stat. § 09.17.020(f) (Westlaw 2010). However, if the defendant's action is motivated by financial gain, punitive damages are limited to the greater of four times compensatory damages, four times the aggregate amount of financial gain, or $7,000,000. *See id.* § 09.17.020(g).

In Colorado, punitive damages may not exceed actual damages or, if there are aggravating circumstances, three times actual damages. Colo. Rev. Stat. Ann. § 13-21-102 (Westlaw 2010).

In Kansas, a punitive award, with certain exceptions, may be no more than $5 million or the gross income of the defendant, whichever is less. *See* Kan. Stat. Ann. § 60-3701(1)(e)–(f) (Westlaw 2010).

In Texas, except when conduct violates selected rules in the state penal code, "[e]xemplary damages awarded against a defendant may not exceed an amount equal to the greater of: (1) (A) two times the amount of economic damages; plus (B) an amount equal to any noneconomic damages found by the jury, not to exceed $750,000; or (2) $200,000." Tex. Civ. Prac. & Rem. Code § 41.008 (Westlaw 2010).

In Connecticut, damages awarded to punish may not exceed litigation expenses less taxable costs. *See Triangle Sheet Metal Works, Inc. v. Silver*, 154 Conn. 116, 222 A.2d 220 (1966).

A Nebraska constitutional provision precludes an award of punitive damages. *See* Neb. Const. art. VII, § 5 (Westlaw 2010). In Washington State, a similar rule was judicially created. *See Spokane Truck & Dray Co. v. Hoefer*, 25 P. 1072 (Wash. 1891).

Illinois expressly bans awards of punitive damages in legal malpractice cases. A state statute provides:

> In all cases, whether in tort, contract or otherwise, in which the plaintiff seeks damages by reason of legal, medical, hospital, or other healing art malpractice, no punitive, exemplary, vindictive or aggravated damages shall be allowed.

735 ILCS 5/2-1115 (Westlaw 2010).

c. Partial Forfeiture to the State

Some states have passed laws requiring part of any punitive damages award to be forfeited to the state. For example, an Iowa statute requires forfeiture of at least 75% of a punitive award, unless the defendant's conduct was directed specifically at the claimant. *See* Iowa Code Ann. § 668A.1(2)(b) (Westlaw 2010).

2. Constitutional Limitations

a. Due Process and the Amount of Punitive Damages

The two key decisions of the United States Supreme Court limiting awards of punitive damages are *BMW of North America, Inc. v. Gore*, 517 U.S. 559, 116 S. Ct. 1589, 134 L. Ed. 2d 809 (1996), and *State*

Farm Mutual Automobile Ins. Co. v. Campbell, 538 U.S. 408, 123 S. Ct. 1513, 155 L. Ed. 2d 585 (2003). The latter case ultimately gave rise to a legal malpractice claim, *Christensen & Jensen, P.C. v. Barrett & Daines*, 613 Utah Adv. Rep. 3, 194 P.3d 931 (Utah 2008). (*See* Chapter 3 Part C.) Subsequent cases have explored the meaning of *Gore* and *Campbell*. These various decisions are discussed in the sections that follow.

(1) BMW of North America, Inc. v. Gore

In *Gore*, Justice John Paul Stevens explained for the Supreme Court:

> Elementary notions of fairness enshrined in our constitutional jurisprudence dictate that a person receive fair notice not only of the conduct that will subject him to punishment, but also of the severity of the penalty that a State may impose.

517 U.S. at 574.

With this principle in mind, *Gore* then identified three guideposts for determining whether a punitive award complies with the demands of due process. In reviewing awards, courts must consider: (1) the degree of reprehensibility of the defendant's misconduct; (2) the disparity between the actual or potential harm suffered by the plaintiff and the punitive damages award; and (3) the difference between the punitive damages awarded by the jury and the civil penalties authorized or imposed in comparable cases.

(2) State Farm Mutual Automobile Insurance Co. v. Campbell

In *Campbell*, the Supreme Court explored the meaning of *Gore*. Addressing the first guidepost, Justice Anthony Kennedy wrote for the Court that:

> "[T]he most important indicium of the reasonableness of a punitive damages award is the degree of reprehensibility of the defendant's conduct." ***. We have instructed courts to determine the reprehensibility of a defendant by considering whether: the harm caused was physical as opposed to economic; the tortious conduct evinced an indifference to or a reckless disregard of the health or safety of others; the target of the conduct had financial vulnerability; the conduct involved repeated actions or was an isolated incident; and the harm was the result of intentional malice, trickery, or deceit, or mere accident ***. The existence of any one of these factors weighing in favor of a plaintiff may not be sufficient to sustain a punitive damages award; and the absence of all of them renders any award suspect. It should be presumed a plaintiff has been made whole for his injuries by compensatory damages, so punitive damages should only be awarded if the defendant's culpability, after having paid compensatory damages, is so reprehensible as to warrant the imposition of further sanctions to achieve punishment or deterrence ***. 538 U.S. at 419.

Justice Kennedy then made the following points, which are paraphrased here from the opinion of the Court:

- ■ A State cannot base an award of punitive damages on conduct that was lawful where it occurred; or, generally, on unlawful conduct that was committed outside the State's jurisdiction; or on dissimilar acts of the defendant that occurred independent of the acts upon which liability is premised; or on hypothetical claims involving injuries to third parties; and

- ■ A defendant should be punished for conduct that harmed the plaintiff, not for being an unsavory individual or business.

538 U.S. at 421-23.

Elaborating on the relevance of events that occurred outside the jurisdiction to a punitive damages award, Justice Kennedy explained:

- ■ Lawful out-of-state conduct may be probative when it demonstrates the deliberateness and culpability of the defendant's action in the State where it is tortious, but that conduct must have a nexus to the specific harm suffered by the plaintiff.

538 U.S. at 422.

Addressing the significance of harm to others, Justice Kennedy acknowledged that "evidence of other acts need not be identical to have relevance in the calculation of punitive damages." 538 U.S. at 423. He further explained:

- Although "[o]ur holdings that a recidivist may be punished more severely than a first offender recognize that repeated misconduct is more reprehensible than an individual instance of malfeasance," in the context of civil actions courts must ensure the conduct in question replicates the prior transgressions.

538 U.S. at 423.

The *Campbell* court then turned to the second guidepost, namely the relationship between the actual or potential harm suffered by the plaintiff and the size of the punitive damages award. In terms paraphrased from the language of Justice Kennedy:

- While there are no rigid benchmarks, few awards exceeding a single-digit ratio will comply with the demands of due process.

- Greater ratios may pass constitutional muster if particularly egregious conduct has resulted in only a small amount of economic damages.

- However, if compensatory damages are substantial, a lesser ratio of punitive damages (perhaps only 1:1), will be the maximum that due process allows.

- The wealth of a defendant, and the fact that the defendant may be punished only in rare cases, cannot justify an otherwise unconstitutional punitive damages award.

The Court's single-digit ratio maxim suggests that there may be a great difference between a 9:1 ratio and a 10:1 ratio of punitive to compensatory damages.

Nine to one is a single-digit ratio; ten to one is a double-digit ratio.

The third guidepost articulated in *Gore*—namely, the disparity between a punitive damages award and the civil penalties authorized or imposed in comparable cases—is typically the least useful in determining whether a punitive damages award violates due process. No clear rule-of-thumb has emerged. Thus, in *Campbell*, the Supreme Court said little about this consideration. Justice Kennedy wrote simply that:

> The existence of a criminal penalty does have bearing on the seriousness with which a State views the wrongful action. When used to determine the dollar amount of the award, however, the criminal penalty has less utility ***.

In overturning a multimillion dollar punitive damages award, the *Campbell* court merely noted that the award dwarfed the most relevant civil sanction under state law for the wrong in question, a $10,000 fine.

Campbell was remanded for further proceedings consistent with the standard announced by the Supreme Court, which had opined that, in light of the substantial compensatory damages award of $1 million, the facts "likely would justify a punitive damages award at or near the amount of compensatory damages." 538 U.S. at 429. However, the Utah Supreme Court ultimately approved a generous $9,018,780.75 in punitive damages, an amount barely within the single-digit ratio articulated the by the United States Supreme Court. *See Christensen &*

Jensen, P.C. v. Barrett & Daines, 613 Utah Adv. Rep. 3, 194 P.3d 931, 936 (Utah 2008).

(3) Subsequent Supreme Court Cases

Subsequent to *Campbell*, the Supreme Court emphasized that an award of punitive damages may not be based, even in part, on a jury's desire to punish a defendant for harming nonparties. In *Philip Morris USA v. Williams*, 549 U.S. 346, 127 S. Ct. 1057, 166 L. Ed. 2d 940 (2007), the jury, in response to the plaintiff's argument that many other smokers had been killed by the defendant's cigarettes, made a large punitive damages award to the estate of a heavy smoker. In remanding the case for further proceedings, Justice Stephen Breyer's opinion for the court explained:

> [T]he Due Process Clause prohibits a State from punishing an individual without first providing that individual with "an opportunity to present every available defense." ***. Yet a defendant threatened with punishment for injuring a nonparty victim has no opportunity to defend against the charge, by showing, for example ***, that the other victim was not entitled to damages ***.
>
> *** [T]o permit punishment for injuring a nonparty victim would add a near standardless dimension to the punitive damages equation. How many such victims are there? How seriously were they injured? Under what circumstances did injury occur? The trial will not likely answer such questions as to nonparty victims. The jury will be left to speculate ***.

*** [W]e can find no authority supporting the use of punitive damages awards for the purpose of punishing a defendant for harming others ***.

Respondent argues that she is free to show harm to other victims because it is relevant to a different part of the punitive damages constitutional equation, namely, reprehensibility. ***. Yet for the reasons given above, a jury may not go further than this and use a punitive damages verdict to punish a defendant directly on account of harms it is alleged to have visited on nonparties.

***. We *** conclude that the Due Process Clause requires States to provide assurance that juries are not asking the wrong question, *i.e.*, seeking, not simply to determine reprehensibility, but also to punish for harm caused [to] strangers.

549 U.S. at 353-55.

More recently, in *Exxon Shipping Co. v. Baker*, 128 S. Ct. 2605, 171 L. Ed. 2d 570 (2008), a case arising from an Alaskan oil spill, the Court held that, under federal maritime law, an award of punitive damages could not exceed the jury's substantial compensatory damages award of $507.5 million.

(4) Limitations on Punitive Awards in Legal Malpractice Cases

Like other forms of tort litigation, legal malpractice cases are subject to the limitations announced in the *Gore-Campbell* line of cases. This means, among other things, that punitive awards are unlikely to exceed compensatory damages by a factor of ten or more even in cases of highly egregious conduct, such as intentional overbilling of clients or facilitation of a Ponzi scheme that defrauds investors.

b. Vicarious Liability for Punitive Damages

If a law firm or its principals are held vicariously liable for a punitive damages award based on the conduct of a lawyer in the firm, there is a risk that persons actually punished by the award will be innocent of any wrongdoing. Nevertheless, the United States Supreme Court has held that vicarious liability for punitive damages does not violate the Constitution. In *Pacific Mutual Life Ins. Co. v. Haslip*, 499 U.S. 1, 111 S. Ct. 1032, 113 L. Ed.2d 1 (1991), a case not involving legal malpractice, the Court explained:

> Imposing exemplary damages on the corporation when its agent commits intentional fraud creates a strong incentive for vigilance by those in a position "to guard substantially against the evil to be prevented." ***. If *** [an entity] were liable for such damages only upon proof that it was at fault independently, it would have an incentive to minimize oversight of its agents. Imposing liability without independent fault deters fraud more than a less stringent rule. It therefore rationally advances the State's goal [in allowing awards of punitive damages].

499 U.S. at 14.

Some states have passed statutes addressing the issue of vicarious liability for punitive damages. For example, Alaska law provides:

In a civil action in which an employer is determined to be vicariously liable for the act or omission of an employee, punitive damages may not be awarded against the employer under principles of vicarious liability unless

(1) the employer or the employer's managerial agent (A) authorized the act or omission and the manner in which the act was performed or omission occurred; or (B) ratified or approved the act or omission after the act or omission occurred; or

(2) the employee (A) was unfit to perform the act or avoid the omission and the employer or the employer's managerial agent acted recklessly in employing or retaining the employee; or (B) was employed in a managerial capacity and was acting within the scope of employment. ***.

Alaska Stat. §09.17.020(k) (Westlaw 2010).

3. Liability for "Lost Punitive Damages"

A lawyer's negligence at trial may cause the plaintiff to lose not only compensatory damages, but a punitive award that would have been assessed in that litigation. This raises the question as to whether lawyers who commit litigation-related malpractice are liable for "lost punitive damages."

Some states allow malpractice plaintiffs to recover lost punitive damages as an element of compensation. However, other courts reject this approach. *See Tri-G, Inc. v. Burke, Boselman &Weaver,* 222 Ill. 2d 218, 856 N.E.2d 389, 305 Ill. Dec. 584 (2006). The courts in the latter group generally reason that there is no entitlement to punitive damages; that making a merely negligent lawyer liable for a lost punitive award would punish the wrong party and exacerbate the costs of legal services and legal malpractice insurance; and that efforts to assess the size of a lost punitive award would amount to sheer speculation. *See generally Restatement (Third) of the Law Governing Lawyers* § 53 cmt. h (2000).

C. RESTITUTION

Restitution is a remedy which measures the plaintiff's entitlement to redress based not on what the plaintiff lost (damages), but on what the defendant improperly gained. Thus, a restitutionary remedy is designed to prevent unjust enrichment.

In many cases, a lawyer who commits malpractice enjoys no benefit at the plaintiff's expense. For example, the misdrafting of a will may mean that a portion of the decedent's estate goes not to A, but to B; it does not mean that the legacy in question goes to the lawyer. In this type of case, there is no basis to talk about restitution. Even though the lawyer was paid a fee for legal services, the payment was presumably made by the decedent rather than by the disappointed legatee. The lawyer has not been unjustly enriched at the expense of A, so as to give A a right to restitution.

However, in some situations, a lawyer wrongly benefits at the plaintiff's expense. This may be true if confidential client information is misused and the lawyer thereby usurps a valuable business opportunity. In such a case, the client should be entitled to recover the value of what the lawyer gained, even though the client suffered no "out of pocket" losses.

For many years, the law of restitution was neglected by courts and scholars. However, the completion of the new *Restatement (Third) of Restitution and Unjust Enrichment* (2010) seems certain to catalyze a revival of this area of the law. Undoubtedly, restitutionary principles will find increased application in legal malpractice case. An excellent illustration of how the law may develop is the increased prominence of actions for total or partial fee forfeiture if a lawyer commits a clear and serious breach of duty. (*See* Chapter 4 Part D.) Fee forfeiture is a remedy designed to prevent unjust enrichment. As noted earlier, forfeiture is generally available even if the plaintiff has not suffered provable damages.

CHAPTER SEVEN

DEFENSES AND OBSTACLES TO RECOVERY

With respect to lawyer liability, defenses are every bit as important as causes of action. Even if a lawyer has blatantly violated the standard of care and caused serious damages, a defense may defeat the plaintiff's claim or limit the extent of the defendant's liability. There are three broad categories of defenses relevant to legal malpractice claims.

The first category deals with *conduct on the part of the plaintiff*. This includes carelessness (*see* Part A-1) or unlawful conduct (*see* Part B) which contributes to the harm for which recovery is sought, as well as the plaintiff's failure to mitigate damages (*see* Part A-2). Also within this category is the plaintiff's signing of an arbitration agreement (*see* Part H) or settlement documents (*see* Part F), and previous allegations in earlier litigation (*see* Part J).

The second category of malpractice defenses relates to *conduct on the part of the defendant*, such as lawful representation of a client or participation in litigation. These types of conduct may give rise to a qualified or absolute privilege which will defeat liability, if the lawyer is sued by a nonclient. (*See* Part G.)

The third category of malpractice defenses concerns *obstacles to recovery that arise by operation of law*. This category encompasses statutes of limitations (including the discovery rule, the continuing representation doctrine, and statutes of repose) (*see* Part C), the rules governing joint and several liability and related matters, such as indemnity, contribution, and credits for payments by other tortfeasors (*see* Part E), and the general nonassignability of malpractice claims (*see* Part D). Also within this third category are certain immunities, such as those which sometimes bar actions against public defenders or court-appointed lawyers (*see* Part G-4) or arise under special statutes (*see* Part I).

These various topics, and their application to legal malpractice actions, are discussed below.

A. CONTRIBUTORY NEGLIGENCE, COMPARATIVE NEGLIGENCE, AND COMPARATIVE FAULT

In the vast majority of states with comparative negligence or comparative fault regimes, the plaintiff's recovery in a malpractice action may be reduced based on the plaintiff's own carelessness, if that conduct contributed to the harm for which recovery is sought. On appropriate facts, such carelessness might consist of the plaintiff's failure to read a document, supply accurate factual information, or carry out a lawyer's request for action needed to protect the client's interests.

In states with "modified," rather than "pure," system of comparative negligence or comparative fault, a plaintiff is totally barred from recovery, rather than allowed a reduced recovery, if the plaintiff's share of the negligence or fault is greater than 50%. Whether a plaintiff who is exactly 50% responsible is entitled to a reduced recovery, or no recovery at all, depends on the wording of the applicable comparative negligence or comparative fault rule.

A few states have never adopted comparative negligence or comparative fault, and continue to adhere to the doctrine of contributory negligence. Under that rule, any negligence on the part of the plaintiff is a total bar to an action for negligence. Thus, in legal malpractice actions, any carelessness on the part of a client or other plaintiff will preclude recovery from a lawyer for professional negligence. In *Lyle, Siegel, Croshaw & Beale, P.C. v. Tidewater Capital Corp.*, 249 Va. 426, 457 S.E.2d 28 (1995), the Supreme Court of Virginia found that there was a question of fact as to whether the actions and knowledge of a partner in the defendant law firm, who was also a 50% shareholder of the plaintiff client, could be imputed to the client. If so, the client would be barred from recovery by the state's contributory negligence rule.

Carelessness (*i.e.*, negligence) on the part of a malpractice plaintiff is never a defense to an intentional tort claim. Therefore, a lawyer who steals a client's money cannot argue that the client was careless in entrusting the money to the lawyer or in monitoring the lawyer's conduct. Carelessness is also not a defense to a breach of contract claim.

1. Carelessness by the Plaintiff Contributing to the Harm

In a recent case, a former professional athlete, who was represented by a law firm in the purchase of a jet, alleged that he did not understand the changing terms of the deal and that the law firm did not advise him that he would be liable for a $7 million loan. A jury returned a verdict in favor of the plaintiff, but reduced his recovery because he bore some responsibility for entering into the ill-advised deal. *See* Karen Sloan, "Former NBA Star Wins $2 Million Legal Malpractice Judgment," *Nat'l L.J.* (July 2, 2010).

2. Avoidable Consequences and Failure to Mitigate Damages

A lawyer ordinarily is not liable for damages that a malpractice plaintiff could have avoided through the exercise of reasonable care after the lawyer's breach of duty caused harm. This avoidable consequences principle is sometimes referred to as the plaintiff's duty to mitigate damages.

For example, if a lawyer's negligence results in the entry of default judgment against a client, the cost of the judgment is not compensable if it was feasible for the client to have moved to vacate the default judgment and the motion would have been granted. However, in *Grochocinski v. Mayer Brown Rowe & Maw LLP*, 2007 WL 1875995, *5 (N.D. Ill.), a federal court in Illinois found that these issues were so legally and factually complex that they could not be decided on a motion for summary judgment.

Alternatively, suppose that a lawyer's malpractice subjects a client's successor-in-interest to claims by a third party, and that the successor settles those claims at an inflated price. If the defendant law firm can prove at trial that there was a collusive settlement of the underlying demands, that evidence "would presumably negate causation and/or mitigate damages on the [successor's] legal malpractice claim." *Smith v. O'Donnell*, 288 S.W.3d 417, 422 (Tex. 2009).

Failure to mitigate damages is now treated as a form of comparative fault in many jurisdictions. *See* Uniform Comparative Fault Act §1(b), 12 U.L.A. 123 (Westlaw 2010).

a. Mitigation Versus Judicial Estoppel

In *Dashiell v. Meeks*, 396 Md. 149, 913 A.2d 10, 24 (2006), a lawyer was allegedly negligent in omitting an alimony waiver provision from a prenuptial agreement, and in counseling his client to sign the agreement without reading it. The error was not discovered until the client later separated from his wife. In the ensuing divorce, the court granted *the client's request* to enforce the agreement as executed, and awarded the client's spouse rehabilitative alimony. The client then sued the lawyer who misdrafted the agreement. The Maryland Court of Appeals ruled that, on a more fully developed record, the defendant lawyer could plausibly assert that the plaintiff was judicially estopped from basing a malpractice action on an award of alimony which the plaintiff had requested the divorce court to grant. Under Maryland law, judicial estoppel exists if (1) one of the parties to a lawsuit takes a factual position that is inconsistent with a position it took in previous litigation, (2) the previous position was accepted by a court, and (3) the party who is maintaining the inconsistent position is intentionally misleading the court to gain an unfair advantage. (*See* Part J of this Chapter.)

Another way of looking at the *Dashiell* case would be to say that the client, upon discovering the omission of the critical provision from the prenuptial agreement, had a duty to mitigate damages by seeking to avoid enforcement of the agreement. If that was reasonably possible—perhaps because there had been a mutual mistake by the parties to the agreement, both of them believing that the agreement contained a waiver of alimony provision—compensatory damages for the amount of the alimony could not be collected from the errant lawyer.

B. UNLAWFUL CONDUCT

In recent years, many states have legislatively enacted or judicially recognized, in a wide range of circumstances, what amounts to an unlawful conduct defense. The defense goes by various names. However, in general terms, it bars recovery for damages that are the direct result of knowing participation in serious criminal or tortious conduct.

The unlawful conduct defense plays an important role in legal malpractice cases. Thus, a client who is found to have lied under oath cannot sue the lawyer who advised the client to commit perjury. Likewise, a business involved in defrauding investors may not be able to sue its lawyers for having negligently facilitated the transactions. *See* Vincent R. Johnson, "The

Unlawful Conduct Defense in Legal Malpractice," 77 *UMKC L. Rev.* 43 (2008).

1. A Defense in Many Guises

In some cases, the unlawful conduct defense is really an attack on the causation element of a legal malpractice claim. Courts hold that the plaintiff's criminal conduct makes it impossible to prove that the alleged malpractice caused damages.

For example, in *Fang v. Bock*, 305 Mont. 322, 28 P.3d 456 (2001), a university legal aid office's representatives were allegedly negligent in advising the plaintiff that he would not be deported if he pleaded guilty to assaulting a family member. Nevertheless, after the plaintiff entered a plea, he was deported to China. Although the plaintiff's initial guilty plea was eventually withdrawn, and a conviction pursuant to a second guilty plea was expunged, the Supreme Court of Montana rejected the plaintiff's malpractice claim. The plaintiff had alleged that as a result of the bad legal advice he was exposed to the possibility of removal from the country and had to spend large sums of money. However, the court found that the plaintiff's legal expenses and deportation predicament were the result of his own unlawful conduct, which he had admitted on two separate occasions. He would have been exposed to removal from the country, based on his conduct, with or without the allegedly negligent advice. In cases like *Fang*, the plaintiff's unlawful conduct is not an affirmative defense that needs to be pleaded and proved by the defendant, but rather a matter which negates the causation element of the plaintiff's *prima facie* case.

On other occasions, the plaintiff's unlawful conduct is treated as an affirmative defense. Thus, in some suits, the plaintiff is said to be barred from seeking recourse in the courts because the plaintiff is "*in pari delicto*" with the defendant (equally at fault) or has "unclean hands." However, there is so much imprecision and questionable precedent surrounding these equitable doctrines, that it is better to talk, as some courts do, in straight-forward terms about an unlawful conduct defense with clear requirements. One of the better definitions of the defense was offered in *Barker v. Kallash*, 63 N.Y.2d 19, 468 N.E.2d 39, 479 N.Y.S.2d 201 (1984), a case not involving legal malpractice. There, the New York State Court of Appeals explained that "when the plaintiff has engaged in activities prohibited, as opposed to merely regulated, by law, the courts will not entertain the suit if the plaintiff's conduct constituted a serious violation of the law and the injuries for which he seeks recovery were the direct result of that violation." 468 N.E.2d at 41. (*Barker* held that a fifteen-year-old boy who was injured while constructing a "pipe bomb" was precluded from recovering from the nine-year-old boy who supplied the gunpowder.)

It is important to remember that any formulation of the unlawful conduct defense which too readily closes the court house doors to legal malpractice claims threatens to undercut the deterrent force of tort law and its ability to discourage bad professional practices. Comparative fault principles already make it possible to reduce a plaintiff's recovery based on the plaintiff's own fault. Consequently, recognition of a total bar to recovery based on unlawful conduct is only needed if there are interests at stake so significant that they warrant full denial of judicial relief.

In general, this means only the most serious forms of unlawful conduct, knowingly committed by the plaintiff, should suffice as the predicate for an unlawful conduct defense in a legal malpractice action. The plaintiff's commission of fraud, perjury, or another grievous felony readily falls within this category. Of course, the plaintiff's *knowing* perpetration of serious unlawful conduct must be convincingly proven, either by prior adjudication in a criminal or civil proceeding, or in the legal malpractice action itself. Finally, the plaintiff's unlawful conduct should be a total defense to liability only if that conduct is both a factual and proximate cause of the plaintiff's injury, judged according to ordinary tort principles. To satisfy the demands of factual causation, the plaintiff's conduct must normally have been such a substantial factor that it made an indispensable contribution to the production of the harm (*i.e.*, was a but-for cause). Further, to meet the requirements of proximate causation, the harm for which the plaintiff seeks recovery must have been a foreseeable result or a direct consequence of the plaintiff's unlawful conduct.

Nevertheless, there are many cases which apply the unlawful conduct defense in a largely freewheeling fashion. When that happens, the defense may threaten to immunize large classes of lawyers from malpractice liability. As discussed below, this is true in numerous states with respect to malpractice arising from representation of persons accused of crime.

2. Exoneration or Innocence Requirement in Criminal-Defense Malpractice

In the legal malpractice field, the unlawful conduct defense finds its clearest endorsement in the
decisions requiring persons alleging defective criminal
representation to first overturn their convictions and,
in some states, also prove their innocence of the
crimes for which they were prosecuted. Although
these cases do not use the term "unlawful conduct
defense," they clearly seize upon the defendant's
unlawful conduct to insulate lawyers from liability.

What is most striking about state exoneration or
innocence requirements is how broadly they sweep.
Any kind of criminal conduct (misdemeanors as well
as felonies), however established (whether by plea or
conviction), wholly bars an action for professional
negligence (regardless of the gravity of the lawyer's
misconduct). It is easy to doubt the wisdom of these
formidable obstacles to recovery for lawyer wrongdoing. Not surprisingly, exoneration and innocence
requirements have been widely criticized.

To begin with, these obstacles to recovery—which
are not affirmative defenses, but additional requirements in the plaintiff's *prima facie* case—are simply
doctrinal overkill. If the concern is that an undeserv-
ing claim will succeed, there is little cause for worry.
It is difficult for even appealing and sympathetic
plaintiffs with good facts to prevail on legal malpractice claims. Presumably, it is all the more challenging
for one carrying the stigma of actual or apparent
criminality to do so. The difficulty of finding an

attorney to initiate a malpractice action, the nature of the jury system, the demanding requirements of the "trial within a trial" causation analysis, and the rules that protect a lawyer's exercise of discretion, all conspire to defeat a malpractice claim raised by one charged with or convicted of a crime.

In addition, exoneration or innocence requirements are of dubious value from the standpoint of legal deterrence. In the sphere of criminal defense work, there are virtually no formal legal mechanisms for enforcing the standards of conduct that should be observed by lawyers. Requests for post-conviction relief based on ineffective assistance of counsel seldom succeed. Disciplinary sanctions against errant criminal defense lawyers are a rarity. Motions for disqualification or disgorgement of fees are essentially unheard of in the world of criminal representation.

One explanation for the rush by states to adopt exoneration and innocence requirements is that this is just another effort to limit the rights of criminals and those suspected of crimes. In other words, one might argue, these requirements are just another part of the ongoing "war on crime." However, a more convincing explanation is that proponents of these rules were concerned about the risk of criminal defense attorneys, often appointed by courts and poorly compensated, being deluged with malpractice claims filed by prisoners.

A plaintiff's unlawful conduct should bar recovery in a tort action only in cases where the plaintiff's fault is great and only if that misdeed is related to the attorney's negligence in such a way that it is fair to totally foreclose recovery. The cases imposing an exoneration or innocence requirement on plaintiffs suing for malpractice arising from criminal defense work sweep much too broadly to honor these important factors.

a. Lesser Included Offenses

Some courts hold that a plaintiff suing with respect to malpractice committed during criminal representation must prove not only innocence of the charge directly related to the malpractice, but also innocence of lesser included offenses. For example, in *Sangha v. La Barbera*, 146 Cal. App. 4th 79, 52 Cal. Rptr. 3d 640 (2006), the defendant lawyer was allegedly negligent in advising the plaintiff to plead guilty to felony vandalism. Subsequently, that plea was set aside when the plaintiff retained new counsel and admitted guilt to a misdemeanor vandalism charge. The California Court of Appeal rejected the plaintiff's argument that he only needed to prove innocence of the offense to which the malpractice was directly related. Consequently, the plaintiff's misdemeanor plea was an insuperable obstacle to his malpractice claim. The court quoted with approval an earlier decision which opined that "damages should only be awarded to a person who is truly free from any criminal involvement." 52 Cal. Rptr. 3d at 647.

b. Sentencing Errors

Some jurisdictions otherwise requiring proof of actual innocence hold that the requirement does not apply to malpractice claims based on sentencing errors. For example, in *Jones v. Link*, 493 F. Supp. 2d 765 (E.D. Va. 2007), a lawyer improperly failed to object to a five-level enhancement when his client was sentenced. Thereafter, the client proved that he had received ineffective assistance of counsel, and his sentence was reduced by 36 months. In a subsequent malpractice action, the court held, in line with other jurisdictions, that it is not necessary to prove actual innocence in this kind of case because "the improper sentence was not the direct result of the plaintiff's criminal behavior, but rather, it was the proximate result of his attorney's negligence." 493 F. Supp. 2d at 770.

C. MALPRACTICE STATUTES OF LIMITATIONS

In every case, it is vitally important for the lawyers to identify the applicable statute of limitations. Even if a defendant's malpractice is egregious, the untimely filing of a claim will wholly defeat the plaintiff's cause of action.

In some instances, the filing period for legal malpractice is governed by a statute expressly applicable to claims against lawyers. For example, a Louisiana statute provides:

> No action for damages against any attorney ***, whether based upon tort, or breach of contract, or otherwise, arising out of an engagement to provide legal services shall be brought unless filed *** within one year from the alleged act, omission, or neglect, or within one year from the date the alleged act, omission or neglect is discovered or should have been discovered ***.

La. Rev. Stat. 9:5605(A) (Westlaw 2010).

However, in other cases, a general statute of limitations governs. For example, in *Channel v. Loyacono*, 954 So. 2d 415, 421 (Miss. 2007), the Mississippi Supreme Court found that the operative statute for a legal malpractice claim was one that provided:

All actions for which no other period of limitations is prescribed shall be commenced within three (3) years after the cause of such action accrued, and not after.

954 So. 2d at 420.

In some circumstances, a special statute of limitations applies based on the nature of the malpractice claim. Thus, the Louisiana statute quoted above does not apply "in cases of fraud." La. Rev. Stat. 9:5605(E) (Westlaw 2010).

1. Accrual of the Cause of Action

The statute of limitations begins to "run" when the plaintiff's cause of action "accrues." In each jurisdiction, accrual is normally governed by either of two different rules: the "occurrence rule" or the "damage rule."

a. Occurrence Rule

States following the occurrence rule say that the plaintiff's cause of action accrues, and the statute of limitations begins to run, when the negligent act or omission occurs. Thus, a Connecticut statute provides that:

No action founded upon a tort shall be brought but within three years from the date of the act or omission complained of.

Conn. Gen. Stats. § 52-577 (Westlaw 2010). In *Abdelsame v. Foden de Castro*, 2007 WL 2036849 (Conn. Super. Ct.), a court held that, under this statute, a malpractice claim alleging negligence related to the obtaining of a passport stamp to travel was untimely. More than three years had passed since the lawyer's allegedly wrongful acts and omissions, and there was no basis for tolling the running of the statute that would make the filing of the action timely. (Tolling is discussed in Part C-2 of this Chapter.)

b. Damage Rule

Some states adhere to a "damage rule," which holds that the statute of limitations does not begin to run until the lawyer's malpractice causes damage. The idea underlying this view is that until damage has occurred, it would be impossible for the plaintiff to successfully litigate a malpractice claim because proof of damages is essential.

In *Warnock v. Karm Winand & Patterson*, 376 Ill. App. 3d 364, 876 N.E.2d 8 (2007), the substantive issue was whether the drafting of certain letter agreements amounted to malpractice. In rejecting the defendant's statute of limitations defense, an Illinois appellate court applied the state's damage rule for determining when a cause of action accrues. The court found that damage did not occur, and the statute of limitations did not begin to run, until an adverse judgment was entered against the plaintiffs in a suit related to the letter agreements. The court reaffirmed an earlier holding that "a cause of action for legal malpractice will rarely accrue prior to the entry of an adverse judgment, settlement, or dismissal of the underlying action in which the plaintiff has become entangled due to the purportedly negligent advice of his attorney." 876 N.E.2d at 15. Moreover, the court rejected the malpractice defendant's argument that the statute of limitations began to run when, prior to the entry of the adverse judgment, the clients were sued and had to hire counsel to defend them, becoming liable for additional attorney's fees. The court reasoned that "the incurring of additional attorney fees may trigger the running of the statute of limitations for legal malpractice purposes, *but only where it is clear, at the time the additional fees are incurred, that the fees are directly attributable to former counsel's neglect (such as through a ruling adverse to the client to that effect)." Id.* at 14 (emphasis in original). The court found that the specified condition was not satisfied.

Nevertheless, other cases have found that "damage" can occur before the entry of an adverse court ruling. For example, in *Antone v. Mirviss*, 720 N.W.2d 331 (Minn. 2006), a lawyer was allegedly negligent in preparing a prenuptial agreement that failed to protect his client's interest in appreciation of his premarital property. The Supreme Court of Minnesota held that the client's legal malpractice action against the lawyer accrued when the agreement took effect. Therefore, the statute of limitations began to run upon the client's marriage, rather than when the client's wife was later awarded a portion of the appreciation in a marital dissolution proceeding. Finding that the plaintiff's claim was barred because it was filed outside the six-year statute of limitations, the majority rejected the dissent's argument that damage did not occur until the dissolution of the marriage. As the majority explained: "At the time of his marriage, Antone [the client] lost the legal right to unfettered ownership in his premarital property. This loss was not a mere seed planted when Antone said 'I do'; rather, it was a fully-matured briar patch." 720 N.W.2d at 338. The fact that the full extent of the damage was not ascertainable did not mean that no damage had occurred.

2. Tolling

The running of the statute of limitations may be "tolled," which is to say temporarily suspended, by certain types of special circumstances. This may be true, for example, for the period during which the plaintiff is under the age of majority or suffers from mental incapacity. *See DeLuna v. Burciaga*, 223 Ill.2d 49, 857 N.E.2d 229, 306 Ill. Dec. 136 (2006). However, it is not easy to generalize. Even with regard to these types of disability, the law varies from state to state.

Of particular relevance to legal malpractice actions are tolling based on lack of discovery of the lawyer's errors, continuation of the lawyer-client relationship, an agreement of the parties, or pendency of other litigation, such as a client's pursuit of post-conviction relief. These issues and related topics are discussed in the following sections.

a. Discovery Rule

Most states apply a discovery rule to legal malpractice claims. In these jurisdictions, the statute of limitations generally does not begin to run until the plaintiff has discovered, or reasonably should have discovered, the lawyer's malpractice.

For example, in *Widom v. Egenberg*, 2006 WL 3432552 (N.J. Super. Ct. App. Div.), a lawyer was allegedly negligent in representing multiple parties to a real estate transaction and in failing to explain to the plaintiffs the consequences, under the Statute of Frauds, of not documenting in writing a side agreement for the buyers to reconvey the property to the sellers on certain terms at a future date. Although there was a six-year statute of limitations, and the malpractice action was not filed until almost eight years after the closing, a New Jersey appellate court found that, under the applicable discovery rule, the suit was not untimely. There was no reason for the plaintiffs to have known until long after the closing that they should have had independent counsel and that the side agreement should have been put into writing.

Similarly, in *Viglione v. Farrington*, 2007 WL 2302342, *5 (N.J. Super. Ct. App. Div.), the court found that the mere fact that the plaintiff had expressed disappointment with a final divorce settlement did not mean that she had discovered that the defendant lawyer's representation of her was significantly flawed.

In *Ross v. Ihrie*, 2006 WL 3446897 (E.D. Mich. 2006), a lawyer allegedly committed malpractice by incorrectly telling a client that recovery for a personal injury claim was capped by a Nevada statute at $50,000. The lawyer argued that the client had discovered the malpractice because he was dissatisfied with the lawyer's representation from "Day One." However, a federal court in Michigan rejected that contention because the "statute of limitations for legal malpractice does not begin to run just because a client is unhappy with his attorney's work." *Id.* at *6.

For purposes of a dispute with another party to a contract, a person is presumed to have read and understood the terms of the contract at the time of execution. However, that does not mean that the statute of limitations on a malpractice claim begins to run on the date the contract was signed. In a state with a discovery rule, the defendant lawyer must still prove that the plaintiff actually discovered, or should have discovered, the error or omission related to the contract giving rise to malpractice liability. *See Dashiell v. Meeks*, 396 Md. 149, 913 A.2d 10, 20-21 (2006).

In some cases, a client's threat to sue or file a grievance has been found to establish that the plaintiff "discovered" the lawyer's malpractice, and to commence the running of the statute of limitations. *Serou v. DeLaup*, 2006 WL 3759555, *3 (E.D. La.), *aff'd* 244 Fed. Appx. 588 (5th Cir. 2007).

However, something less than a threat to initiate litigation may also amount to discovery. For example, in *Franklin Financial, Inc. v. Sandoz*, 956 So.2d 143 (La. Ct. App. 2007), the court found that a client discovered its lawyer's malpractice, and the statute of limitations began to run, when it sent the lawyer a letter detailing the lawyer's errors. This was true, the Louisiana Court of Appeal held, even though the client argued that its continuing relationship with the lawyer meant that it did not realize the full extent of the lawyer's errors.

In *Channel v. Loyacono*, 954 So. 2d 415, 422 (Miss. 2007), a law firm represented clients in a mass tort action, some of whom later sued the firm for malpractice. The Mississippi Supreme Court concluded that the statute of limitations began to run once the clients suspected wrongdoing and contacted another lawyer for advice, or when the clients were approached by disaffected lawyers, who had previously been involved in the case and wanted to take over the representation.

The application of a discovery rule is often a fact-intensive process. This means that while a lawyer may ultimately prevail in asserting a statute of limitations defense, it may not be possible to bring the plaintiff's malpractice action to an early termination.

For example, in *General Nutrition Corp. v. Gardere Wynne Sewell, LLP*, 2008 WL 4411951 (W.D. Pa. 2008), a federal court in Pennsylvania refused to grant a motion to dismiss. Although there was evidence that the client had discovered the defendant's malpractice, because it had received an "expert report from a law professor," there was also conflicting evidence that the defendant law firm had continued to assure the client that its analysis of the client's potential liability to a third-party was correct, and that the firm had covered up its original error. *Id.* at *4. The court concluded that it could not determine at that early stage of the proceedings that the plaintiff's claim was untimely, in light of applicable law tolling the running of the statute of limitations "when the client, despite the exercise of due diligence, cannot discover the injury or its cause." *Id*.

Of course, the prospect of prolonged litigation increases the settlement value of a malpractice claim. The longer litigation continues, the greater the costs of mounting a successful defense, and the more a defendant may be willing to pay to resolve the claim. Thus, the plaintiff's ability to plausibly invoke the discovery rule may increase the likelihood of settlement.

(1) Statutes of Repose

Some states have statutes of repose which are applicable to legal malpractice actions. A statute of repose provides that, regardless of the other calculations related to the applicable statute of limitations, a claim is barred after the passage of a certain period of time. Statutes of repose are not subject to tolling based on non-discovery. Thus, a statute of repose can extinguish a plaintiff's cause of action before the plaintiff is even aware of the need to sue.

In certain jurisdictions, the statute of repose is part of the same legislative provision that establishes the statute of limitations for a malpractice claim. For example, legislation in Montana provides that a legal malpractice action:

> must be commenced within 3 years after the plaintiff discovers or through the use of reasonable diligence should have discovered the act, error, or omission, whichever occurs last, but in

no case may the action be commenced after 10 years of the date of the act, error, or omission.

Mont. Code Ann. § 27-2-206 (Westlaw 2010).

In *Snyder v. Love*, 335 Mont. 49, 153 P.3d 571 (2006), the statute quoted above was applied to a case where a lawyer was allegedly negligent in drafting the terms of a will. The testator's will was executed on February 24, 1987; the testator died on November 18, 1992; the will was admitted to probate on November 25, 1992; and the malpractice complaint was filed on August 21, 2002. The Supreme Court of Montana held that the suit was time-barred because the ten-year statute of repose began to run on February 24, 1987. The court expressly rejected arguments that the running of the statute of repose was tolled by a discovery rule or by the fact that no cause of action accrued prior to the testator's death.

b. Continuous Representation Rule

Many states hold that the running of the statute of limitations is tolled for the period during which a lawyer continues to represent a client in the matter giving rise to the alleged malpractice. The reason for this rule is that it normally would be unreasonable to require a client, who is the victim of malpractice, to sue the client's lawyer while the representation is still in progress. If the client were compelled to file suit, the client would need to retain other counsel to present the malpractice claim. That, in itself, can be difficult, time-consuming, and expensive. In addition, the commencement of such litigation, with its attendant threat of liability and reputational harm to the defendant lawyer, would so harm the professional relationship between the client and malpractice defendant as to make further representation difficult or impossible. Thus, the client might be forced to also hire new counsel for the underlying matter. Not only would that be burdensome, but any opportunity for the defendant lawyer to "cure" the malpractice through remedial actions and good lawyering would probably be lost. The continuous representation rule alleviates these problems by delaying the necessity of filing suit.

Of course, a finding that there was no attorney-client relationship between the plaintiff and defendant (*see* Chapter 3 Part A) undercuts any attempt by a plaintiff to rely on the continuous representation rule. For example, in *International Strategies Group, Ltd. v. Greenberg Traurig, LLP*, 482 F.3d 1 (1st Cir. 2007), the First Circuit concluded that there was no attorney-client relationship between a corporate investor and the corporation's lawyer. Therefore, the investor's claims against the lawyer for conversion, and for aiding and abetting fraud and breach of fiduciary duty, were time-barred. The applicable statute of limitations was three years, and more than that amount of time had passed since the investor knew or should have known of the improper transfer of funds on which the claims were based.

Moreover, the continuous representation rule does not toll the statute of limitations with respect to any period of time after the lawyer-client relationship has ended. Thus, there is an issue in many cases about whether the professional relationship terminated. (*See* Chapter 3 Part A.) Conduct reflecting serious tensions in a lawyer-client relationship may be found

to raise a fact question about whether legal representation ended.

For example, in *Thayer v. Fuller & Henry, Ltd.*,
503 F. Supp. 2d 887 (N.D. Ohio 2007), a lawyer was
alleged to have committed malpractice by failing to
secure, as part of an employment severance package,
a release of the client's personal guaranty of a loan.
Although the client later consulted another lawyer
regarding whether the defendant lawyer and law firm
had committed malpractice, and sent the individual
defendant a letter saying that he had lost confidence
in him and did not intend to pay an outstanding bill,
it was not clear that the representation had terminated. The defendants had not performed legal
services for the plaintiff for a period of time, but upon
receiving the plaintiff's letter responded by seeking
clarification as to whether the firm should "cease any
further legal work." 503 F. Supp. 2d at 890. Moreover,
the costs of the plaintiff's hiring and bringing substitute counsel "up to speed" were substantial. *Id.* at 890.
Therefore, it was for the jury to determine when the
representation ended, and summary judgment on
statute of limitations grounds could not be granted.

Interestingly, the *Thayer* court noted that the
defendant lawyer, upon receiving the "no confidence"
letter, could not have unilaterally terminated the
attorney-client relationship. This was true because a
lawyer must give notice of an intention to withdraw,
and the plaintiff was never notified of such an intent.
Cf. Model Rules of Prof'l Conduct R. 1.16(d) (2010).
Therefore, the question was whether the client's
actions (not the lawyer's), or some other developments, had ended the relationship.

States differ in how they articulate the continuous representation rule. In some jurisdictions, the formulation of the rule is highly nuanced. For example, in Connecticut, a plaintiff may invoke the doctrine, and thus toll the running of the statute of limitations, only "when the plaintiff can show: (1) that the defendant continued to represent him with regard to the same underlying matter; and (2) either that the plaintiff did not know of the alleged malpractice or that the attorney could still mitigate the harm allegedly caused by that malpractice during the continued representation period." *DeLeo v. Nusbaum*, 263 Conn. 588, 821 A.2d 744, 749-50 (Conn. 2003).

In *Abdelsame v. Foden de Castro*, 2007 WL 2036849, *5 (Conn. Super. Ct.), a court interpreting Connecticut's continuous representation rule found that the plaintiff's filing of a grievance against an attorney unequivocally indicated that the plaintiff had ceased relying on the defendant's professional and legal judgment.

Some states do not recognize a continuous representation rule as a basis for tolling. *See Channel v. Loyacono*, 954 So. 2d 415, 421 (Miss. 2007). The Supreme Court of South Carolina refused to adopt the rule in *Epstein v. Brown*, 363 S.C. 372, 610 S.E.2d 816 (2005). Therefore, a surgeon's legal malpractice action against the lawyer who represented him in a wrongful death and survival action was governed by the state's discovery rule. The court held that, on the facts of the case, which involved alleged errors before and during trial, the surgeon knew or should have known that a legal malpractice action existed when an adverse verdict was entered against him in the underlying tort litigation. There was no basis for tolling while an appeal was being taken.

(1) Determining Continuity

The continuous representation rule, by its very terms, necessitates proof that representation of the client "continued." A lawyer's handling of discrete matters for a client at different times may fail to meet this requirement. Thus, the Second Circuit wrote that:

> New York's continuous representation doctrine does not apply to a client's "continuing general relationship with a lawyer." ***. Rather, it tolls the statute of limitations "only where the continuing representation pertains specifically to the matter in which the attorney committed the alleged malpractice."

Bastys v. Rothschild, 154 Fed. Appx. 260, 262 (2d Cir. 2005).

However, some courts are more lenient in determining that there has been continuation of representation sufficient to trigger the tolling rule. For example, in *Williams v. Maulis*, 2003 S.D. 138, 672 N.W.2d 702, 707-07 (2003), the Supreme Court of South Dakota held that a lawyer's continued representation of the estate of a widow's deceased husband was a continuation of related services that the lawyer had rendered for the widow in negotiating a contract for deed, which was the focus of the alleged malpractice.

A lawyer who is discharged by a client, but later resumes the client's representation, may decide that it would have been better not to return. By resuming representation after being discharged, a lawyer may be found to have extended the statute of limitations. Thus, in *Dodson v. Fishman*, 2006 WL 3639746, *3 (Cal. Ct. App.), a California appellate court held that a two-month hiatus during an initial discharge did not mean that the lawyer's resumption of representation was not "continuous."

c. Fraudulent Concealment

Fraudulent concealment by a lawyer is sometimes deemed to toll the running of the statute of limitations on a malpractice claim. However, this basis for tolling is often narrowly construed. In general, it is not sufficient that the lawyer merely failed to disclose the errors or omissions that allegedly constitute malpractice. Rather, the lawyer must have taken affirmative steps to conceal the malpractice by preventing its discovery.

In *Bomar v. Moser*, 369 Ark. 123, 251 S.W.3d 234, 242 (2007), the Supreme Court of Arkansas stated that "in order to toll the statute of limitations on the basis of fraudulent concealment, there must be (1) a positive act of fraud (2) that is actively concealed, and (3) is not discoverable by reasonable diligence." The *Bomar* court found that the first two elements of the test were satisfied because the defendant lawyers had allegedly set up entities as shell corporations and eliminated the plaintiff's access to various accounts and financial records. As to the third element, there was a question of fact, because it was unlikely that the plaintiff, even if he had exercised his rights as a shareholder, could have discovered the fraud. Therefore, it was improper for the trial court to grant summary judgment for the defendant lawyers on statute of limitations grounds. This was true even though the plaintiff admitted that he commenced the malpractice action more than six years after a certain business deal failed, well beyond the applicable three-year statute of limitations.

d. Agreement of the Parties

Within reasonable limits, persons may contractually agree to lengthen or shorten the statute of limitations. If the agreement is valid, a party thereto is estopped from asserting the statute of limitations as a defense.

(1) Tolling Agreements

A contract which lengthens the filing period may do so to allow more time for investigation of the facts or settlement negotiations, in the hope of avoiding the bad publicity that attends the filing of a lawsuit. That type of arrangement is referred to as a "tolling agreement."

(2) Shortening the Filing Period

An agreement purporting to shorten the filing period for disputes is only valid if it allows an aggrieved party an adequate opportunity to seek legal redress. For example, in *Charnay v. Cobert*, 145 Cal. App. 4th 170, 51 Cal. Rptr. 3d 471 (2006), a client alleged that she had been misled by her lawyer about her exposure to liability for attorney's fees in litigation. In a malpractice action alleging fraud, negligent misrepresentation, and breach of fiduciary duty, the defendant argued that the action was barred by a provision in the lawyer-client contract stating that the client would be billed monthly, and that if the client did not object to a bill within ten days, the law firm would assume that the client did not dispute the bill's accuracy. Rejecting that contention, the California Court of Appeal wrote:

> [I]f the notice provision were interpreted to be an agreement to shorten the applicable limitations period, it would be unreasonable as a matter of law and thus unenforceable ***. Whatever the outside limit may be for shortening a limitations period ***, we have no doubt requiring a client to assert a claim for breach of contract against her attorney within 10 days of receipt of a billing statement is inherently unreasonable.

51 Cal. Rptr. 3d at 481. The court further noted that "no decision upholding the validity of a contractually shortened limitation period has done so in the context of an action against a professional or skilled expert where breach of a duty is *** difficult to detect." *Id.* at 481-82. The court also observed that allowing the notice provision to bar the plaintiff's suit "would abrogate *** [California's] well-established delayed discovery rule applicable to actions asserting breach of fiduciary duty." *Id.* at 482.

In *Williams v. Kublick*, 41 A.D.3d 1193, 837 N.Y.S.2d 803 (2007), a lawyer, who was unaware that the language of an insurance contract shortened the statute of limitations from six years to two years, filed suit after the two-year deadline had passed. As a result, the client's claim was time-barred. In a subsequent malpractice action against the lawyer, a New

York appellate court held that the late filing was "negligence as a matter of law." 837 N.Y.S.2d at 730.

e. Pendency of Other Litigation

Considerations relating to judicial efficiency sometimes warrant the tolling of a malpractice statute of limitations. This is why some (but not all) states hold that a person alleging malpractice in connection with criminal representation may delay the initiation of the malpractice claim until judicial review of the underlying conviction has become final. (*See* Part B of this Chapter.) For example, in *McKnight v. Office of Public Defender*, 197 N.J. 180, 962 A.2d 482 (2008), a public defender failed to advise a client of the risk that he might be deported if he plead guilty to certain charges. The Supreme Court of New Jersey held that the two-year statute of limitations ran from the date that the client received post-conviction relief setting aside his guilty plea.

Similar considerations arise outside of the criminal practice context. In *Fontanella v. Marcucci*, 89 Conn. App. 690, 877 A.2d 828 (2005), *certification granted in part*, 275 Conn. 907, 882 A.2d 670 (2005), *certification withdrawn* (Mar. 13, 2006), the victims of an auto accident alleged that their lawyers were negligent in failing to obtain and preserve evidence of alleged seatbelt failure. The court held that "because of the complexity of the legal and factual issues arising out of the spoliation of evidence relating to the product liability claim, the legal malpractice claim was not capable of being adjudicated by the judicial power until the underlying product liability claim was resolved by final judgment." 877 A.2d at 830. Therefore, the running of the statute of limitations on the plaintiff's legal malpractice and breach of contract claims was tolled during the pendency of the underlying action.

Texas applies a bright-line tolling rule to a broad category of legal malpractice cases: "When an attorney commits malpractice in the prosecution or defense of a claim that results in litigation, the statute of limitations on a malpractice claim against that attorney is tolled until all appeals on the underlying claim are exhausted or the litigation is otherwise finally concluded." *Apex Towing Co. v. Tolin*, 41 S.W.3d 118, 119 (Tex. 2001). The *Apex Towing* court concluded that, on the facts of the case, the two-year statute of limitations began to run when the court of appeals issued an order dismissing an appeal in the litigation that was the basis for the malpractice claim. This was true despite the fact that the plaintiff had previously hired a new attorney and ultimately settled the litigation.

f. Equitable Estoppel

Some courts will toll the running of the statute of limitations under the doctrine of equitable estoppel. Generally, the defendant must have intended to deceive the plaintiff, made misrepresentations, or engaged in bad faith tactics to delay the commencement of litigation. In *Abdelsame v. Foden de Castro*, 2007 WL 2036849, *3 (Conn. Super. Ct.), the plaintiff was deported from the United States after traveling to Egypt, allegedly as the result of the defendant lawyer's failure to properly advise him about travel and to have his passport stamped correctly. The court found the equitable tolling doctrine inapplicable to the facts of the case because there was no evidence that "the defendant intended to induce or deceive the plaintiff into believing that he could travel in and out of the United States, or that the defendant lulled the plaintiff into believing that it was not necessary for him to commence litigation, or that it was impossible for him to file a timely claim from Egypt." *Id*. at *3.

3. Continuing Torts

The "continuing tort" doctrine occasionally plays a role in legal malpractice litigation. A continuing tort is one that is inflicted over a period of time and involves wrongful conduct that is repeated until desisted.

It is not sufficient that there are continual ill effects arising from a completed violation of the plaintiff's rights. There is only a continuing tort if the tortious conduct persists.

In cases involving a continuing tort, the plaintiff's cause of action accrues, and the statute of limitations begins to run, on the date of the last injury, or when the tortious conduct ceased. As interpreted by some courts, if suit for a continuing tort is timely filed, a jury may award damages for all of the wrongs committed during the progress of the continuing tort, even if those actions occurred many years earlier.

In *Pierce v. Cook*, 992 So.2d 612 (Miss. 2008), a lawyer represented a husband, wife, and son on a medical malpractice claim. During the course of the representation, the lawyer had an adulterous affair with the wife. In affirming a $1.5 million award for the husband on a variety of legal theories, the Mississippi Supreme Court held that the husband's claim for intentional infliction of emotional distress was not barred by a one-year statute of limitations because the lawyer had committed a continuing tort which lasted until the couple's divorce. Not only had the lawyer taken the wife on a trip to New Orleans, during which he had sexual relations with her, he also flaunted his involvement with the wife in front of her husband at a restaurant, coached the wife on what to say to her husband during a phone call, and called the husband on the phone to apologize about the situation. The court found that there was repeated wrongful conduct by the lawyer.

D. NONASSIGNABILITY OF LEGAL MALPRACTICE CLAIMS

Most states hold that, for reasons of public policy, a legal malpractice claim is not assignable. Thus, a client cannot settle with an adversary by assigning to the adversary the client's right to sue the client's lawyer. If such an assignment is made and a malpractice claim is initiated by the adversary, the defendant lawyer can usually defeat the claim by arguing nonassignability.

Legal malpractice claims cannot be transferred because permitting that practice would pose a serious threat to the justice system. An adversary could drive a wedge between a client and lawyer by offering a favorable settlement to the client at the expense of the lawyer. Ultimately, lawyers might become reluctant to represent certain types of clients, such as those who are underinsured or judgment-proof.

Moreover, if a malpractice claim were assigned, the client would lose control over the litigation, but the client's lawyer would have the right to defend against the claim by revealing confidential client information. (*See* Model Rules of Prof'l Conduct R. 1.6(b)(5) (2010).)

In *Kim v. O'Sullivan*, 133 Wash. App. 557, 137 P.3d 61, 64-65 (2006), the Washington State Court of Appeals refused to permit circumvention of the nonassignment rule by an agreement that the client would prosecute the malpractice claim in his own name for the benefit of the client's former adversary. The court held that the agreement was invalid and therefore the malpractice action was subject to dismissal because the adversary was the real party in interest.

Most applications of the nonassignment rule are straightforward. Thus, a malpractice claim cannot be sold or given away. However, the rule against assignment sometimes is recognized in surprising ways. In *Johnson v. Hart*, 279 Va. 617, 692 S.E.2d 239 (2010), the Supreme Court of Virginia considered whether the sole testamentary beneficiary of an estate, *in her individual capacity*, could maintain a legal malpractice action against the estate's lawyer for negligence in representing the estate. The court answered that question in the negative reasoning that to allow such a claim would violate the principle that legal malpractice claims are not assignable.

There is a difference between assigning a malpractice claim and assigning rights under a malpractice insurance policy. A law firm may settle a claim for malpractice by assigning to the plaintiff its rights against a malpractice insurer which denied coverage for the claim. *See C. Ingram Co. v. Philadelphia Indemnity Insurance Co.*, 303 Ga. App. 548, 694 S.E.2d 181, 183 (2010). Malpractice insurance is discussed in Chapter 11.

E.   JOINT LIABILITY AND REIMBURSEMENT

The principles of joint and several liability that apply in other tort actions typically govern responsibility for damages in legal malpractice cases. However, it is difficult to generalize about this area of the law because, in recent years, states have greatly modified the common law rules on governing the liability of joint tortfeasors. The law now differs substantially from one jurisdiction to the next. *See generally Restatement (Third) of Torts: Apportionment of Liability* (2000).

1.   Allocation of Fault to Other Persons

In many situations, tort defendants are now subject only to "several liability," which is individual and proportional, rather than "joint and several liability," under which a defendant may be liable for the wrongdoing of others in addition to personal wrongdoing. If liability is several, a defendant may seek to limit its responsibility for damages by having a portion of the fault which caused the plaintiff's losses allocated to one or more other persons.

In *Dennerline v. Atterholt,* 886 N.E.2d 582 (Ind. Ct. App. 2008), a law firm allegedly failed to advise a healthcare insurance trust that it had discovered that the trust was insolvent and needed to cease operations. Thereafter, the state insurance commissioner sued the firm for legal malpractice to recover millions of dollars in losses that the commission incurred when it liquidated the trust. The law firm argued that the losses were caused in whole or in part by various nonparties, including actuaries, a third-party administrator, the trust's management, trustees, member associations, and even the company from whom the trust purchased a computer system. The Indiana Court of Appeals recognized the theoretical viability of the law firm's comparative fault argument. However, it concluded that the jury had properly allocated 100% of the fault to the law firm because the firm failed to prove that alleged breaches of duty by the various nonparties had caused any of the damages.

2. Contribution

If liability is several, there is generally no need to talk about reimbursement. No defendant pays more than its fair share because several liability is proportional.

However, where liability is joint and several, contribution and indemnity may be important issues. While these principles do not reduce the defendant's liability to the plaintiff, they sometimes allow a defendant to obtain reimbursement for amounts paid to the plaintiff as a result of a malpractice claim. Contribution is partial reimbursement; indemnity is total reimbursement.

As explained in basic law school courses, states award contribution on either a proportional or a *pro rata* basis. In proportional states, a person liable for contribution must pay the person entitled to contribution an amount equivalent to the percentage of the plaintiff's losses caused by the liable party. In *pro rata* states, contribution is calculated by counting heads. If there are four joint tortfeasors, each can be made to reimburse a party entitled to contribution for one-fourth of the plaintiff's losses.

Intentional tortfeasors generally have no right to contribution. In addition, many states hold that contribution cannot be obtained from a settling joint tortfeasor. In these jurisdictions (but not in all states), settlement of claims is encouraged by the fact that a tortfeasor who pays a settlement is sure that its exposure to liability is extinguished. This is true even though denying other joint tortfeasors contribution from the settling joint tortfeasor may ultimately result in an allocation of liability disproportionate to fault.

Except by settling with a potential defendant, a plaintiff cannot determine whether a defendant can assert contribution rights against another joint tortfeasor. Thus, in *Connell, Foley & Geiser, LLP v. Israel Travel Advisory Service, Inc.*, 377 N.J. Super. 350, 872 A.2d 1100 (App. Div. 2005), a New Jersey appellate court held that a contribution claim was validly stated against co-counsel, even though co-counsel was not admitted to practice in the state and was not named as a defendant in the malpractice action.

In every state, detailed rules govern the assertion of contribution rights. It is essential for a legal malpractice lawyer to become familiar with applicable statutory provisions and related precedent.

Contribution is available only from a person who qualifies as a joint tortfeasor. This means that if the person from whom contribution is sought owed no duty to the plaintiff in the underlying action, contribution will be denied. For example, *Breen v. Law Office of Bruce A. Barket, P.C.*, 52 A.D.3d 635, 862 N.Y.S.2d 50, 53 (2008), was a legal malpractice action arising from a divorce. The former wife sued her lawyers, as well as her former husband's lawyer. The former wife's lawyers then sued the former husband's lawyer for contribution or indemnification. A New York appellate court rejected the reimbursement claims because there was no theory under which the former husband's lawyer owed a duty of care to the wife or to her lawyers. (*See* Chapter 5 Part I.) Thus, with respect to whatever harm the wife allegedly suffered as a result of her own lawyers' wrongful conduct, the husband's lawyer was not a joint tortfeasor.

3. Indemnity

The ascendency of proportionality principles in American tort law during the past half century means that indemnification (total reimbursement) is now available only in a limited range of situations. Two such occasions are where an innocent person is held vicariously liable for the tortious conduct of another or where one person has granted another person a contractual right to indemnity. A firm's governing agreement may entitle principals within the firm to indemnity from the firm under specified circumstances. However, lawyers practicing in limited liability entities (*see* Chapter 8 Part C) may be personally immunized from reimbursement claims by applicable statutory provisions. For example, the Tennessee limited liability partnership act provides that, except with respect to liability for any person under a partner's direct supervision and control:

> a partner in a registered limited liability partnership is not liable, directly or indirectly (including by way of indemnification, subrogation, contribution, assessment or otherwise), for debts, obligations and liabilities of or chargeable to the partnership or another partner, whether in tort, contract, or otherwise, arising from omissions, negligence, wrongful acts, misconduct or malpractice committed while the partnership is a registered limited liability partnership and in the course of the partnership business by another partner or an employee, agent, or representative of the partnership.

Tenn. Code Ann. § 61-1-306 (Westlaw 2010).

Common law indemnity is not available to a joint tortfeasor who was personally at fault. A blameworthy joint tortfeasor has rights to reimbursement only if such rights are granted by the law of contribution. For example, in *Spencer v. Gavin*, 400 N.J. Super. 220, 946 A.2d 1051 (App. Div. 2008), a lawyer acting as executor and administrator of three estates misappropriated their assets. A second lawyer, who did a small amount of work for one of the estates, allegedly knew about the misappropriation, but failed to disclose it. In a malpractice action by the estates, the second lawyer tried unsuccessfully to assert claims for indemnity and contribution against the first lawyer (and the first lawyer's estate, since the first lawyer had died). A New Jersey appellate court found that the second lawyer had no common law right to indemnification, presumably because this was not a case of innocent vicarious liability. The court held that if the second lawyer had actual knowledge of the wrongdoing, he had a duty to disclose that information. Furthermore, the contribution claim failed because the estate of the first lawyer had settled with the plaintiffs, and applicable state law barred contribution claims against settling joint tortfeasors. The *Spencer* court noted that the second lawyer might be entitled to a credit against any judgment eventually entered against him recognizing the fault of the settling defendants.

States differ with regard to how they calculate such credits. Some jurisdictions reduce the plaintiff's judgment on a dollar-for-dollar basis calculated by reference to the exact amount previously paid by a settling joint tortfeasor. If the settling joint tortfeasor paid the plaintiff $10,000, another joint tortfeasor against whom a judgment is subsequently entered will be given credit for the plaintiff's having already received $10,000. Other states hold that by settling with one of several tortfeasors, the plaintiff gives up the right to enforce a portion of a subsequent judgment equivalent to the percentage of the settling joint tortfeasor's share of the fault. This percentage is not determined until the eventual trial of the case. Therefore, under this type of system, a plaintiff cannot be sure about what is being given up by entry into a pretrial settlement. This uncertainty may discourage the plaintiff from settling, particularly with seemingly peripheral parties. In some states, there are other types of rules for calculating credits in cases where some, but not all, of the responsible parties settled before trial.

In *Powell v. Wood County Com'n*, 209 W. Va. 639, 550 S.E.2d 617, 620-21 (2001), the Supreme Court of Appeals of West Virginia held that a statute conferring immunity on court-appointed criminal defense counsel logically required a county to indemnify appointed counsel from costs incurred in defending against a malpractice claim.

4. Claims Involving Successive Counsel or Co-counsel

In many states, a lawyer responsible for malpractice may obtain contribution or indemnity from another lawyer involved in the client's representation. This is true regardless of whether the other lawyer served as predecessor counsel, co-counsel, or successor counsel. *See, e.g.*, *Bolton v. Weil, Gotshal & Manges, LLP*, 9 Misc. 3d 1105(A), 806 N.Y.S.2d 443, 2005 WL 2185470, *3 (N.Y. Sup.). Thus, if a law firm is vicariously liable for the malpractice of outside co-counsel (*see* Chapter 8 Part D), the outside lawyer may be obliged to pay contribution or indemnity. *See Restatement (Third) of the Law Governing Lawyers* § 58 cmt. e (2000).

However, a few jurisdictions have barred some types of reimbursement claims because of perceived conflicts of interest or threats to client confidences. For example, California prohibits a negligent initial lawyer from seeking reimbursement from a negligent *successor lawyer*. As the California Supreme Court explained in *Musser v. Provencher*, 28 Cal. 4th 274, 48 P.3d 408, 408, 121 Cal. Rptr. 2d 373 (2002):

> The threat of an indemnification action would arguably create a conflict of interest between the successor attorney and the client because the greater the award the successor attorney managed to obtain for the client in the malpractice action, the greater the exposure [of the successor attorney] to the [claim of the] predecessor attorney in the indemnification action. ***. [Moreover, in] order to defend against an indemnification action, the successor attorney might be tempted to compromise the confidentiality of communications with the client.

48 P.3d at 412. However, California holds that whether reimbursement claims should be permitted *between co-counsel* should be decided on a case-by-case basis. Because the *Musser* court concluded that, on the facts of the case before it, there was no danger of conflict of interest or risk to client confidences, it allowed a family law lawyer to assert a reimbursement claim against a bankruptcy lawyer who had provided erroneous information which the family lawyer then relied upon in the client's representation.

F.   RELEASES AND COVENANTS NOT TO SUE

Under traditional rules, now modified in many jurisdictions, there were two important types of settlement documents. A "release" given to one tortfeasor extinguished the plaintiff's rights against all joint tortfeasors. However, a "covenant not to sue" a tortfeasor was enforceable only by the person to whom it was given, and did not affect the plaintiff's rights against other joint tortfeasors.

There was often confusion as to the legal effect of a document which, although denominated a "release," purported to reserve rights against some joint tortfeasors. This sometimes meant that a plaintiff, who thought that rights had been reserved, was unexpectedly barred from litigating a case against one wrongdoer because of an earlier settlement with another person involved in the relevant events.

To avoid ensnaring plaintiffs in the legal traps inherent to this area of the law, the *Restatement* embraces a sensible position: "A valid release of one tortfeasor *** does not discharge others liable for the same harm, unless it is agreed that it will discharge them." *Restatement (Second) of Torts* (§ 885) (1979). Under the *Restatement*, the plaintiff's intent to reserve rights need not be written and can be proved by parol evidence.

Some states go even further than the *Restatement* in attempting to prevent the inadvertent release of legal claims. For example, in *McMillen v. Klingensmith*, 467 S.W.2d 193 (Tex. 1971), the Texas Supreme Court held that a settlement document releases from liability only those tortfeasors named or otherwise specifically identified in the document, and no others.

1.   Settlement with a Third Person

In *Channel v. Loyacono*, 954 So. 2d 415, 427 (Miss. 2007), the Mississippi Supreme Court held that a client's release of claims against the defendant in a lawsuit did not bar a subsequent malpractice action against the client's lawyers. This was true because the lawyers were not named as released parties in the document executed when the underlying case was settled.

Nevertheless, some states still require a settling plaintiff to specifically reserve rights against tortfeasors not involved in the settlement. In *Prince v. Buck*, 969 So.2d 641 (La. Ct. App. 2007), the plaintiff hired lawyers (including Buck) to represent him in a worker's compensation dispute. When Buck withdrew, the plaintiff filed a motion for sanctions against him. Before that motion was resolved, other lawyers for the plaintiff settled his worker's compensation claim. The release executed incidental to that settlement did not contain a reservation of rights against Buck (nor did it, apparently, expressly release Buck). The Louisiana Court of Appeal held that the plaintiff's subsequent malpractice action against Buck was barred by the release that he signed in the worker's compensation dispute. The case illustrates that, even today, lawyers must exercise great care with respect to the drafting and signing of settlement documents. Failure to do so is itself a basis for a legal malpractice claim.

2. Settlement with the Defendant

Sometimes a malpractice claim is barred because there has been a related settlement of claims with the same defendant in another proceeding. For example, in *Liberty Associates v. Etkin*, 69 A.D.3d 681, 893 N.Y.S.2d 564 (2010), a client sued a lawyer for legal malpractice. Later, while the malpractice claim was pending, the lawyer's firm commenced a separate proceeding against the plaintiff for unpaid fees. After the fee dispute was settled, the lawyer successfully moved to dismiss the malpractice claim. A New York appellate court wrote:

> This action to recover damages for legal malpractice against Etkin, as a member of the Ravin Firm, arises out of the same series of transactions as the fee dispute action asserted by the Ravin Firm against the plaintiff herein for legal fees. Upon resolution of the fee dispute action, the parties, by their attorneys, executed a stipulation of dismissal with prejudice and without costs. A stipulation of discontinuance with prejudice without reservation of right or limitation of the claims disposed of is entitled to preclusive effect under the doctrine of *res judicata*.

893 N.Y.S.2d at 565.

Lawyers may not secure from a client a relinquishment of claims without complying with applicable rules of legal ethics. In general, it is unethical for a lawyer to make an agreement *prospectively limiting* the lawyer's liability to a client for malpractice unless the client is represented by independent counsel in making the agreement. Further, a lawyer may not *settle an existing claim* with an unrepresented client or former client without advising that person *in writing* of the desirability of obtaining independent counsel, and allowing that person a reasonable opportunity to do so. *See* Model Rules Prof'l Conduct R. 1.8(h) (2010). A release obtained in violation of these rules will subject a lawyer to discipline, and may be deemed unenforceable by a court.

G. PRIVILEGES AND IMMUNITIES

Privileges or immunities generally fall within two broad categories: absolute and qualified. Conduct coming within the terms of an absolute privilege or immunity is wholly insulated from the risk of liability. The defendant's state of mind and the reasonableness of the defendant's conduct are irrelevant. In contrast, a qualified privilege or immunity is conditional, which is to say defeasible. Depending on what the defendant knows, or how or why the defendant acted, the protection of a qualified privilege or immunity may be lost.

1. The Absolute Judicial Proceedings Privilege (Litigation Privilege)

The judicial proceedings privilege, which is sometimes called the litigation privilege, bars a wide variety of claims arising from statements made by participants in lawsuits, such as lawyers, clients, and witnesses. The privilege is absolute, so long as the statement in question, in a broad sense, is related to the litigation. Thus, the privilege applies not only to what is said in a courtroom, but also to depositions and pleadings, as well as certain other out-of-court utterances. This includes some statements made by lawyers before a suit is filed. *See Restatement (Second) of Torts* § 586 (1977).

Finding that courts apply an "extremely liberal" test in determining what statements are pertinent to litigation, and therefore protected, the Second Circuit held that allegedly defamatory statements in an e-mail message relating to a fee dispute arising from litigation could not serve as the basis for a cause of action. *See Cassuto v. Shulick*, 313 Fed. Appx. 448 (2d Cir. 2009).

Nevertheless, courts sometimes find that statements connected to litigation are not protected by the absolute judicial proceedings privilege. For example, in *Bochetto v. Gibson*, 580 Pa. 245, 860 A.2d 67 (Pa. 2004), a lawyer (Bochetto) was sued for malpractice based on conduct related to the defense of a client in quiet-title actions. In the legal malpractice action, the client (the malpractice plaintiff) was represented by a new lawyer (Gibson). The malpractice complaint alleged that Bochetto had breached fiduciary obligations by failing to disclose an expert report to the client and by misconduct related to the procurement of a substitute expert report. After filing the legal malpractice complaint for his client, Gibson faxed a copy to a reporter with the *Legal Intelligencer* (Dudick). The result was the publication of a story which Bochetto claimed was false and defamatory. In Bochetto's defamation action against Gibson and his law firm, the defendants argued that the claim was barred by the judicial proceedings privilege. The Supreme Court of Pennsylvania held that absolute immunity extends only to communications which are issued in the regular course of judicial proceedings and are pertinent and material to the redress or relief the plaintiff seeks. Under this standard, Gibson's publication of the complaint to the trial court was clearly protected by the privilege. However, because Gibson's act of sending the complaint to Dudick was an extrajudicial act that occurred outside of the regular course of judicial proceedings, and was not relevant in any way to those proceedings, it plainly was not protected by the judicial proceedings privilege. The court noted, however, that liability for faxing the complaint to the reporter might be barred by qualified immunity. (Qualified immunities are discussed later in this Chapter.)

Importantly, the judicial proceedings privilege applies only to claims arising from *statements* pertinent to litigation. A garden-variety malpractice claim by a client, based on a lawyer's acts or omissions during the course of a lawsuit, is not barred by the privilege. As the California Court of Appeal observed, there is "no sound reason why litigators should be exempted from malpractice liability." *Kolar v. Donahue, McIntosh & Hammerton*, 145 Cal. App. 4th 1532, 52 Cal. Rptr. 3d 712, 719 (2006).

2. Qualified Privileges

A qualified privilege arises when there is good reason for the law to encourage or permit certain types of conduct. *See Restatement (Second) of Torts* §§ 593-598A (1977). However, such a privilege is lost by "abuse," which may occur if a person acts with an improper purpose, with knowledge of a statement's falsity, or publishes a statement excessively by disseminating a statement to improper recipients. *See Restatement (Second) of Torts* §§ 599-605A (1977).

A lawyer has a qualified privilege to represent his or her client. Thus, a lawyer for one co-defendant can make an argument on that client's behalf even if the lawyer knows that doing so may cause harm to another, separately represented, co-defendant. *See*

Maynard v. Caballero, 752 S.W.2d 719, 721 (Tex. App. 1988).

3. Truth

An allegedly defamatory statement may be privileged because it is substantially true. In *Pitcock v. Kasowitz, Benson, Torres & Friedman LLP*, 74 A.D.3d 613, 614, 903 N.Y.S.2d 43 (2010), a trade publication reported that a partner had "jump[ed] ship" from the defendant law firm. In response, the law firm issued a press release stating that the ex-partner had been terminated because of "extremely inappropriate" behavior, which news reports said included suggestive comments, gender-specific jokes, and obscene gestures. 903 N.Y.S.2d at 44. A New York appellate court ruled that the firm did not defame the ex-partner because the statements were substantially true.

4. Immunity of Public Defenders and Court-Appointed Lawyers

Public defenders are often protected from malpractice liability by some form of absolute or qualified statutory immunity. For example, in *Osborne v. Goodlet*, 2005 WL 1713868, *1 (Tenn. Ct. App.), the plaintiff alleged that his public defender committed malpractice by failing to interview a co-defendant and subpoena him for trial, preventing the plaintiff from testifying in his own defense, and otherwise not providing adequate representation. The Tennessee Court of Appeals found that the defendant lawyer was absolutely immune under a state statute which provided:

>   State officers and employees are absolutely im-
>   mune from liability for acts or omissions within
>   the scope of the officer's or employee's office or
>   employment, except for willful, malicious, or
>   criminal acts or omissions or for acts or omissions
>   done for personal gain. ***.

Id. Moreover, the defendant was further immune
from suit because another statute provided in relevant part:

>   No court in this state has any power, jurisdiction
>   or authority to entertain any suit against *** any
>   public defender *** with a view to reach the ***
>   funds or property of any public defender *** for
>   any act of negligence arising from the execution of
>   *** official duties as an employee of the district
>   public defenders conference.

Id.

However, some states have expressly ruled that
public defenders *are not* immune from suit. *See
Barner v. Leeds*, 24 Cal. 4th 676, 13 P.3d 704,
705-714, 102 Cal. Rptr. 2d 97 (2000).

Court-appointed lawyers often face greater
exposure to malpractice liability than their public
defender counter parts. A "majority of states permit
legal malpractice actions against attorneys appointed
to represent criminal defendants *** [and only] a
small minority of states have statutes that provide
immunity to attorneys appointed to represent indigent criminal defendants." *Mooney v. Frazier*, 225 W.
Va. 358, 693 S.E.2d 333, 343 (2010).

Federal law does not provide immunity to a
private lawyer appointed by a federal judge in a

criminal case. *See Ferri v. Ackerman*, 444 U.S. 193, 202-05 100 S. Ct. 402, 62 L. Ed. 2d 355 (1979). However, immunity may be conferred *by state law*. In *Mooney*, the Supreme Court of Appeals of West Virginia held that "an attorney appointed by a federal court to represent a criminal defendant, in a federal criminal prosecution in West Virginia, has absolute immunity from purely state law claims of legal malpractice that derive from the attorney's conduct in the underlying criminal proceedings." 693 S.E.2d at 345.

H. ARBITRATION AGREEMENTS

Mandatory arbitration provisions in lawyer-client contracts are sometimes held to be valid and enforceable. However, courts have occasionally refused to enforce an arbitration clause on the ground that, on the particular facts, it constituted an adhesion contract. *See LaFleur v. Law Offices of Anthony G. Buzbee, P.C.*, 960 So. 2d 105, 110 (La. Ct. App. 2007).

The Supreme Court of Texas Professional Ethics Committee concluded that a lawyer's use of a malpractice arbitration clause in a fee agreement is not *per se* an unethical attempt to limit malpractice liability. Tex. Eth. Op. 586, 2008 WL 5680298. However, the committee noted three important constraints on the use of arbitration agreements:

- First, use of an arbitration clause that prohibits the recovery of certain otherwise allowable damages for legal malpractice would be an impermissible and unethical limitation on a lawyer's malpractice liability.

■   Second, a lawyer may not include clearly
    unfair terms in an arbitration agreement,
    such as language giving the lawyer the sole
    right to select an arbitrator, requiring arbitra-
    tion in a remote location, or entailing exces-
    sive costs that would effectively foreclose the
    client's use of arbitration.

■   Third, a client must receive sufficient infor-
    mation about the differences between litiga-
    tion and arbitration to permit the client to
    make an informed decision about the wisdom
    of agreeing to binding arbitration. A lawyer
    should normally advise an individual or
    small-business client about relevant costs and
    time savings and the fact that choosing arbi-
    tration may entail waiver of significant rights,
    such as the right to a jury trial, reduced
    availability of discovery, inapplicability of the
    rules of evidence, and great restrictions on
    the right to appeal an adverse decision.

In many respects, the principles of legal malpractice law protect lawyers from liability. Consider, for
example, the rules that permit lawyers to reasonably
exercise discretion without risk of liability (*see* Chapter 3 Part B-2) or that impose demanding causation
requirements on malpractice plaintiffs that necessi-
tate a "trial within a trial" (*see* Chapter 3 Part C). A
lawyer who elects to include a malpractice claim
arbitration provision in a lawyer-client contract
cannot be sure that the usual substantive rules will be
followed by the arbitrator. Moreover, if the arbitrator
departs from well-establish malpractice principles,
there will be little opportunity to appeal a resulting

adverse ruling. Consequently, choosing arbitration over litigation has risks. Arbitration may not minimize a lawyer's exposure to liability.

I. SLAPP LAWS

Lawsuits are often filed not to win, but to silence critics who may be coerced to back down rather than face the inconvenience, expense, and uncertainties of litigation. Not surprisingly, many states have sought to curb such abuses, at least insofar as they threaten to diminish discussion and resolution of public issues. These states have passed what are called "SLAPP" laws. The acronym is short for "Strategic Lawsuits Against Public Participation." SLAPP laws provide for early dismissal of unmeritorious claims filed to interfere with the valid exercise of the Constitutional rights of free speech and petition.

Occasionally lawyers assert that a malpractice claim is barred by a SLAPP law. However, this type of defense seldom succeeds.

For example, in *Kmart v. Lewis Brisbois Bisgaard & Smith LLP*, 2010 WL 2804360 (Cal. Ct. App.), the court found that although "malpractice claims challenging the competency of legal counsel typically reference protected litigation activities," such claims are rarely subject to dismissal under California's SLAPP statute. The *Kmart* malpractice action alleged that the defendant lawyers had improperly represented and disclosed information to a party with adverse interests. The court found that the act giving rise to the plaintiff's breach of loyalty and confidentiality claims was not the defendant lawyers' filing of suit on behalf of the adverse party, but their decision to undertake a representation that allegedly violated ethical standards. Consequently, California's SLAPP law was inapplicable.

J. JUDICIAL ESTOPPEL

A malpractice claim may be barred by judicial estoppel. That doctrine prohibits a party from deliberately taking inconsistent factual positions in different cases involving related matters or in different phases of the same case.

In *Jackson v. Hancock & Canada, L.L.P.*, 245 S.W.3d 51 (Tex. App. 2007), a Texas appellate court found that former clients who had failed to identify a potential legal malpractice action as an asset in their bankruptcy proceeding were thereafter precluded from prosecuting the malpractice claim.

Judicial estoppel sometimes does not bar an action because a party's later position is not "clearly inconsistent" with its former position. For example, in *Pike v. Mullikin*, 158 N.H. 267, 965 A.2d 987 (2009), a client, who feared that his antenuptial agreement with his wife was unenforceable, negotiated a division of assets with his wife. The couple then certified to the divorce court that they were each satisfied that the agreement was a fair and equitable resolution of the divorce. The Supreme Court of New Hampshire held that the client's subsequent legal malpractice action against the lawyers who drafted the antenuptial agreement was not barred by judicial estoppel. The court reasoned that, during the divorce proceedings, the client never asserted any claims or took any position with respect to the validity of the antenuptial agreement or the adequacy of the legal services the client's lawyer rendered in connection with its drafting. The client's acknowledgment that the division of assets was fair and equitable was not "clearly inconsistent" with his claim that the defendants committed malpractice.

CHAPTER EIGHT

VICARIOUS LIABILITY

A. LIABILITY OF LAW FIRMS

A malpractice plaintiff may seek to sue any of several possible defendants, including among others: (1) the lawyer who committed the malpractice, (2) that lawyer's law firm, (3) other lawyers who are members of the law firm, and perhaps even (4) lawyers practicing law in other firms. Mindful of these possibilities, this chapter focuses on issues of *vicarious liability*. It also addresses related issues of direct or *personal liability*.

Part A considers when a law firm is liable for harm caused by its lawyers and nonlawyer employees or agents. Part B deals with the liability of law firm principals (partners and shareholders) who practice law in firms that have not organized themselves as "limited liability" entities. Part C then explores the extent to which the organization of a law firm as a limited liability entity reduces a principal's exposure to vicarious liability. Finally, Part D discusses other types of arrangements which expose lawyers to liability for the wrongful conduct of other lawyers, such as referring clients to lawyers or office sharing.

1. The Benefits and Costs of Operating as a Law Firm

Lawyers often organize themselves into law firms. *See Restatement (Third) of the Law Governing Lawyers* § 9 (2000). This is done for a variety of reasons.

It is often easier for a law firm to take advantage of the economies of scale (relating, for example, to office space and facilities), to handle complex matters, or to compete for business from clients unwilling to entrust their affairs to a single lawyer.

The law firm structure also facilitates the monitoring of lawyer performance. Senior lawyers (such as partners, shareholders, or senior associates) supervise the performance of more junior lawyers. This tends to ensure a quality product and produce client satisfaction.

In addition, newer members of a law firm usually have an incentive to work hard and excel at their chosen profession because firms often defer a significant amount of compensation and confer it only on the winners of the promotion-to-partnership "tournament." *See* Vincent R. Johnson, "On Shared Human Capital, Promotion Tournaments, and Exponential Law Firm Growth," 70 *Tex. L. Rev.* 537 (1991).

The structure of law firms can offer other advantages related to client protection. In order to enhance and safeguard the firm's reputation, and reduce exposure to liability, law firms frequently create peer review committees and adopt other mechanisms that tend to ensure that the delivery of legal services is rendered in a manner consistent with the lawyers' legal and ethical obligations. *See* Susan Saab Fortney,

"Am I My Partner's Keeper? Peer Review in Law Firms," 66 *U. Colo. L. Rev.* 329 (1995).

Of course, if lawyers personally benefit from operating as law firms, they should have to internalize the costs of that form of doing business. Thus, issues regularly arise about the vicarious liability of law firms and their principals for harm caused by lawyers and non-lawyer employees of the firm.

2. Vicarious Liability of Law Firms

In *National Union Fire Insurance Co. of Pittsburgh, PA v. Wuerth*, 122 Ohio St.3d 594, 913 N.E.2d 939 (2009), the Supreme Court of Ohio, by a divided vote, held that because a firm does not engage in the practice of law, it cannot commit legal malpractice directly. Further, according to the court, a law firm cannot be vicariously liable for malpractice unless one of its principals or associates is liable for malpractice. Whether all courts would agree with this analysis is open to doubt. Lawyer-client contracts often name the law firm, not individual lawyers within the firm, as the party responsible for providing legal services. Moreover, a law firm undoubtedly will be liable for malpractice if a paralegal, not licensed to practice law, tarries on the way to the courthouse and arrives too late to file a lawsuit before the statute of limitations elapses. This is true even if it was entirely reasonable (*i.e.*, not negligent or in any other way tortious) for the lawyers in the firm to entrust the filing of the suit to the paralegal, and regardless of the fact that the lawyers may have been in no way personally responsible for untimely filing.

Nevertheless, the fact remains that vicarious liability is the chief, if perhaps not exclusive, theory under which law firms are held liable for malpractice. It is often essential to prove that a particular lawyer in the firm breached professional duties owed to the plaintiff.

However, the fact that a lawyer in the firm engaged in tortious conduct and could be held personally liable is not, in itself, enough to make the law firm vicariously responsible. The law firm will be accountable only if the tort was sufficiently related to the business of the law firm to make it fair to require the firm to pay damages.

It is generally agreed that:

A law firm is subject to civil liability for injury legally caused to a person by any wrongful act or omission of any principal or employee of the firm who was acting in the ordinary course of the firm's business or with actual or apparent authority.

Licette Music Corp. v. Sills, Cummis, Zuckerman, Radin, Tischman, Epstein & Gross, P.A., 2009 WL 2045259, *7 (N.J. Super. A.D. 2009) (quoting *Restatement (Third) of the Law Governing Lawyers* § 58(1) (2000)). Thus, there are three different avenues to establishing a law firm's vicarious responsibility: ordinary course of business, actual authority, and apparent authority. These bases for liability are discussed below.

a. Ordinary Course of Business

The vicarious liability of law firms is based on traditional principles of *respondeat superior* and enterprise liability. *See Restatement (Third) of the Law Governing Lawyers* § 58 cmt. b (**2000**). Thus, the precedent that has emerged in other areas of tort law relating to these principles plays a role in determining whether malpractice occurred in the "ordinary course" of a law firm's business.

According to the *Restatement*:

> The ordinary course of business of a law firm includes the practice of law and various activities normally related to it. Thus, liability is imposed for legal malpractice *** by any firm lawyer; ***; misapplication of funds in the custody of the firm or its personnel ***; and torts committed by a principal or employee while acting in the scope of employment, for example for the negligent driving of an employee who is on firm business.

Restatement (Third) of the Law Governing Lawyers § 58 cmt. d (2000).

Conduct that is unrelated to a firm's practice of law or ancillary activities is not within the firm's ordinary course of business. Thus, a law firm is not liable for harm that arises from the operations of a principal's independent business partnership. *Id.* The same is true with respect to acts of non-principals that are outside the scope of their employment. Consequently, a law firm is not responsible for losses caused by the misdrafting of a will that is written by a nonlawyer firm librarian acting with no authority to undertake that task. *Id.*

The breadth of the ordinary course of business differs from firm to firm. A firm that routinely makes investments for clients from settlement proceeds may therefore have broader exposure to vicarious liability than a firm that does not undertake such tasks. *Id.*

There are different ways of interpreting the phrase "ordinary course of business." One possibility is to focus on whether the alleged malpractice was part of the normal risks of operating a law firm. Another approach is to focus on whether the conduct was intended to benefit the firm. These ideas, which are sometimes complementary and other times at odds, are discussed below.

(1) Normal Risks Incidental to the Practice of Law

It is fair to hold a law firm responsible for harm resulting from normal risks that are incidental to the practice of law. Thus, some types of malpractice, such as the misdrafting of a document or the late filing of a lawsuit, are routinely found to fall within the ordinary course of business. They are the type of errors that may occur when persons working for a law firm fail to exercise care when performing common tasks. These types of mistakes are incidental to law practice. Except for the errors, the drafting and the filing of the lawsuit were routine firm activities. It is therefore fair to hold the firm liable for these types of losses. If the firm enjoys the benefits of a certain mode of doing business, it should also bear the losses which are, more or less, normal incidents of that type of operation.

(2) Abnormal Risks

Some malpractice cases involve special risks which might be thought of as "abnormal" in the sense that they are not an inevitable or necessary part of the practice of law. Most lawyers represent clients without lying, stealing funds or property, or sexually abusing individuals. The risk of these types of harm is extra-ordinary. Cases involving these types of conduct often pose difficult questions as to whether a law firm should be liable for resulting losses. Two ways of approaching these kinds of issues are to focus on whether the conduct was intended, at least in part, to benefit the firm, or on whether the conduct violated the standards of conduct applicable to the practice of law in general or the law firm in particular. These factors are considered below.

(a) Conduct Intended to Benefit the Law Firm

Intent to benefit the law firm is often an important factor in determining whether conduct will be imputed to a firm. This is not surprising because vicarious liability will be imposed under *respondeat superior* principles only if an agent's conduct was intended, at least in part, to further the business purposes of the principal. *Cf. Restatement (Third) of Agency* § 7.07(2) (2006).

The second *Restatement of Agency* contained a list of factors for ascertaining whether conduct was within the scope of employment. That list emphasized the importance of the tortfeasor's intent to benefit the party the plaintiff seeks to hold vicariously liable.

According to the second *Restatement*, the conduct of a servant is within the scope of employment if, but only if:

> (a) it is of the kind he is employed to perform;
>
> (b) it occurs substantially within the authorized time and space limits;
>
> (c) it is actuated, at least in part, by a purpose to serve the master; and
>
> (d) if force is intentionally used by the servant against another, the use of the force is not unexpectable by the master.

Restatement (Second) of Agency § 228 (1958). Although the second *Restatement* has been superseded, the factors enunciated in § 228 are part of the law in many jurisdictions. The third *Restatement* uses different language to discuss scope of employment, but is consistent in important respects:

> (2) An employee acts within the scope of employment when performing work assigned by the employer or engaging in a course of conduct subject to the employer's control. An employee's act is not within the scope of employment when it occurs within an independent course of conduct not intended by the employee to serve any purpose of the employer.

Restatement (Third) of Agency § 7.07(2) (2006).

(b) Conduct Not Intended to Benefit the Law Firm

Conduct not intended to benefit a law firm is often found to fall outside the ordinary course of business.

For example, in *O'Toole v. Carr*, 175 N.J. 421, 815 A.2d 471 (N.J. 2003), the Supreme Court of New Jersey held that a law firm was not responsible for an auto accident involving one of its partners who was on his way to a part-time job as a municipal judge. The plaintiff argued that the law firm indirectly benefitted from the partner's service as a judge, even though no income from the judgship was paid to the firm. In rejecting this claim, the court wrote:

> [The parties] argue that we should consider the broad articulation of enterprise liability adopted in California, which states that the "'modern and proper basis of vicarious liability of the master is not his control or fault but the risks incident to his enterprise.'" *** In other words, "'[t]he losses caused by the torts of employees, which as a practical matter are sure to occur in the conduct of the employer's enterprise, are placed upon that enterprise itself, as a required cost of doing business.'" ***.

> *** [W]e have thus far declined to adopt that view, retaining instead the *Restatement* as our vicarious liability standard ***. Further, even if we were inclined to adopt the broadest view of enterprise liability, it would not alter the outcome in this case ***. Carr's commutation to his job as a municipal court judge is, as a legal matter, unrelated to his law firm activity. Accordingly, the accident could in no event be considered a risk incident to that enterprise.

815 A.2d at 474.

If a law firm receptionist misuses client information to commit identity theft for personal gain it can be argued (probably successfully) that the misconduct does not fall within the ordinary course of the law firm's business. Presumably, there was no intent on the part of the receptionist to benefit the law firm by misusing the clients' personal information. (Of course, even if the firm is not *vicariously* liable for the receptionist's commission of identity theft, the firm might be liable for *negligent* failure to protect client information from unauthorized access, if such harm was foreseeable and could have been prevented.)

(c) Conduct Violative of Professional Standards of Conduct

Some courts have focused on the unethical and professionally prohibited nature of a lawyer's conduct as a reason to conclude that it did not occur within the ordinary course of law firm business. However, whether that factor should amount to a hard-and-fast rule is open to question.

In every state, ethics rules prohibit the over-billing of clients. *See* Model Rules of Prof'l Conduct R. 1.5(a) (2010). However, if over-billing by a partner enriches not only the partner (who receives an increased share of the firm's profits), but the firm (which enjoys the balance of the profits resulting from the over-billing), it can be argued that the firm should be subject to vicarious liability. The over-billing was intended, at least in part, to benefit the firm because the partner knew with substantial certainty that the firm would benefit. (*See Restatement (Third) of Torts: Liability for Physical and Emotional Harm* § 1(b)

(2010) (defining intent).) Indeed, on the assumed facts, not only was benefit intended, but the partner's conduct resulted in such a benefit. Moreover, the over-billing related directly to the business of the firm. Many persons would argue that those considerations are sufficient to bring the over-billing within the ordinary course of the firm's business. Nevertheless, some cases take a different path, focusing not on the tortfeasor's intent and the conduct's relationship to the firm's business, but on professional standards of conduct.

For example, in *Goodman v. Holmes & McLaurin Attorneys at Law*, 192 N.C. App. 467, 665 S.E.2d 526 (2008), the question was whether fraudulent conduct by a partner occurred in the ordinary course of a law firm's business. In *Goodman*, a lawyer (McLaurin) voluntarily dismissed a personal injury claim without the permission of the client, failed to re-file the claim before the statute of limitations lapsed, and then made misrepresentations over a period of years in order to conceal that misconduct from the client. In a subsequent malpractice action against the lawyer, his partner (Holmes), and the firms with which the two lawyers had been associated (the other "Holmes defendants"), a North Carolina appellate court found that claims for professional negligence and malpractice were barred by the state's statute of repose. As to the remaining claim for fraudulent concealment of professional negligence, the court held that the innocent partner and the law firms could not be vicariously liable. The court quoted the state's disciplinary rule which requires lawyers to keep clients reasonably informed about the status of their representation, then explained its reasoning as follows:

[T]he representation of a plaintiff in a personal injury action is clearly within the normal range of activities for a typical law partnership. However, fraud associated with such representation, including the failure to keep a client informed about the status of his or her case and the active concealment of the true state of affairs, in violation of the standards of the legal profession, is not in the ordinary course of the partnership business. There is nothing in plaintiff's complaint to suggest that the Holmes defendants authorized, participated in, or even knew about McLaurin's fraudulent conduct.

665 S.E.2d at 533.

The *Goodman* court cited with approval an earlier decision which held that, in view of the state's disciplinary rule prohibiting lawyers from engaging in malicious or harassing litigation, a partnership could not be vicariously liable for one partner's institution of a malicious prosecution. According to that court, malicious prosecution was not within the ordinary course of business of a law partnership.

At one level, decisions like *Goodman* make sense. How could conduct that is unethical and professionally prohibited be part of the "ordinary course" of business? Yet, on another level, decisions which place too much weight on the prohibited nature of the principal tortfeasor's conduct threaten to undercut the goals of vicarious liability. Those goals are discussed in the following section.

(d) The Goals of Vicarious Liability

Vicarious liability is a form of strict liability, liability without fault. In various areas of the law, strict liability is imposed for a variety of reasons. In some cases, the goal of strict liability is to deter future losses by making the party who is subject to strict liability especially vigilant with respect to loss prevention. Arguably, a law firm that is subject to strict liability for a principal or employee's misconduct will be more inclined to devote limited resources to making sure that such conduct does not occur again in the future. This is probably true even if the law firm could be sued for negligent supervision of the partner or associate (*see* Part B-3). As any shopkeeper knows, it is more effective to put up a sign saying, "If you break it, you bought it," than a sign advising customers, "If you break it, you bought it, if you failed to exercise care."

In other situations, the goal of strict liability is to shift a loss from an innocent victim to the enterprise whose operations created the risks that led to the victim's injury. Doing so forces the enterprise to internalize the risk as part of the costs of doing business. As a result, the enterprise will be likely to engage in an honest calculation of whether certain modes of operation are worth it. In the case of a law firm, this might mean that the firm will consider whether it is really worth having a lawyer operate a branch office in a distant city without adequate supervision.

In other instances, the purpose of strict liability is to spread losses broadly by placing them on an enterprise that can distribute the loss through marginally increased prices for goods and services, or perhaps through the purchase of insurance. In the case of law firms, imposing vicarious liability on a firm for harm caused to one client means that other clients of the firm may need to pay a bit more for the firm's legal services, or that the firm may need to pay higher premiums if it has malpractice insurance. However, spreading the loss broadly would ensure that the entire weight of a loss arising from the law firm's operations would not fall solely on one unfortunate victim or group of victims.

The merits of these arguments for strict vicarious liability are open to debate. Nevertheless, it is clear that American law has emphatically embraced the idea of strict vicarious liability in the business context. Enterprises are regularly held liable for a wide range of torts committed by their principals, employees, and other agents.

(e) Conduct Violative of the Law Firm's Own Rules

The idea that conduct violative of the legal profession's ethics rules is outside the ambit of the ordinary course of business is akin to the idea that an employer cannot be held liable for conduct of an employee that violates the employer's own rules. However, the latter proposition has been rejected by American law, and that rejection casts doubt on the viability of the former idea.

Employers are routinely subject to vicarious liability under *respondeat superior* principles even though they had "rules" which prohibited an employee from doing just the sort of thing that gave rise to tort liability. The reasoning of the courts in these cases is that an employer cannot undercut the policy foundations of strict vicarious liability (deterrence, internalization of costs, and spreading of losses) by simply placing a rule in the employee handbook. Thus, the fact that an employer has a rule prohibiting employees from driving fast, leaving dangerous equipment unattended, or neglecting important matters, does not mean that the employer cannot vicariously be held liable for such misconduct.

The American legal profession is governed by many rules derived from a variety of sources. Those rules prohibit such things as conflicts of interest, misuse of confidential information, and misrepresentation. Yet, it would be far too broad to say that a law firm can never be subject to vicarious liability for conduct involving conflicts of interest, breaches of confidentiality, and misleading statements.

The unethical and professionally prohibited nature of a lawyer's misconduct, or the fact that the law firm had a rule against such conduct, may be entitled to weight in the assessment of whether the conduct falls within the ordinary course of business. However, if so, the prohibited nature of the conduct is only one of many considerations relevant to the determination of whether a law firm should be subject to strict vicarious liability.

The fact that a law firm has malpractice-avoidance rules and procedures, does not remove malpractice from the ordinary course of a law firm's business.

Restatement (Third) of the Law Governing Lawyers § 58 cmt. d (2000).

(3) Enterprise Liability

It is often easier to raise questions about vicarious liability than to answer them. Suppose that a partner steals money from clients by lying to them about the resolution of their cases, forging their names on settlement checks, depositing those funds into the partner's own account, and then spending the money on personal matters. Is the law firm liable for the partner's misdeeds?

In resolving these types of issues, some court decisions downplay, or perhaps ignore, the question of whether the firm benefitted from the tortious conduct of one of its lawyers. (*See* Part A-2.) For example, in *Vanacore v. Kennedy*, 86 F. Supp. 2d 42 (D. Conn. 1998), *aff'd* 208 F.3d 204 (2d Cir. 2000), a federal court acknowledged that, under Connecticut law, for conduct to fall within the ordinary course of a law firm's business, the acts "must have: (1) been the kind of thing a law partner would do; (2) occurred substantially within the authorized time and geographic limits of the partnership; and (3) been motivated at least in part by a purpose to serve the partnership." 86 F. Supp. 2d at 51. However, the court concluded that under this standard the defendant law firm was liable for the harm that resulted when a partner stole a client's funds because the partner, in the "ordinary course" of serving as the client's lawyer, received trust funds from a third party in connection with the client's sale of a business. Instead of depositing those funds into the firm's trust account, they were misappropriated by the partner. It is difficult to see how the partner's conduct benefitted the law firm, unless one considers not just the misappropriation that harmed the client, but the larger set of facts which indicated that the partner had been serving the client on behalf of the firm for many years.

(a) Uncertain Focus of the Inquiry

Unfortunately, court decisions typically provide little guidance with respect to how narrowly or broadly one should focus in deciding whether conduct was within the ordinary course of business. Some decisions holding law firms liable are better explained not by the fact that the errant lawyer intended to benefit the firm, but by the fact that the firm had profited in the past from a mode of delivering legal services which created certain risks, including the risk of the tortious conduct that occurred.

(b) Liability for Sex-Related Injuries

Law firms sometimes escape liability for harm caused by sexual relationships between a lawyer and a client on the ground that such conduct by an employee was not intended to further the business purposes of the law firm. However, other cases have imposed liability, occasionally on the ground that such risks are incidental to the operation of a law firm. The grounds for holding a law firm vicariously liable are stronger in cases where the plaintiff is a client of the firm and the existence of a lawyer-client relationship facilitated the commission of the tort. *See Restatement (Third) of the Law Governing Lawyers* § 58 cmt. d (2000).

Some sex-related claims against law firms are filed not by clients, but by lawyers who were allegedly victims of conduct perpetrated by other employees of the firm. *See* Brian Baxter, *Former Bingham Associate Files Date Rape Suit Against Firm*, www.law.com, July 1, 2009.

In one recent case, a law firm clerical employee alleged that she was raped on the firm's premises by a lawyer in the firm. The plaintiff asserted that she was not merely an employee (and therefore a business invitee), but also a client of the firm because the firm provided *pro bono* legal services to her by advising her on child custody and appearing on her behalf in court. In an action against the law firm and the lawyer who allegedly committed the battery, the Louisiana Court of Appeal refused to grant summary judgment in favor of the firm because there were unresolved issues of fact as to the plaintiff's legal status and whether the firm had been negligent. *See Doe v. Hawkins*, 2010 WL 2291867 (La. Ct. App. 2010).

Of course, rather than talk about *vicarious* liability for the conduct of the lawyer who engaged in the sexual relationship, it may be possible to argue that the firm was *negligent* in not taking reasonable steps to prevent such a relationship from occurring. (*See* Part B-3.)

b. Actual Authority and Apparent Authority

If a law firm principal or employee commits a tort while acting with actual or apparent authority, the law firm is subject to vicarious liability, even if the tortious conduct was not within the ordinary course of the law firm's business. *Cf. Restatement (Third) of the Law Governing Lawyers* § 58 cmt. d (2000).

Actual authority derives from a communication *between the principal and the agent* which empowers an agent to undertake a particular sphere of action. In contrast, apparent authority arises from communications *between the principal and the third party*. If the principal has cloaked the putative agent with the trappings of authority (for example, the use of an office, a phone, business cards, and a receptionist), and a third person therefore believes that the putative agent has authority to act for the principal, there is a basis for holding the principal liable to the third party for harm caused by the putative agent. However, unauthorized statements made by a putative agent to a third party cannot create apparent authority. *See generally Restatement (Third) of Agency* § 2.03 cmt. c (2006).

In *Licette Music Corp. v. Sills, Cummis, Zuckerman, Radin, Tischman, Epstein & Gross, P.A.*, 2009 WL 2045259 (N.J. Super. A.D. 2009), a lawyer who represented companies in a recording industry dispute joined a law firm that had previously been employed, and fired, by the companies. The lawyer handled the representation as a private consulting matter, and no fees were shared with the law firm. In addressing the question of whether the law firm was liable for the lawyer's alleged malpractice, a New Jersey appellate court found that the asserted malpractice did not arise in the ordinary course of the firm's business because *respondeat superior* principles condition a firm's liability on the agent's intention, at least in part, to benefit the firm. There was no such intention with respect to the private consulting matter since only the lawyer would financially benefit. Further, the law firm was not liable under actual authority principles because the lawyer had never asked the firm to approve acceptance of the representation, and no such approval ever occurred. Finally, the law firm was not liable under apparent authority principles. Although the lawyer used the defendant law firm's resources (offices, letterhead, and staff time) in representing the companies, there was no evidence that the companies relied on the firm (which they had previously fired) to ensure the success of the representation. Rather, the evidence showed that the companies were impressed with the lawyer's services rendered before he joined the law firm, and that it made no difference to the companies whether he was practicing on his own or as a member of a firm. The companies did not entrust their affairs to the lawyer because he appeared to be working for the firm.

B. LIABILITY OF LAW FIRM PRINCIPALS

Historically, corporations were barred from practicing many professions. Therefore, at one time, lawyers could practice law only as solo practitioners or partners. Beginning in the 1960s, legislatures allowed firms to organize themselves as a professional corporation (PC), professional association (PA), or limited partnership (LP). More recently, it has become possible for lawyers to practice law as a limited liability corporation (LLC) or limited liability partnership (LLP). The subject of limited liability law firms is discussed below in Part C.

A principal in a law firm (whether a partner or a shareholder) is not vicariously liable for acts or omissions that occurred before the lawyer became a principal. *See Restatement (Third) of the Law Governing Lawyers* § 58 cmt. i (2000). Similarly, with limited exceptions, a lawyer is not vicariously liable for acts or omissions that occur after the lawyer ceases to be a principal.

1. Vicarious Liability of Partners

The partners of a law firm organized as a general partnership without limited liability are subject to joint and several liability along with their firm. *See Restatement (Third) of the Law Governing Lawyers* § 58(2) (2000). Under generally applicable principles of partnership law, each partner is liable for all partnership debts and obligations, including those arising from wrongful acts or omissions, including malpractice. Thus, in *Dennerline v. Atterholt*, 886 N.E.2d 582, 586 n.1 (Ind. Ct. App. 2008), the court referred to the defendant partner and his law firm interchangeably because their liability, for harm caused by failure to properly advise a client about legal issues, was "coextensive."

The rights and liabilities of a partner are normally governed by the relevant state's version of the Uniform Partnership Act (1914) or Revised Uniform Partnership Act (1993).

Unless individual partners are named and served as parties in a malpractice lawsuit, they are not liable for a judgment and their personal assets are not subject to execution. The failure to name law firm partners as defendants in a legal malpractice action may itself be malpractice because many law firms are thinly capitalized and carry little or no malpractice insurance.

However, malpractice litigation can be simplified by not naming law firm principals as defendants. In one recent suit against a large Chicago-based firm, filed in a Texas state court, the plaintiff named only the law firm and none of its lawyers as a defendant. The plaintiff was convinced that the firm was liable for the alleged malpractice, and that the firm had adequate malpractice insurance. *See* Brenda Sapino Jeffreys, "Plaintiff Alleges Firm Didn't Properly Perfect Security Interests," *Tex. Law.* June 8, 2009, at 7.

Partnership assets usually must be exhausted before an innocent partner's individuals assets can be reached. Of course, a partner's withdrawal from a partnership does not terminate the partner's responsibility for liabilities that arose prior to the withdrawal. A "partner cannot escape liability simply by leaving the partnership after the malpractice is committed but before the client wins or settles a malpractice claim." *In re Keck, Mahin & Cate*, 274 B.R. 740, 745 (Bankr. N.D. Ill. 2002).

2. Vicarious Liability of Shareholders

When a law firm is organized as a corporation, the liability of shareholders depends upon state law. In general, states have taken one of three approaches. Some states impose very limited vicarious liability which is roughly equivalent to the liability of shareholders in other corporations. A second group imposes extensive liability similar to the liability of partners. In some instances, joint and several liability in these states has statutory limits. A third group of states has taken a middle course, imposing supervisory liability in addition to personal liability.

3. Negligent Supervision

In many cases, the *vicarious* liability of a partner or shareholder is not an issue because partners and shareholders are *personally* liable for their own malpractice. This includes liability for negligent hiring, negligent training, and negligent supervision.

a. Disciplinary Rules Dealing with Supervision

Both the *Restatement* and the Model Rules of Professional Conduct lay out in significant detail provisions indicating that, under some circumstances, lawyers are *subject to discipline* based on failure to supervise the conduct of other lawyers or nonlawyer assistants. *See Restatement (Third) of the Law Governing Lawyers* § 11 (2000); Model Rules of Prof'l Conduct R. 5.1 & 5.2 (2010). These rules are finely honed and contain a considerable degree of nuance. However, viewed from the perspective of *civil liability*, two observations may be made about these *disciplinary* provisions.

First, the fact that discipline may be imposed with regard to lack of supervision is important evidence that the standard of care for lawyers includes, under some circumstances, a duty to supervise the work and actions of other persons with whom one practices law. Such arguments are routinely asserted in litigation. For example, in *Cecala v. Newman*, 2007 WL 2530369 (D. Ariz.), a former client alleged that a law firm "breached its duty of supervision" as well as "applicable attorney ethical rules" in failing to detect a firm lawyer's "sexualization of the attorney-client relationship." *Id.* at *2.

Second, at least three different theories of supervisory liability can be discerned in the disciplinary rules: (a) partners have a duty to ensure that a firm has in place measures giving reasonable assurance that the firm will operate in a manner consistent with each lawyer's ethical obligations; (b) lawyers with supervisory authority over other lawyers must exercise care to ensure that supervised lawyers act ethically; and (c) lawyers with partnership status or supervisory authority, and other lawyers working with nonlawyer assistants, must take reasonable steps to ensure that nonlawyers act in a manner compatible with each lawyer's ethical obligations.

However, it is essential to remember that negligent supervision is garden-variety tort liability. Defendants have been liable under this theory, in numerous contexts, for decades. Presumably, the question put to juries in these kinds of cases is often nothing more complex than simply whether the defendant acted reasonably in light of the foreseeable risks. If there is some twist or turn in the disciplinary rules that seems to absolve a lawyer from the duty to pay attention to how persons within the firm are practicing law or assisting those efforts, or from the duty to take remedial action or make disclosures when problematic facts are learned, it is useful to remember that every lawyer working for a client ordinarily has a broadly applicable duty to exercise reasonable care.

Consider, for example, the case of a young associate who, while participating in a client's representation, learns that a partner dealing with same matter is cheating the client by over-billing. The associate is not a partner in the firm, and may not have the authority to supervise anyone. Yet because there is an attorney-client relationship between the associate and the client, the associate has a duty to the client to exercise reasonable care to prevent, mitigate, rectify, and disclose the harm to the client.

One advantage of a negligent supervision theory of liability is that it may allow a plaintiff to state a claim against a lawyer who was involved in the client's representation, but not personally involved in the misconduct, and not subject to liability as a principal in the law firm (either because the lawyer was an associate or, although a principal, was shielded from responsibility by a limited liability law (*see* Part C)). For many reasons—some relating to insurance and others to the vicarious liability of a law firm and its principals—negligent supervision is a valuable theory of liability to plaintiffs.

b. The Duty to Supervise Principals

There is a duty to supervise not only the conduct of underlings, but also the conduct of law firm principals. This means that a law partnership must have in

place the systems and mechanisms that allow a firm
to detect fraudulent conduct by a partner.

In *Vanacore v. Kennedy*, 86 F. Supp. 2d 42 (D.
Conn. 1998), *aff'd* 208 F.3d 204 (2d Cir. 2000), a
partner in a two-lawyer firm misappropriated client
funds. The client thereafter commenced various
malpractice claims, including a suit against the
"innocent" partner and the law firm for negligence. In
finding that the defendants' conduct (characterized as
legal malpractice and breach of fiduciary duty) proximately caused the plaintiff's losses, a federal court in
Connecticut noted that the law firm's lack of financial
controls had prevented the firm from discovering the
existence of a secret checking account that was used
to facilitate the misappropriation of funds. 86 F. Supp.
2d at 49. Further, the court observed that the defendants, upon previously learning that the partner who
eventually stole the funds had allowed the statute of
limitations to lapse on another client's claim, failed to
review the partner's handling of other cases, including
the representation of the plaintiff. *Id.* In an attempt
to excuse their inaction, the defendants argued that
the plaintiff was exclusively a client of the partner
who stole the funds and never a client of the firm, and
that therefore the defendants owed no duty to the
plaintiff. Legally, this was not a bad argument, but it
had no support in the facts of the case. The court held
that the two lawyers were a partnership, as evidenced
by their partnership tax return, records indicating
that *the firm* represented the client, and entry of a
firm appearance on behalf of the client in a lawsuit.
Id. at 48-49.

In one case, at least $35 million in escrow money held by a New York law firm seemed to be missing. During the search for the funds, lawyers in the firm scoured the firm's books, which until then had been the exclusive preserve of the firm's sole equity partner. According to the *New York Times*, the lawyers discovered, to their dismay, that "bills had not been paid in months." The partner had also allowed the firm's malpractice insurance to lapse, exposing the lawyers "to enormous risk" if they were sued by the partner's victims. Alison Leigh Cowan *et al*, "A Lawyer Seen as Bold Enough to Cheat the Best of Investors," *N.Y. Times*, Dec. 14, 2008, at A1.

Failure to scrutinize the conduct of law firm principals can also give rise to disciplinary sanctions. In a recent New York case, a lawyer was suspended from practice for three years for ignoring multiple warning signs that his partner was committing a $17 million fraud. *See In re Fonte*, 75 A.D.3d 199, 905 N.Y.S.2d 173 (2010).

C. SPECIAL RULES FOR LIMITED LIABILITY LAW FIRMS

Many lawyers practice law today as part of limited liability entities, most notably limited liability corporations and limited liability partnerships. *See* Robert R. Keatinge, "Are Professional Partnerships Really Partnerships? Vicarious Liability Protection and Limitations," 60 *Consumer Fin. L.Q.* Rep. 518 (2006).

To some extent, these forms of limited liability organization narrow the exposure of lawyers in a firm to *vicarious* liability. However, the protections from liability afforded by state legislation authorizing the use of limited liability entities are not as extensive as might first appear. *See* Ethan S. Burger, "The Use of Limited Liability Entities for the Practice of Law: Have Lawyers Been Lulled into a False Sense of Security," 40 *Tex. J. Bus. L.* 175, 176-77 (2004). This is a particularly important issue if a lawyer practices in a law firm that has no malpractice insurance, or if a claim is likely to exceed policy limits or be excluded from coverage. *Id.* at 182. Malpractice insurance is discussed in Chapter 11.

1. Firm Liability and Personal Liability Survive

Organization as a limited liability law firm does not affect the *personal* liability of lawyers who commit malpractice, nor the *vicarious* liability of any law firm in which those lawyers practice. The lawyer remains accountable to those harmed by the lawyer's malpractice. Indeed, there is no type of organizational structure that will protect a lawyer from that kind of liability. Moreover, regardless of the form of organization, a lawyer's firm remains responsible for the wrongful acts and omissions of its principals and employees occurring in the ordinary scope of firm business. *See Restatement (Third) of the Law Governing Lawyers* § 58 cmt. b (2000).

2. Liability of Principals in Limited Liability Firms

The legislation authorizing the use of limited-liability entities for the practice of law usually contains language immunizing principals from vicarious liability for conduct which they did not participate in or supervise. *See Restatement (Third) of the Law Governing Lawyers* § 58 cmt. c (2000). The supervision exception to limited liability is discussed below. (*See* Part C-2-c.)

The effect of legislation that limits the liability of law firm principals is sometimes constrained by rulings of the state's supreme court or by statutory provisions dealing with professional regulation. *See Restatement (Third) of the Law Governing Lawyers* § 58 cmt. c (2000).

In *Ross v. Ihrie*, 2006 WL 3446897 (E.D. Mich. 2006), a lawyer (Scarfone), who was sued for malpractice, argued that he was protected by his professional corporation from vicarious liability based on the conduct of another lawyer (Ihrie). Scarfone contended that there was no partnership between himself and Ihrie, and that, on the facts of the case, "the only possible partnership in existence was between Richard R. Scarfone, P.C. and Robert D. Ihrie, P.C." *Id.* at *6. Michigan law then provided that a professional services corporation:

> shall be liable up to the full value of its property for any negligent or wrongful acts or misconduct committed by any of its officers, shareholders, agents or employees while they are engaged on

behalf of the corporation in the rendering of professional services.

Mich. Comp. Laws Ann. § 450.226(6). However, any "officer, shareholder, agent or employee" of the professional services corporation was only personally and individually liable for "any negligent or wrongful acts committed by him," or for the misconduct of anyone under "his direct supervision and control." *Id.* The court ruled that because the plaintiff did not allege that Scarfone personally engaged in any negligent or wrongful acts, nor that he supervised or controlled Ihrie, Scarfone could not be individually liable for any malpractice committed by Ihrie. The court further ruled that although there was no evidence of an actual partnership between Scarfone and Ihrie, there was a question of fact as to whether the doctrine of partnership by estoppel applied to Richard R. Scarfone, P.C. and Robert D. Ihrie, P.C. Partnership by estoppel is discussed in Part D-5.

a. Pre-Conditions to Limited Liability

Applicable rules of law, in some states, require lawyers practicing in limited liability law firms to give notice to the clients about the true nature of their firm and to maintain a certain amount of malpractice insurance. *See Restatement (Third) of the Law Governing Lawyers* § 58 cmt. c (2000).

b. Misleading Clients About Limited Liability

Law firms must not mislead clients by their adoption or use of a limited liability form of doing business. Otherwise clients may assert claims under common law and equitable principles. *See* Susan Saab Fortney, "Professional Responsibility and Limited Liability Issues Related to Limited Liability Partnerships," 39 *S. Tex. L. Rev.* 399, 430-39 (1997-98).

If clients are not adequately informed about a firm's change to LLP or LLC status, the inadequate disclosure may be regarded as a breach of fiduciary duty. If a firm's existing limited liability status is not fully disclosed, the nondisclosure may be treated as a conflict of interest, actual or constructive fraud, or negligent misrepresentation. A firm's entitlement to limited liability may be lost if the lawyers practicing in a *limited liability corporation* refer to one another as "partners." In addition, statements that partners stand behind each other's work may equitably estop a law firm from asserting limited liability.

c. Supervisory Liability Exception to Limited Liability

As noted above, legislation conferring limited liability on the principals of certain entities sometimes provides that a principal is vicariously liable for the misconduct of other lawyers and employees supervised by the principal. For example, the Tennessee Limited Liability Partnership Act expressly provides that the act:

> does not affect the liability of a partner in a registered limited liability partnership for such partner's own omissions, negligence, wrongful acts, misconduct or malpractice, or that of any

person under such partner's direct supervision and control.

Tenn. Code Ann. § 61-1-306(d) (Westlaw 2010).

However, some state laws contain no exception for supervisory-based vicarious liability. For example, the Illinois statute provides simply:

An obligation of a partnership incurred while the partnership is a limited liability partnership, whether arising in contract, tort, or otherwise, is solely the obligation of the partnership. A partner is not personally liable, directly or indirectly, by way of contribution or otherwise, for such an obligation solely by reason of being or so acting as a partner ***.

805 Ill. Comp. Stat. Ann. 206/306 (Westlaw 2010).

In cases where supervisory-based vicarious liability is allowed by state legislation, it is often unclear what constitutes the type of supervisory authority or conduct that will trigger vicarious liability. Some experts suggest that plaintiffs can potentially name as malpractice defendants all managing partners, section leaders, and other partners who participated in the plaintiff's representation. Indeed, absent specific guidance to the contrary, either in legislation or court decisions, a plaintiff might even consider naming as defendants every principal in the law firm, on the theory that every principal has a duty to monitor the performance of the firm's work.

Of course, most legal malpractice insurance policies are self-liquidating (*see* Chapter 11). Amounts spent on the defense of a case reduce the amount of coverage available to pay a settlement or judgment.

Therefore, it is important to consider whether naming a broad class of defendants under a supervisory-liability theory will adversely impact the availability of insurance coverage for the alleged malpractice.

In states where legislation governing limited liability entities creates an exception for cases where the lawyer was acting in a supervisory capacity, it is important to see that there are two paths to supervisory liability. A lawyer can always be held *personally* accountable for negligent supervision. (*See* Part B-3.) In addition, the exception in the statute governing limited liability entities means that a lawyer, based on his or her supervisory role, can be *vicariously* liable for the conduct of others, regardless of whether the lawyer was *negligent*.

D. VARIOUS ASSOCIATIONS EXPOSING LAWYERS TO LIABILITY FOR THE CONDUCT OF OTHERS

There are numerous ways in which lawyers may be subject to liability based on the misconduct of other lawyers who are not members of the same law firm. A lawyer who refers a case to another lawyer may become liable under the terms of the fee-splitting agreement (*see* Part D-1) or for forwarding a case to an incompetent lawyer (*see* Part D-2). In a limited range of situations, the actions of outside co-counsel may impose on a lawyer a duty to prevent or disclose the threat of harm to the client posed by co-counsel (*see* Part D-3). Law firms and their principals are routinely held liable for conduct of lawyers serving in "of counsel" relationships to the firm (*see* Part D-4).

Careless office sharing may give rise to vicarious liability based on "partnership by estoppel" (*see* part D-5). Of course, lawyers may also be sued for harm caused by assisting non-lawyers in the unauthorized practice of law (*see* Part D-6). In some cases, a law firm and its principals are liable for the misconduct of temporary lawyers working for the firm (*see* Part D-7) and for breach of nondelegable duties (*see* Part D-8).

1. Referral Fee Arrangements

Ethics rules in every state specify the conditions under which a lawyer can collect a fee for referring a case to another lawyer. In most instances, a fee cannot be divided other than in proportion to the services performed by each lawyer, unless each lawyer assumes "joint responsibility" for the representation. *See* Model Rules of Prof'l Conduct R. 1.5(d) (2010). Joint responsibility means that the lawyers agree to be financially and ethically responsible for the representation in the same way that they would be if they were associated in a partnership. *Id.* R. 1.5 cmt. 7. This means that each lawyer can be held liable for the malpractice of the other to the same extent as could partners in a traditional partnership. *See Restatement (Third) of the Law Governing Lawyers* § 47 cmt. d. (2000). This type of exposure to liability deters lawyers from forwarding cases to other lawyers who are likely to commit malpractice, even if those lawyers would pay a large referral fee. *Id.*

A fee-splitting arrangement with a lawyer in another firm can make the referring lawyer vicariously liable for the receiving lawyer's malpractice, even if that malpractice was not reasonably foreseeable. Liability does not depend on showing that the referral was negligently made. *See Noris v. Silver*, 701 So.2d 1238, 1241 (Fla. Dist. Ct. App. 1997).

2. Negligent Referral

Recommending that a client or prospective client engage the services of another lawyer may give rise to negligence-based liability if the recommender knew or should have known that the other lawyer was likely to commit malpractice. *See Restatement (Third) of the Law Governing Lawyers* § 58 cmt. e (2000). Thus, it may be risky to refer a client to another lawyer who has been disciplined for unethical conduct or sued for malpractice on colorable grounds. The same is certainly true of referring a client to a lawyer known to abuse drugs or alcohol. In these types of cases, possible harm to the client is, to some extent, foreseeable.

Of course, a lawyer cannot be liable for negligent referral if the lawyer had no knowledge that the person to whom the case was referred might commit malpractice. *See Noris v. Silver*, 701 So.2d 1238 (Fla. Dist. Ct. App.1997).

Some jurisdictions have not recognized a claim for negligent referral in the legal malpractice context. *See Knighton v. Goldenberg*, 1998 WL 1990426, *3 (Mich. Ct. App.).

3. Co-Counsel Arrangements and Other Outside Counsel

A law firm ordinarily is not *vicariously* liable for the misconduct of a lawyer in another firm who is serving as co-counsel on a case. This is true because

outside co-counsel is usually an independent agent of
the client and the firm has no right to control the
actions of that lawyer. *See Restatement (Third) of the
Law Governing Lawyers* § 58 cmt. e (2000). However,
this basic rule is limited in several ways by principles
of concerted action and agency.

A firm is subject to vicarious liability for the
misconduct of outside lawyers if its principals or
employees directed, or otherwise substantially assisted, the acts or omissions that constitute malpractice. *See Restatement (Third) of the Law Governing
Lawyers* § 58 cmt. e (2000). Further, if the firm,
rather than the client, employed the outside lawyer to
work on the case, the outside lawyer is a subagent of
the law firm. The law firm is therefore subject to
liability, either vicariously or for negligent supervision.

For example, in *Whalen v. DeGraff, Foy, Conway,
Holt-Harris & Mealey*, 53 A.D.3d 912, 863 N.Y.S.2d
100 (2008), a New York law firm, which had won a
judgment for a client, hired a Florida lawyer (Cagan)
and his law firm (Bailey) to collect the judgment from
an estate (Gerzof). Because the claim was not timely
filed, the estate withdrew all settlement offers, and
ultimately the client was unable to satisfy any part of
the judgment from the substantial assets of the
estate. In holding that the New York law firm was
liable for the malpractice of the Florida lawyer, a New
York appellate court wrote:

> [D]efendant [the New York law firm] solicited
> Cagan and Bailey and obtained their assistance
> without plaintiff's knowledge. Although plaintiff
> was later advised that Bailey had been retained

by defendant, she had no contact with Bailey and did not enter into a retainer agreement with that firm. Defendant concedes that plaintiff completely relied on defendant to take the necessary steps to satisfy her judgment against Gerzof. Under these circumstances, defendant assumed responsibility to plaintiff for the filing of the Florida estate claim and Bailey became defendant's subagent ***. Therefore, defendant had a duty to supervise Bailey's actions.

863 N.Y.S.2d at 102.

As the above excerpt suggests, voluntary assumption of duties related to outside counsel may form the predicate for negligence-based liability. If a firm undertakes to assist a client by supervising the work of outside counsel engaged by the client, but fails to perform that task carefully, liability may be imposed for resulting losses. *See Restatement (Third) of the Law Governing Lawyers* § 58 cmt. e (2000).

There are other theories under which a lawyer may be held liable for the malpractice of a lawyer in a different firm. For example, in *Estate of Spencer v. Gavin*, 400 N.J. Super. 220, 946 A.2d 1051 (N.J. Super. Ct. App. Div. 2008), a terminally ill lawyer, while acting as executor and administrator, looted three inter-related estates that he was representing. After the lawyer's death, his misfeasance was discovered, and actions to recoup the losses were commenced against various persons, including the defendant lawyer. The defendant was not a partner of the deceased lawyer, but had had an office in his building and a close relationship which resulted in frequent referrals. The defendant lawyer had done a small amount of work related to one of the estates, and may have been aware of the deceased lawyer's misappropriation of funds while that misconduct was in progress. In addressing a multi-count claim against the defendant, an appellate court in New Jersey held that a lawyer "who has a close and interdependent business relationship with another lawyer, and who is performing legal work for a common client at that lawyer's request, has a duty to report that lawyer if he or she develops actual knowledge that the lawyer has been stealing funds from their common client." 946 A.2d at 1069.

The *Spencer* court stressed that it was "not declaring that a lawyer who received a routine, arms-length referral from another lawyer automatically exposes himself or herself to civil liability if he or she fails to intercede after learning that the referring lawyer has somehow harmed a client." *Id.* at 1070. Moreover, the court left open the possibility that a lawyer might fulfill the obligation to report wrongdoing by notifying not the client, but disciplinary authorities. *Id.* However, the court found it unnecessary to resolve that question because the defendant had failed to notify anyone at all. The case was remanded to determine the disputed issue of whether, in fact, the defendant lawyer had actual knowledge of the other lawyer's theft of client funds, and if so, whether breach of that duty caused damage.

4. "Of Counsel" Arrangements

A lawyer is "of counsel" to a law firm if the lawyer has a regular and continuing relationship to the firm, even though the lawyer is neither a principal in the firm, nor employed on a full-time basis. *See Restatement (Third) of the Law Governing Lawyers* § 123 cmt. c(ii) (2000).

A law firm and its principals are liable for the acts and omissions of lawyers serving in "of counsel" positions, provided that such conduct occurs within the scope of that relationship. *See Restatement (Third) of the Law Governing Lawyers* § 58 cmt. c (2000).

Moreover, an "of counsel" affiliation of a lawyer with a firm may subject the firm to liability under principles of apparent authority. (*See* Part A-2-b.) For example, in *Staron v. Weinstein*, 305 N.J.Super. 236, 701 A.2d 1325 (1997), a lawyer serving as "of counsel" to the defendant law firm allowed the statute of limitations to expire on a personal injury claim that he had agreed to handle for a client. The lawyer was listed on the law firm's stationary (which he used) as being "of counsel," and the retainer agreement signed by the client named the defendant law firm as the contracting party. In view of this evidence, a New Jersey appellate court found that the client raised a triable issue of fact as to whether the "of counsel" lawyer acted with sufficient apparent authority to make the firm liable for his malpractice. This was true even though it was undisputed that the firm did not know of the client's personal injury case until it was sued by the client for malpractice, and that the malpractice did not occur until more than a year after the firm and the "of counsel" lawyer had severed their relationship. The law firm had never notified the client of the termination of its relationship with the "of counsel" lawyer because it had no record of the client in its filing system.

5. Office-Sharing Arrangements

It is a basic rule of legal ethics that "[l]awyers may state or imply that they practice in a partnership or other organization only when that is the fact." Model Rules of Prof'l Conduct R. 7.5 (2010). "Lawyers sharing office facilities, but who are not in fact partners, may not denominate themselves as, for example, 'Smith and Jones' for that title suggests partnership in the practice of law." Wis. Sup. Ct. Rule 20:7.5(d) cmt. 2 (Westlaw 2010). Similarly, "if solo attorney *A* is renting space and services from law firm *B*, *C* & *D* and the only sign in the vicinity of the office identifies the facilities as 'The Law Firm of *B*, *C* & *D*,' then the public would quite naturally assume that attorney *A* is affiliated with the law firm of *B*, *C* & *D* *** [and] would be misled as to the true nature of the relationship among these attorneys." D.C. Bar Ethics Op. 303 (2001).

Lawyers who improperly hold themselves out as partners are subject not only to professional discipline, but to malpractice liability. This may be true of lawyers who share office space, but fail to take precautions with regard to the structure of the relationship and what clients are likely to perceive.

a. Partnership by Estoppel

In some cases, liability is imposed on office-sharers under the theory of "partnership by estoppel." Thus, lawyers who have led clients to believe that they were members of the same firm are estopped from denying the existence of a partnership, and therefore subject to vicarious liability.

To prevail under the doctrine of partnership by estoppel, which is codified in some states, a plaintiff generally must prove: (1) that a lawyer held himself out as a partner; (2) that the holding out was done by the lawyer directly or with the lawyer's consent; (3) that the plaintiff had knowledge of such holding out; and (4) that the plaintiff relied on the ostensible partnership to his or her prejudice. *See Gosselin v. Webb*, 242 F.3d 412, 415 (1st Cir. 2001).

In *Gosselin*, the First Circuit found that there were many facts which potentially supported a finding of partnership by estoppel. For example, one lawyer told the clients that he was "with" the other lawyers; that lawyer's name was listed alongside the other lawyers' names on a lobby directory; the lawyer used the office of the other lawyers to meet with the clients; and the other lawyers sometimes talked with the clients about their cases and assisted with aspects of their representation. 242 F.3d at 417.

Suppose, for example, that three lawyers with individual practices share an office suite, use a common, fictitious name for the "firm," and do not clarify to clients that only one lawyer is solely responsible for each representation. If one of the lawyers disappears, and important deadlines are missed, the other two lawyers will be subject to liability on the ground that there was a partnership by estoppel. This is true if there was nothing disclosed, in an engagement agreement or otherwise, to disabuse the aggrieved client of the idea that there was a law firm. If the two lawyers wanted to limit the risk of vicarious liability, they could have formed a limited liability partnership or corporation that included all three lawyers (*see* Part C of this Chapter) or could have taken steps to make clear to clients that there was no partnership between the lawyers.

In *Ross v. Ihrie*, 2006 WL 3446897 (E.D. Mich. 2006), a federal court in Michigan found that a malpractice plaintiff had raised a fact issue regarding partnership by estoppel. The three lawyers had listed all of their names on common stationary and had used a joint name ("Ihrie, Scarfone & O'Brien") on business cards, in answering the phone, and in lawyer-client agreements.

In some legal malpractice cases, the plaintiff is unable to prove the reliance element of partnership by estoppel. For example, in *Glazer v. Brookhouse*, 471 F. Supp. 2d 945, 950 (E.D. Wis. 2007), the plaintiff added a retired lawyer to a pending malpractice action only upon learning that the retired lawyer was listed on firm letterhead years earlier, at the time when a trust was allegedly negligently amended. In rejecting the partnership by estoppel claim, the court found that there was insufficient evidence that the plaintiff had relied on the retired lawyer's alleged participation in the partnership.

b. Partnership in Fact

The fact that there is no written partnership agreement does not necessarily mean that there is not a partnership. A partnership may exist as a result of the conduct, intention, and relationship of the parties. However, a promise or intention to share profits is usually treated as an indispensable element of partnership in fact. In *Community Capital Bank v.*

Fischer & Yanowitz, 47 A.D.3d 667, 850 N.Y.S.2d 508 (2008), a New York appellate court held that a lawyer was entitled to summary judgment in a malpractice action because there was no evidence that he agreed to share profits with another lawyer and no basis for finding a partnership by estoppel.

In *Estate of Holmes ex rel. Webb v. Ludeman*, 2001 WL 1198638 (Ohio Ct. App. 2001), a malpractice plaintiff argued that certain defendants were liable under the doctrines of partnership in fact and partnership by estoppel. The evidence showed that:

> [A]ll four attorneys, as well as the support staff, had access to all client files in the office; the attorneys would decline to represent any individual with an interest adverse to that of an established client; new clients were "equitably divided" among the four attorneys by the office staff; the attorneys would cover for one another if the primary attorney on a case were unavailable; fee-sharing occurred if more than one attorney worked on a case; there was a "firm account" at Key Bank for office expenses; much of the office furnishings and supplies were commonly owned and the attorneys each had authority to bind the others contractually with respect to the purchase of such items; the resources of the support staff were shared; the attorneys applied jointly for professional malpractice insurance ***; the letterhead, fax cover sheets and paper used for billing *** [were imprinted] "Czerniakowski, Errington, Huffman and Ludeman;" when support staff answered the phone they stated "Czerniakowski, Errington, Huffman and Ludeman;" *** at least

one of the attorneys testified that they were "associated for the practice of law;" the attorneys referred to themselves as partners to clients and other members of the public; and one application for insurance was signed "John G. Ludeman Partner."

Id. at *7. The Ohio Court of Appeals concluded that, in view of this evidence, there were questions of fact as to whether the lawyers were conducting business as a partnership or holding themselves out as partners. The court reversed a grant of summary judgment in favor of the lawyers and remanded the case for further proceedings.

6. Assisting Non-Lawyers in the Practice of Law

There is considerable debate as to what constitutes the practice of law. Presumably not everything that lawyers do is so complex that performing those tasks requires a law license. Nor do activities by nonlawyers that touch upon subjects of law or legal institutions necessarily constitute law practice. Thus, a nonlawyer may publish a book about a legal subject. Nevertheless, at a certain point, what nonlawyers do amounts to the unauthorized practice of law, and that has several consequences.

Practicing law without is license is normally a crime. *See Restatement (Third) of the Law Governing Lawyers* § 4 cmt. a (2000). It can also give rise to civil liability. A nonlawyer who causes harm to a "client" while engaging in unauthorized practice may be sued for malpractice. It is no defense in an action for damages for the unauthorized practitioner to plead that he or she was really not a lawyer. For example, in *Buscemi v. Intachai*, 730 So.2d 329, 330 (Fla. Dist. Ct. App. 1999), the court affirmed a judgment for $675,000 against a financial planner despite the fact that the defendant had disclosed that he was not licensed to practice law.

Courts have applied the standard of care that is applicable to lawyers to "malpractice" actions against nonlawyer insurance claim adjusters, real estate brokers, paralegals, persons assisting divorces, and escrow agents. *See* Sande L. Buhai, "Act like a Lawyer, Be Judged like a Lawyer: The Standard of Care for the Unlicensed Practice of Law," 2007 *Utah L. Rev.* 87, 88-89. (*See* Chapter 3 Part B-4-e.)

Various provisions of law and ethics prohibit a lawyer from assisting a nonlawyer in the practice of law. *See Restatement (Third) of the Law Governing Lawyers* § 4 (2000); Model Rules of Prof'l Conduct R. 5.5 (2008). A lawyer who violates these strictures is subject to discipline. For example, in *In re Hrones*, 2010 WL 3505381 (Mass.), the Supreme Judicial Court of Massachusetts held that the conduct of a law school graduate, who had not passed the bar examination but was employed as a paralegal at a law firm, constituted the practice of law. A lawyer who assisted the graduate's unauthorized practice was suspended from practicing law for one year and a day.

In addition, lawyers who facilitate the unauthorized practice of law may be held responsible for damages caused by a nonlawyer's malpractice on an aiding and abetting theory of liability.

7. Temporary Lawyers

A temporary lawyer is a lawyer who works for a law firm on a short term basis. Temporary lawyers are often procured through a placement agency to handle particular projects, such as issues related to specialized areas of law, or to help a law firm cope with a crush of business, tight deadlines, or temporary vacancies.

The law firm may pay the placement agency, rather than the temporary lawyer, for the services provided. However, a temporary lawyer is a subagent of the law firm. By assigning a client's work to the temporary lawyer, a law firm becomes liable for his or her acts and omissions. *See Restatement (Third) of the Law Governing Lawyers* § 58 cmt. e (2000).

8. Nondelegable Duties

Law firms are ordinarily not liable for the conduct of independent contractors they employ. However, such liability may arise if the independent contractor is engaged in performing a nondelegable duty. *See Restatement (Third) of the Law Governing Lawyers* § 58 cmt. e (2000).

Few courts have attempted to state a general rule as to when a duty cannot be delegated. *See Restatement (Second) of Torts*, note preceding § 416 (1965). Therefore, this theory of liability can be dangerous because it is unpredictable.

Presumably, "nondelegable" duties includes those obligations which, if not performed properly, threaten to cause great harm. In the legal malpractice context, a lawyer's duty to disclose to the client that the lawyer is withdrawing from representation may fall within this category. *Cf. Staron v. Weinstein*, 305 N.J.Super. 236, 701 A.2d 1325, 1328 (1997).

In *Whalen v. DeGraff, Foy, Conway, Holt-Harris & Mealey*, 53 A.D.3d 912, 863 N.Y.S.2d 100, 102 (2008), a malpractice plaintiff argued that a law firm was liable for the failure of an outside lawyer it employed to file a notice of claim with an estate because the duty was nondelegable. In finding for the plaintiff, a New York appellate court did not expressly rule on the nondelegable duty argument because it concluded that the defendant law firm had a duty to supervise the actions of the outside lawyer and that it had taken no steps whatsoever to fulfill that obligation.

The existence of a nondelegable duty might also make one lawyer liable for the conduct of another lawyer, even in the absence of an employment relationship. Suppose that lawyers from different law firms are working on a case as co-counsel, and would not ordinarily be vicariously responsible for each other's malpractice (*see* Part D-3). If one of the lawyers has a nondelegable duty to convey important information to the client, that lawyer may be found to have acted at his or her peril in relying on the other lawyer to make the communication. If the matter in question is so important that it qualifies as "nondelegable," the lawyer who entrusted the task to outside co-counsel should be responsible for the nonperformance of the task in just the same way as if he or she had hired the other lawyer to carry out that function. Indeed, it would be a strange legal system that would hold persons liable for the conduct of other persons they pay to perform a nondelegable duty, but not for the conduct of other persons they rely upon to perform the same function gratuitously.

In some cases, issues arise as to whether duties were divided up between co-counsel in a way sufficient to save one or more of the lawyers from liability for malpractice that occurred in the handling of the case. However, this is a difficult argument on which to prevail, perhaps because some duties are nondelegable.

For example, in *Global NAPs, Inc. v. Awiszus*, 457 Mass. 489, 930 N.E.2d 1262 (2010), two lawyers involved in the handing of a case, as well as their law firms, were sued for malpractice based on failure to file timely notice of appeal from an adverse judgment in an employee's action against the plaintiff client under the state maternity leave law. With respect to the appeal, the one lawyer (Awiszus), who had handled the representation of the client at trial, was told by the client's general counsel that the client (Global) had hired appellate counsel (Kerman). Awiszus was instructed that she was to assist Kerman "in any way that Kerman requested." 930 N.E.2d at 1266. In the subsequent malpractice suit, Awiszus and her firm asserted that they should bear no liability for professional negligence because they played an "extremely limited role" in the post-trial representation of Global. More specifically, Awiszus argued that the tasks assigned to her by Kerman did not include any work pertaining to the filing of the notice of appeal. However, when the untimely notice of appeal was filed, it contained a facsimile of Awiszus's signature, which had been placed there by Kerman with Awiszus's permission. The Supreme Judicial Court of Massachusetts found that this was a sufficient indication that Awiszus was participating in the litigation. Therefore, the court held, the two lawyers and their law firms all bore responsibility for professional negligence with respect to the representation of the client.

Regardless of whether a law firm is *vicariously liable* for the conduct of an independent contractor, the firm may be liable for *negligently* selecting or supervising the independent contractor. *See Restatement (Third) of the Law Governing Lawyers* § 58 cmt. e (2000). Presumably, a lawyer also cannot negligently entrust a important task to an unpaid volunteer.

CHAPTER NINE

IMPORTANT MALPRACTICE ISSUES

A. CONFLICTS OF INTEREST

1. Basic Principles

Conflict of interest is, in many respects, the most difficult and important subject within the law of legal malpractice. It is easy for an unhappy client or former client, or even for an affected third party, to charge that a lawyer acted improperly because the lawyer had a "conflict." It is much more difficult to examine alleged conflicts carefully and to assess fairly and reliably whether a lawyer's conduct complied with the many intricate conflict of interest rules that apply to the delivery of legal services. This is particularly true because many alleged conflicts involve multiple persons and entities, as well as events that played out over a long period of time. Except in the simplest cases, it is often necessary to diagram the actors, competing interests, and key developments, and to analyze the various arguments, claims, and defenses. This is required simply to understand what, if anything, was in conflict with the interests of the alleged victim.

a. Recurring Issue in Malpractice Litigation

Many legal malpractice cases—perhaps half or more of all claims that are filed—include allegations of conflicts of interest. It is therefore essential for a malpractice lawyer to have a confident grasp of this area of the law.

Conflicts of interest arise in many ways, such as through joint representation of multiple clients, business transactions between a lawyer and client, or actions that adversely affect former clients. There is no single rule that governs conflicts of interest. Rather, a number of rules focus, either broadly or specifically, on conflicts of interest issues.

b. Four Kinds of Conflicts

Generally speaking, there are four types of conflicts of interest in the field of legal representation: (1) conflicts between the interests of multiple current clients; (2) conflicts between the interests of a present client and a former client; (3) conflicts between the interests of a lawyer and a client; and (4) conflicts between the interests of a client and a third person who is neither a client nor a former client. It is important to identify the conflict of interest subcategory or subcategories that pertain to a particular case. That makes it possible to identify the operative legal standards.

The initial sections in this Chapter examine general principles related to conflicts of interest in legal representation. The four types of conflicts mentioned above are considered later in Parts A-2 to A-5 of this Chapter.

c. Disciplinary Rules are a Key Point of Reference

Conflict of interest analysis typically relies heavily on the terms of relevant disciplinary rules, such as the state law provisions which parallel, but may differ in some respects from:

- Model Rule 1.7 (dealing generally with conflicts of interest that affect current clients);

- Model Rule 1.8 (dealing with specific types of conflicts of interest that affect current clients); and

- Model Rule 1.9 (dealing with conflicts of interest related to former clients).

See Model Rules of Prof'l Conduct R. 1.7–1.9 (2010).

For example, in cases involving an alleged conflict of interest related to the simultaneous representation of multiple clients, experts testifying about the standard of care, or a judge dealing with issues of law, may refer to the general principles set forth in the state's version of Rule 1.7 or, if the case involves an aggregate settlement of the claims of multiple clients, the specific standard embodied in the state rule that parallels Model Rule 1.8. *See id.* R. 1.7(a) & R. 1.8(g). Similarly, a case involving a former client conflict of interest is likely to focus on the applicable version of Model Rule 1.9. *See id.* at R. 1.9.

A few disciplinary rules dealing with conflicts of interest seldom play a role in legal malpractice litigation. These include Model Rule 1.11 (addressing conflicts of interest of former or current public officers or employees), Model Rule 1.12 (dealing with former judges, arbitrators, mediators, and other third party neutrals), and Model Rule 3.7 (relating to advocates who also serve as witnesses). *See id.* R. 1.11, R. 1.12, & R. 3.7.

However, another conflict of interest rule, Model Rule 1.10 (governing imputation of conflicts of interest), plays a vital part in many legal malpractice cases. *See id.* at R. 1.10. As discussed below (*see* Part A-1-f), that provision, to a large extent, defines the limits of the imputed disqualification principle.

Of course, strictly speaking, *disciplinary* rules set the standard for imposition of *disciplinary* sanctions, not malpractice liability. Violation of a disciplinary rule does not automatically create a civil cause of action. (*See* Chapter 3 Part B-6-c.) Moreover, some courts caution against over-reliance on conflict of interest disciplinary rules in malpractice litigation. Nevertheless, it has become common to refer to pertinent disciplinary rules in sorting out malpractice allegations of conflict of interest. (*See* Chapter 3 Part B-3-e.) Through common law adjudication and efforts to restate the holdings of court decisions, standards similar to those found in lawyer disciplinary codes are now part of state and federal malpractice precedent, as well as the *Restatement. See Restatement (Third) of the Law Governing Lawyers* §§ 121-35 (2000).

d. A Conflict is a Threat to the Client's Representation

The most useful starting point in mastering the subject of lawyer conflict of interest is to understand that a conflict is a divergent loyalty or other matter which poses a threat to the representation of the client. If there is some competing interest that is likely to impair the lawyer's exercise of independent professional judgment on behalf of a client, or to cause the lawyer not to be fully faithful to the client, then there is a conflict of interest.

Put differently, in determining whether there is a conflict, it is necessary to focus on what the lawyer should be doing. If facts exist that make it difficult or impossible for the lawyer to consider, recommend, or carry out what should be done on behalf of the client, a conflict of interest exists.

e. Focus on the Scope of the Representation

One cannot determine whether there is a threat to a lawyer's representation of a client without focusing on the scope of the representation. As discussed earlier (*see* Chapter 3 Part A-2), a lawyer's duties to a client extend only so far as the representation's scope. Therefore, in determining whether there was a conflict which threatened the lawyer's performance, it is essential to ask what the lawyer was engaged to do.

For example, suppose that a lawyer is asked to draft a simple will for a client. In determining whether the lawyer has a conflict of interest, the relevant question is whether there is something that threatens to distort the lawyer's exercise of independent judgment or performance of duties in the drafting of the will.

Similarly, suppose that a lawyer is hired to assist *A* and *B* in forming a corporation. Whether the lawyer has a conflict will depend upon what services the lawyer was asked to provide. It is easy to see how a lawyer would have a conflict—that is, could not be fully loyal to both *A* and *B*—if the lawyer's job was to negotiate the allocation of equity and management rights in the new corporation on behalf of both *A* and *B*. In contrast, if the lawyer was asked to advise *A* and *B* on whether they were required to make disclosures to comply with federal securities laws in forming the corporation, it may be difficult to envision a conflict between the interests of *A* and the interests of *B* that would threaten the faithful performance of the assumed duty.

f. Imputed Disqualification

The principle of imputed conflict of interest has immense practical consequences. Under imputed disqualification, a law firm is generally treated as a single lawyer. If one lawyer in the firm has a conflict of interest, all of the firm's lawyers have a conflict. *See* Model Rules of Prof'l Conduct R. 1.10 (2010).

Of course, there are limits to imputed disqualification. First, a few conflict of interest rules, such as Model Rule 3.7, dealing with advocate-as-witness conflicts of interest, expressly provide that a particular kind of conflict is personal and not imputable to members of the lawyer's firm. *See id.* R. 3.7(b). This is true of conflicts that arise from sexual relations between a lawyer and client. *See id.* R. 1.8(j)–(k).

Second, a few conflict of interest rules expressly provide for "screening," a process which isolates the conflicted lawyer from the representation in question, and thereby obviates the risk that the client's representation will be distorted. For example, the rule dealing with prospective clients provides that a conflict is not imputed to other members of a firm if a lawyer, who received information from a layperson who never became a client, is effectively screened. *See id.* R. 1.18(d). Similarly, the rules applicable to former judges, law clerks, arbitrators, mediators, and other third-party neutrals all provide for screening. *See id.* R. 1.11(b) and R. 1.12(c).

Third, the *Restatement* says that screening is permitted if confidential information gained from a former client is unlikely to be significant in a subsequent matter. *See Restatement (Third) of the Law Governing Lawyers* § 124(2) (2000). Some courts have embraced this position.

Fourth, the American Bar Association House of Delegates recently endorsed the use of screening in cases where a lawyer's conflict of interest arises out of the lawyer's association with a prior law firm. *See* Model Rules of Prof'l Conduct R. 1.10 (2010). This change to the model rules is likely to lead to the increased use of screening in some jurisdictions.

Nevertheless, imputed disqualification remains the general rule under American law. In most states, the principle broadly applies to what are, for purposes of malpractice litigation, the most important categories of conflict of interest. These categories include multiple client conflicts (Model Rule 1.7), former client conflicts (Model Rule 1.9), and most categories of lawyer-versus-client conflicts (Model Rules 1.7 and 1.8). *See* Model Rules of Professional Conduct R. 1.7–1.9 (2010).

(1) Lawyers Who are Treated Like a Law Firm

The *Restatement* takes the position that the imputed disqualification principle applies to lawyers who are associated in rendering legal services to others through a law partnership, professional corporation, sole proprietorship, or similar association. *See Restatement (Third) of the Law Governing Lawyers* § 123(1) (2000). This includes not only lawyers who are employed by the firm or have an equity interest (partners or shareholders), but also "temporary lawyers" working for the firm on a short-term basis and, ordinarily, lawyers who are "of counsel." *See id.* §123 cmts. c(i) & c(ii). However, conflicts are not imputed between different firms working together, such as where one firm hires another to serve as "local counsel" or to consult on a matter. *See id.* §123 cmt. c-(iii).

Conflicts are also imputed among lawyers who share offices without taking adequate precautions to ensure that confidential client information is not available to other lawyers in the office. *See id.* § 123(3) & cmt. e.

Similarly, imputed disqualification applies to lawyers who are not members of a law firm, but are employed by an organization to render legal services either to that organization or to others for the purpose of advancing the interests or objectives of the organization. *Id.* § 123(2).

g. Screening is Difficult

Even when screening may be used to avoid a conflict of interest, it is important to remember just how difficult it is to erect an effective screen. The first obstacle is perhaps the most formidable. The conflict must be spotted promptly, before the dangers posed by the conflict have a chance to infect the representation of a client or adversely impact the interests of a former client. Second, the conflicted lawyer must not be allowed to play any role in the client's representation or receive any fee as a direct result of the representation. Third, other lawyers and staff members must be instructed not to share any information about the representation with the conflicted lawyer. Finally, the affected client or former client must be informed that a screen has been erected, so that the client or former client can monitor the effectiveness of the screen. *See Restatement (Third) of the Law Governing Lawyers* § 124 (2000); Model Rules of Prof'l Conduct R. 1.0(k) & 1.10 cmts. 7–10 (2010).

h. Resolving Conflicts Through Informed Consent

(1) Required Disclosures

Many conflicts of interest are not actionable under the law of legal malpractice if the affected client gave informed consent. Informed consent means that the person in question agreed to waive the conflict after the lawyer communicated appropriate information and explained the material risks and available alternatives. *Cf.* Model Rules of Prof'l Conduct R. 1.0(e) (2010).

In general, obtaining informed consent requires a lawyer to disclose, in a meaningful way, the (1) existence, (2) nature, (3) implications, and (4) possible adverse consequences of the conflict of interest. A brief consultation with the client is unlikely to satisfy these demanding requirements. The only safe way to obtain informed consent to a serious conflict of interest is by making detailed written disclosures addressing the four points mentioned above. Consent based on oral disclosures will suffice in many jurisdictions, but proving that such disclosures were, in fact, made will be difficult in the absence of written evidence.

(2) Written Versus Oral

In many states, the disciplinary rules bearing upon conflicts of interest do not require that a client consent in writing to waive a conflict of interest. However, the American Bar Association's model rules dealing with current client and former client conflicts of interest now require that consent to a conflict of interest be "confirmed in writing." *See* Model Rules of Prof'l Conduct R. 1.7(b) & 1.9(a) (2010). That means that the affected client must have given the consent in writing or that the lawyer must have promptly transmitted to the client written confirmation of the client's oral consent. *See id.* R. 1.0(b). As these model provisions influence the development of the law at the state level, it will increasingly become likely that oral consent to a conflict of interest, not confirmed in writing, will fall short of the standard of care in a malpractice action.

With respect to some conflicts of interest, such as business transactions between a lawyer and client, disciplinary rules in most states already require that the client's consent, to the essential terms of the transaction and the lawyer's role in the transaction, must be manifested in a writing signed by the client. *See id.* R. 1.8(a)(3). (*See* Part A-4-b of this Chapter.)

(3) Disinterested Lawyer Standard

The validity of informed consent to a conflict of interest hinges on two tests: one is subjective and the other is objective. The subjective test, discussed above (*see* Part A-1-h-(1)), is whether the affected client in fact agreed to waive the conflict after material facts relating to the conflict were disclosed. The objective test holds that a lawyer may not even ask a client to consent to a conflict of interest if a disinterested lawyer would conclude that consent should not be given.

If the conflict is unconsentable because the facts fail the objective test, it makes no difference what the defendant lawyer told the client or whether the client agreed to the proposed course of representation. Some conflicts are so serious that a lawyer exercising reasonable care cannot ask a client to waive them.

Some conflicts of interest are not consentable as a matter of law. For example, a lawyer or law firm cannot represent both sides of a case in litigation.

In malpractice litigation, an expert addressing the standard of care in light of the facts of the case is normally asked whether there was a conflict and, if so, whether any alleged consent was valid under both prongs of the validity test. Thus, if the expert believes there was a conflict, or is asked to assume *arguendo* that a conflict existed, the expert will normally opine on both whether the lawyer could ask for consent and whether necessary disclosures were made for consent to be valid.

(4) Client Sophistication

Client sophistication plays an important role in determining whether it is reasonable to ask for consent to a conflict of interest and what disclosures are required. The more sophisticated the client, the easier it is for the law to conclude that consent was possible and that sufficient information about risks and alternatives was disclosed. If a large corporation, such as Microsoft, agrees to waive a conflict of interest, it will have a difficult time arguing that it should not have been asked to consent or that it was not given enough information to make an informed decision.

There is no exact list of what factors should be taken into account in judging client sophistication. Cases often make reference to a client's education level, employment background, business experience, and prior use of attorneys. Whether the client has access to other legal counsel, as may be true of a corporation with in-house lawyers, sometimes also factors into the analysis.

Client sophistication is not an all-or-nothing proposition. Thus, there is a spectrum that ranges from highly sophisticated (at one end) to not at all sophisticated (at the other end). Where the client falls on that continuum is an important factor in judging whether valid consent was obtained to a conflict of interest.

(5) Advance Waiver of Conflicts of Interest

Issues persist about the validity of advance waivers of conflicts of interest. This is not surprising given that in many cases a client may have little real understanding of the threats posed by a potential future conflict of interest before that conflict later emerges during the course of representation.

An advance waiver of a conflict of interest is a written document which says that the client waives the right to object to one or more future conflicts. The conflict or conflicts are described, either specifically or generally, in the document. For example, in *Concat LP v. Unilever, PLC*, 350 F. Supp. 2d 796 (N.D. Cal. 2004), a waiver which was part of the engagement letter signed by the client provided that the client agreed that the law firm could continue to represent, or undertake in the future to represent, existing or new clients in any matter, including litigation, "not substantially related" to the firm's work for the client, even if the interests of such clients in those other matters were directly adverse to the client. 350 F. Supp. 2d 796. A federal court in California held that the waiver did not bar the client from seeking to disqualify the firm from conflicting representation. However, other courts, faced with different facts, have upheld written advance waivers of conflicts of interest.

In general, an advance waiver of a conflict of interest is more likely to bar a malpractice claim in cases where the nature of the possible conflict was disclosed with reasonable specificity *and* the consenting client understood the risks of granting an advance waiver. Further, an advance waiver is more likely to be deemed valid in the case of a sophisticated client, such as a business entity accustomed to dealing with lawyers, than in the case of an unsophisticated client, such as an individual who never previously retained a lawyer.

See generally Nathan Crystal, "Enforceability of General Advance Waivers of Conflicts of Interest," 38 *St. Mary's L.J.* 859 (2007).

i. De Minimis Non Curat Lex

The maxim *"de minimis non curat lex"*—meaning "the law does not concern itself with trifles"—plays an important role in many areas of the law, including the law governing conflicts of interest. Weak conflicts of interest are generally ignored. Strong conflicts of interest require careful adherence to applicable rules of professional conduct.

If an alleged conflict is speculative, remote, or hypothetical, it requires nothing more than a modest degree of attention as to whether, as representation progresses, circumstances have changed in a way that makes the purported conflict more serious. Because a weak conflict poses no significant threat to the client's representation, it need not be disclosed to the client, nor is client consent required. *De minimis non curat lex.*

For example, suppose that, in the course of heated negotiations between lawyers representing clients in litigation, opposing counsel threatens to name a defendant's lawyer as a co-defendant in the case. There would obviously be a significant conflict if that were to actually happen. In that case, the lawyer/co-defendant's representation of the client/co-defendant might be threatened by the fact that the lawyer could be tempted to handle the representation in a manner that protected the lawyer, even if that were at the expense of the client.

However, if there is no reason to think that the "threat" to name the lawyer as a co-defendant is anything more than tactical "saber rattling" about a possible action that is ungrounded in the facts and unlikely to occur, the mere receipt of the threat does not create a conflict of interest. Disclosure of the "threat" to the client may not even be required, and informed consent to the "conflict" need not be obtained.

Of course, if the facts change, the analysis might be different. If the "threat" is repeated on several occasions, if there are supporting facts that make the lawyer a viable co-defendant, and if there are grounds for believing that the "threat" may come to pass, then the potential conflict may need to be disclosed to the affected client. In that case, whether the potential conflict is consentable depends on several things. Those facts would likely include the probability that the threat will be carried out and the lawyer named a co-defendant, and whether lawyer and client's interests are substantially congruent. Thus, it will be necessary to consider whether there are critical differences relating to the law or the facts of the case that would save either the lawyer or the client from liability, but not save the other. If so, the conflict may be unconsentable. In contrast, if the interests of the lawyer and client are aligned, so that the arguments that will win for one will also win for the other, then the conflict may be consentable. Further, if the conflict is consentable, then the question will be whether the lawyer disclosed sufficient information about the risks posed by the conflict to enable the client to make an informed judgment about whether to continue the representation.

The *de minimis non curat lex* principle is reflected in the language of Model Rule 1.7, which provides that there is a conflict of interest only if there is a "significant risk" that the representation of a client will be materially limited by a lawyer's duties to other clients or third persons, or by the lawyer's own interests. *See* Model Rules of Prof'l Conduct R. 1.7(a)(2) (2010).

j. A Conflict Must Cause Damage

Legal malpractice actions always require proof of damage. Therefore, even if there is evidence that the defendant lawyer had a serious conflict of interest, uncured by informed consent, the plaintiff must prove that the conflict caused harm. It is often difficult to establish this element of a malpractice case because the plaintiff normally must convince the jury that an unconflicted lawyer would have handled the representation differently and would have achieved a better result.

Put differently, if the conflicted lawyer acted reasonably despite the conflict, a malpractice action will fail. For example, in *Stonewell Corp. v. Conestoga Title Insurance Co.*, 678 F. Supp. 2d 203, 211-13 (S.D.N.Y. 2010), a legal malpractice plaintiff alleged that the lawyer representing him in litigation had an undisclosed conflict of interest arising from his relationship with a title insurance company. A federal court in New York held that the alleged conflict was insufficient to establish a claim for legal malpractice because the defendant lawyer had acted reasonably and appropriately at every stage of the litigation. Therefore, the alleged conflict could not be found to have caused damage.

In one sense, the damage requirement means that adding conflict of interest allegations to a malpractice claim may add little to the merits of the plaintiff's case. The issue is still likely to be whether the defendant lawyer rendered deficient legal services. There is no presumption that a conflict of interest caused harm.

However, in reality, proof that a lawyer had a conflict of interest can be a great advantage to a malpractice plaintiff. First and foremost, if there is colorable evidence that the defendant lawyer had a conflict of interest, the plaintiff's lawyer will be able to repeatedly hammer into the jury's understanding of the case the theme that the defendant lawyer violated basic rules of professional conduct and that the representation was "unethical." Those arguments, if supported by expert testimony and viewed by the jury as meritorious, may influence the jury's resolution not only of the question about whether the lawyer had a conflict, but other issues in the case as well. When in doubt, the jury may decide that a lawyer who violated applicable conflict of interest rules also violated the standard of care in other important respects relating to competence or loyalty.

Proving that a defendant lawyer had a conflict of interest may give the plaintiff an advantage not only with regard to trial tactics, but with respect to legal principles. Many states treat conflicts of interest as a breach of fiduciary duty. Some of those states then apply a relaxed standard of proof for assessing whether the breach of fiduciary duty caused damage. In those states, the plaintiff does not have to show that, "but for" the conflict of interest, harm to the plaintiff would not have occurred, but only that the conflict of interest was a "substantial factor" in causing the plaintiff's losses. (*See* Chapter 4 Part B.)

In addition, some states will "not hold a lawyer liable for failure to disclose a possible malpractice claim [to a client] unless the potential claim creates a conflict of interest that would disqualify the lawyer from representing the client." *Leonard v. Dorsey & Whitney LLP*, 553 F.3d 609, 629 (8th Cir. 2009) (predicting Minnesota law). The duty to disclose malpractice to a client is discussed in Chapter 11 Part D.

k. Standing to Assert a Conflict of Interest

It is difficult for a *nonclient* to successfully assert in a malpractice action that a lawyer had a conflict of interest. The reason this is true is essentially lack of standing. Most conflicts rules are intended to protect *clients* from threats that pose a risk of harm to their representation. *See, e.g.*, Model Rules of Professional Conduct R. 1.7 &.R. 1.8 (2010). Other conflicts rules focus on duties to *former clients* (*see id.* R. 1.9), or *former prospective clients* (*see id.* R. 1.18). Persons who are neither clients, former clients, or former prospective clients are usually well outside the protective ambit of conflict of interest rules.

In *Argoe v. Three Rivers Behavioral Center and Psychiatric Solutions*, 2010 WL 2944729 (S.C.), a woman brought a professional negligence action against a lawyer who had represented her son in his capacity as her attorney-in-fact. The son had transferred certain assets into a trust to prevent the woman from losing them in imprudent transactions as a result of her allegedly impaired mental condition. The Supreme Court of South Carolina rejected the plaintiff's argument that the lawyer had a conflict of interest. The court reached this conclusion, in part, because there was no attorney-client relationship between the plaintiff and the lawyer, and therefore no basis for the plaintiff to complain about a conflict of interest. As the court explained:

> The Durable Power of Attorney at issue in this case was executed by Appellant so that Son could protect her interests from her poor judgment and erratic behavior. This type of arrangement is commonplace and serves a good purpose: the protection of the infirm from their own infirmities. The fact that an infirm principal of a Durable Power of Attorney does not appreciate an action taken by an attorney-in-fact pursuant to the power she willfully gave him *** does not create liability for the attorney facilitating a transaction that is called into question. Recognizing a duty owed to a third-party, even one in privity to an attorney's client, would undermine the good and common practice of executing Durable Powers of Attorney ***.

Id. at *5.

2. Conflicts Between Multiple Current Clients

A lawyer's representation of one client may be materially limited by the lawyer's obligations to other clients. In that case, there is a conflict of interest related to the divergent interests of the multiple clients. *See* Model Rules of Prof'l Conduct R. 1.7(a)(2) (2010).

a. Conflicts Among Jointly Represented Co-Clients

Conflicts of interest often arise when clients are jointly represented in the same matter. For example, the affected clients may be co-defendants in a lawsuit, entrepreneurs seeking to start a business, or several family members injured in a single auto accident.

In any case where a lawyer represents multiple persons with respect to the same matter, it is essential for the lawyer to consider whether the clients are similarly situated or have divergent interests. In the latter case, the lawyer must decline or withdraw from the representation or seek informed consent to the conflict from every affected client. (*See* Part A-1-h of this Chapter.)

In *Call v. Czaplicki*, 2010 WL 3001395 (D.N.J. 2010), a lawyer who was hired to implement a tax shelter simultaneously represented the plaintiff client, two other shareholders, and their three business entities. A federal court in New Jersey found that the plaintiff stated causes of action for legal malpractice, breach of fiduciary duty, and negligence, based in part on conflicts of interest, because the plaintiff adequately alleged that the lawyer had engaged in "simultaneous representation of multiple clients with adverse interests." *Id.* at *7.

In *Sitar v. Sitar*, 50 A.D.3d 667, 854 N.Y.S.2d 536 (2008), a lawyer represented both the buyers and the sellers in the sale of a closely held corporation (Business Computing). An appellate court in New York found that the aggrieved sellers stated claims for legal malpractice against the lawyer based on conflict of interest. The plaintiffs alleged that the conflict of interest caused harm because the lawyer was aware of information critical to determining the purchase price of Business Computing, but withheld that information from them because of allegiance to another co-client.

(1) Conflicts Arising From Claims for Contribution or Indemnity

The interests of clients may diverge if one co-client could assert a claim for contribution or indemnity against another co-client. This is true because the successful prosecution of that claim would be to the advantage of one co-client at the expense of the other co-client. Whether, in such a case, the resulting conflict is consentable will be a function of several factors. Those factors will include, among other things, the strength of the underlying claim that the co-clients are subject to liability, and the likelihood that the reimbursement claim will need to be asserted.

b. Conflicts Among Separately Represented Current Clients

A multiple client conflict of interest may also arise from the simultaneous representation of clients who are not co-clients. This might be true, for example, where a lawyer separately represents two clients seeking to purchase the same piece of land. Successful efforts on behalf of one client would directly and adversely impact the lawyer's ability to accomplish the objectives of the other client.

One way to defeat a conflict of interest claim relating to contemporaneously represented current clients is to prove that one of the "clients" was not a client at all. For example, in *Leonard v. Dorsey & Whitney LLP*, 553 F.3d 609, 628 (8th Cir. 2009), a lower court had found that a law firm breached its fiduciary duty to a client (M & S) by representing it in a lawsuit against Bremer, while Bremer was a current client of the firm. However, the Eighth Circuit concluded that Bremer was not at any time the firm's client, or even a third-party beneficiary of the law firm's services. Therefore, there was no proof of conflicting loyalties that diminished the firm's representation of M & S.

3. Former Client Conflicts of Interest

The disciplinary rules in most states dealing with former client conflicts of interest run parallel to Model Rule 1.9. *See* Model Rules of Prof'l Conduct R. 1.9 (2010). This means that the touchstone for determining if there is a conflict of interest between a lawyer's earlier representation of a former client and new representation of a current client is usually whether the subject matter of the representations is the "same" or "substantially related." Generally, it is obvious whether two representations involve the "same" matter. Therefore, the difficulties that arise with respect to former client conflicts of interest usually relate to the question of whether the matters are "substantially related."

With respect to the rights of former clients, the conflicts analysis focuses on whether the matters are the same or substantially related because it is only in such cases that there is a risk that the lawyer will be tempted to be disloyal to the continuing duty of confidentiality that is owed to a former client. (*See* Chapter 3 Part A-2-e-(1).) If the matters are the same or substantially related, the confidential information entrusted to the lawyer by the former client may be useful.

The assessment of whether matters are substantially related is a fact intensive inquiry, which often focuses on whether the actors, events, dates, claims, defenses, and objectives of the two different representations are so linked that a lawyer's duty of confidentiality to the former client will be in conflict with the duty of candor to a current client. *See Restatement (Third) of the Law Governing Lawyers* § 132 cmt. d (2000). However, even if the matters are the same or substantially related, improper revelation of confidential information will not be presumed.

A former client alleging that a lawyer committed malpractice by undertaking representation of another client in the same or substantially related matter must prove that the subsequent representation caused damages. In this respect, a malpractice claim is very different from a request for disqualification. A lawyer will be disqualified from representing a client in a matter substantially related and materially adverse to the representation of a former client without proof that any confidential information was disclosed or used in the representation of the new client. Disqualification is ordered to avoid the appearance of impropriety. *See NCNB Texas National Bank v. Coker*, 765 S.W.2d 398, 400 (Tex. 1989). However, in a malpractice action, proof that the two matters were substantially related creates no presumption that confidential information was abused. *See City of Garland v. Booth*, 895 S.W.2d 766, 773 (Tex. App.1995).

The damages requirement is sometimes an insuperable obstacle to a malpractice plaintiff alleging that a lawyer violated the former client conflict of interest rules. For example, in *Benaquista v. Burke*, 74 A.D.3d 1514, 902 N.Y.S.2d 235 (2010), a New York appellate court held that an alleged former client's legal malpractice action failed because he did not identify any personal or confidential information used by the defendant, or any damages suffered as a result thereof.

4. Lawyer Versus Client Conflicts of Interest

Conflicts between the interests of lawyers and clients are addressed in most state disciplinary codes by two different rules. Those rules parallel Rules 1.7 and 1.8 in the American Bar Association's Model Rules of Professional Conduct.

Model Rule 1.7 deals with conflicts between the interests of a lawyer and a client in general terms. *See*

Model Rules of Prof'l Conduct R. 1.7(a)(2) (2010). The rule provides that a lawyer shall not undertake or continue to represent a client if there is a significant risk that the representation will be materially limited by the lawyer's own interests.

Model Rule 1.8 supplements Rule 1.7 by addressing a variety of specific situations in which the conflicting interests of a lawyer and client may threaten the lawyer's representation of the client. Thus, Model Rule 1.8 sets forth particular rules relating to business transactions (subsection a); misuse of client information (subsection b); gifts (subsection c); literary and media rights relating to the representation (subsection d); agreements limiting a lawyer's malpractice liability (subsection h); proprietary interests in the subject matter of litigation (subsection i); and sexual relations with clients (subsection j). *See* Model Rules of Prof'l Conduct R. 1.8 (2010).

In many instances, the resolution of lawyer-versus-client conflict of interest charges entails a difficult, multi-layered analysis of the facts. For example, in *On-Line Power Inc. v. Armstrong*, 2010 WL 3064374 (Cal. Ct. App.), the court needed to sort through facts relating to three different actual or potential lawsuits in order to determine whether the plaintiff stated a viable claim. The first lawsuit was the client's underlying litigation with a third-party. The second lawsuit was a resulting malpractice action against one of the lawyers involved in the underlying litigation. Finally, the third lawsuit was a potential malpractice claim against the law firm which had initially represented the plaintiff in the underlying litigation.

In *On-Line Power*, the plaintiff client was initially represented in litigation by a law firm named Haight. Armstrong was a partner in the Haight law firm who continued to represent the client in the same litigation after he left Haight and became "of counsel" to a new law firm. Unhappy with the resolution of the litigation, the client sued Armstrong for breach of fiduciary duty. The client alleged that, based on his prior affiliation with Haight, Armstrong had a conflict of interest which kept him from considering whether the Haight law firm had committed malpractice and from disclosing that information to the client. More specifically, the client alleged that if the Haight law firm's malpractice had been disclosed, the client would have sought other counsel to handle that malpractice claim, and would have litigated the claim against the Haight law firm within the applicable period of limitations.

An appellate court in California affirmed a judgment in favor of lawyer Armstrong. The court reasoned that in order to link Armstrong's alleged violation of the conflict of interest rules to the loss of the purported malpractice claim against the Haight law firm, the client had to demonstrate that the Haight law firm breached a duty of care. However, in the action against Armstrong, the client had failed to designate an expert witness to testify about whether Haight violated the standard of care. Because there was no expert proffered on whether Haight committed malpractice, there was no evidence that the client had a potentially meritorious claim to pursue against Haight. Consequently, the client failed to show that Armstrong's alleged conflict of interest and nondisclosure caused damages.

a. Lawyers Simultaneously Performing Different Roles

Plaintiffs sometimes allege that a lawyer committed malpractice by simultaneously acting in different roles. However, this type of conflict of interest is actionable only if it caused harm because the client misunderstood what the lawyer was doing or the lawyer's performance of the lawyering role was deficient. For example, in *Floyd v. Hefner*, 556 F. Supp. 2d 617 (S.D. Tex. 2008), a federal court in Texas held that a corporate client failed to establish legal malpractice based on a conflict of interest. As the court explained:

Fuller [a lawyer] wore numerous hats during the relevant time period: he was a director of Seven Seas, a lender in the Secured Facility, and an attorney for Seven Seas. However, there is no evidence that the board did not know about Fuller's multiple roles. ***.

*** Seven Seas has not offered the testimony of any person associated with the Company who was dissatisfied with the Lawyers' legal performance. Indeed, the Lawyers accomplished what Seven Seas asked them to do with respect to the Deep Well Transaction.

***. There is no evidence that but for the Lawyers' advice and actions, the Secured Facility would not have been approved or the Deep Well drilled.

556 F. Supp. 2d at 663.

b. Business Transactions with Clients

Business transactions between lawyers and clients are usually treated as conflicts of interest. This is because, in such transactions, there is a risk that the lawyer will benefit at the client's expense. For example, it is apparent that a lawyer and client have differing interests if one makes a loan to the other, or purchases, sells, or leases real or personal property in a transaction with the other. Indeed, if a lawyer and client jointly invest in property, they may be treated as participants in a business transaction.

To protect clients from abuse and overreaching, all states have a disciplinary rule which imposes significant limitations on lawyers doing business with clients. *See* Model Rules of Prof'l Conduct R. 1.8 (2010). For example, Rule 1.8 in the District of Columbia's Rules of Professional Conduct provides that:

(a) A lawyer shall not enter into a business transaction with a client or knowingly acquire an ownership, possessory, security, or other pecuniary interest adverse to a client unless:

(1) The transaction and terms on which the lawyer acquires the interest are fair and reasonable to the client and are fully disclosed and transmitted in writing to the client in a manner which can be reasonably understood by the client;

(2) The client is given a reasonable opportunity to seek the advice of independent counsel in the transaction; and

> (3) The client gives informed consent in writing thereto.

D.C. Rules of Prof'l Conduct R. 1.8 (2010). These types of disciplinary provisions are routinely mentioned in malpractice actions against lawyers involving allegedly unfair business relations.

For example, in *McMahon v. Eke-Nweke*, 503 F. Supp. 2d 598 (E.D.N.Y. 2007), a lawyer leased space in a building from a client on favorable terms. In addressing the client's claim against the lawyer for breach of fiduciary duty, a federal court in New York quoted and discussed the provisions of the New York disciplinary rules governing business transactions between lawyers and clients. Because the court found that there was a question of fact as to whether the client had been informed of all material circumstances related to the lease, the defendant lawyer's motion for summary judgment was denied.

In *Liggett v. Young*, 877 N.E.2d 178 (Ind. 2007), a client who built a home for a lawyer was sued by a material supplier. The client then brought a third-party complaint against the lawyer alleging that the contract for the home violated applicable rules of professional conduct and was void. The Supreme Court of Indiana held that the state's version of the disciplinary rule limiting business transactions between a lawyer and client did not automatically create a civil cause of action. However, the court recognized that, as a matter of common law, transactions entered into by a fiduciary with a client are presumptively fraudulent. Therefore, the lawyer had the burden of proving that the contract related to the construction of the house was fair and reasonable. The court noted that the disciplinary rule dealing with business transactions did not apply to standard commercial transactions. Such dealings are essentially the same for all customers and thus are not a likely source of abuse. Addressing the circumstances of the case, the court held that there was a fact issue as to whether the contract to build the house came within a standard commercial transaction exception to the common law presumption of invalidity, and therefore remanded the case for further proceedings.

As the discussion of *Liggett* suggests, some courts treat many business transactions with clients as presumptively fraudulent. Other courts shift the burden of proof to a defendant lawyer to show that the requirements of the applicable ethics rule were satisfied. An improper business transaction between a lawyer and client may be actionable as negligence or breach of fiduciary duty, and may also entitle the client to seek rescission of the transaction or imposition of a constructive trust to strip the lawyer of ill-gained profits.

c. Stock in Lieu of Fees and Other Equity Investments in Clients

Lawyers representing start-up ventures and other businesses with growth potential are sometimes paid for their legal services with stock in the enterprise. Even if this arrangement is the idea of the client, who may be short on cash, it is easy to see the potential that a lawyer's acquisition of an equity interest in the business has for creating a potentially serious conflict of interest. If the lawyer continues to represent the business in which the investment is held or persons related to the venture, it may later be argued that the lawyer's advice and judgment were distorted by the lawyer's personal interest in protecting the lawyer's equity stake, rather than the product of undivided loyalty to the interests of the client. If the lawyer's equity share is substantial, a jury might conclude that the conflict of interest amounted to malpractice. Moreover, even if the investment is relatively minor, the lawyer's equity stake will complicate the defense of any malpractice claim asserted by the client.

See generally John S. Dzienkowski & Robert S. Peroni, "The Decline in Lawyer Independence: Lawyer Equity Investments in Clients," 81 *Tex. L. Rev.* 405 (2002).

d. Economic Benefit to Lawyer-Related Businesses

If work for a client, such as photocopying and document production, is performed by a business in which the lawyer, or a person related to the lawyer, owns an interest, the lawyer or third person may benefit at the client's expense. The failure to disclose the true nature of such an arrangement is actionable as a conflict of interest. Moreover, even if the client is apprised of the details of the arrangement, the business transaction may not be fair and reasonable if the client is being charged more for services which could be obtained at a lower cost from other sources. Thus, notwithstanding the client's consent, it may be possible for the client to challenge the legal validity of the transaction and recoup profits that exceeded the market rate for the services in question.

e. Modification of Fee Contracts

Changes to the lawyer-client fee contract during the course of the representation are subject to close scrutiny and may be deemed to be unenforceable. The lawyer has the burden of proving that the modification was fair and reasonable to the client and that all material was disclosed to the client. *See Restatement (Third) of the Law Governing Lawyers* § 18 (2000).

f. The Limits of the Term "Business Transaction"

The concept of "business transaction" has limits, and those limits influence the application of conflict of interest principles. An agreement entered into by a client, which benefits the client's lawyer, is not necessarily a "business transaction" for purposes of the rules governing lawyer-client conflicts of interest.

In *Berner Cheese Corp. v. Krug,* 312 Wis. 2d 251, 752 N.W.2d 800 (2008), a cheese manufacturer (Berner) was sued by an outside law firm (Brennan) for unpaid legal fees. The manufacturer then filed a third-party complaint against its former corporation counsel (Krug), who was a member of another law firm. The manufacturer alleged that Krug committed legal malpractice and breach of fiduciary duties relating to an underlying dispute, which the manufacturer had settled with a third-party cheese brokerage (Dairy Source). A release, drafted by the Brennan law firm to implement the settlement, relinquished the manufacturer's claims against various parties, including corporation counsel Krug. According to a member of the Brennan law firm, Krug was released "because '[w]e wanted to make sure that everybody in the civil action that was a party defendant or a possible party defendant' would be insulated from further legal liability." 752 N.W.2d at 808. The release of Krug was never bargained over when the representatives of Berner and Dairy Source, without lawyers present, negotiated the amount of the settlement. Nor did Krug pressure the Brennan law firm to include language in the release releasing him from liability. Seizing upon the fact that the release benefitted Krug, the manufacturer argued that the document constituted a business transaction for purposes of lawyer-client conflict of interest rules, and that Krug had to prove the fairness of the amount paid to settle the underlying litigation. The manufacturer's theory was that Krug's alleged breach of fiduciary duty made him liable for the full costs of the settlement. Addressing the fiduciary duty claim, the Supreme Court of Wisconsin rejected this argument. The court explained its reasoning as follows:

> In all the cases we have located where attorney-client transactions were involved, there was a communication or activity that reciprocally affected the client and the attorney. That is, one party gave up something and the other party received something at the expense of the one who relinquished it. ***.
>
> In contrast, there is no evidence that the Berner-Dairy Source settlement embodies reciprocal activity affecting Berner and Krug. Krug was not involved in Berner's decision to pay Dairy Source in a settlement. That determination was made in a meeting between Berner and Dairy Source. Accordingly, Dairy Source, not Krug, is

the party with whom Berner engaged in reciprocal activity. Berner paid Dairy Source $1.35 million dollars and in return received from Dairy Source its commitment not to "use, distribute or copy" Berner's proprietary information ***. Therefore, Berner gave up nothing to Krug when it agreed to pay Dairy Source $1.35 million as settlement. The settlement negotiation that resulted in the settlement was a transaction between Berner and Dairy Source, not between Berner and Krug.

Furthermore, Brennan [the outside law firm], not Krug, represented Berner in the litigation with Dairy Source. Berner does not dispute that its attorneys at Brennan were engaged with Dairy Source representatives in drafting the settlement document. Moreover, the admissions by *** [Berner's representatives] belie Berner's claim that, because the settlement document releases Krug from all claims, the settlement was the product of undue influence. When asked whether Krug had any input into the settlement amount, *** [a Berner representative] testified that Krug had not. ***.

***. Because the settlement was not a transaction between Berner and Krug, Berner has failed in its proof that it is entitled to the presumption [of unfairness] it seeks. ***.

752 N.W.2d at 812-13.

5. Third-Person Conflicts of Interest

Conflicts of interests threatening the representation of a client may arise from duties that the lawyer owes to a third person. This is why all state disciplinary codes have a provision, similar to Model Rule 1.8(h), barring a lawyer from accepting undisclosed compensation from a third party for representing the client. *See* Model Rules of Prof'l Conduct R. 1.8(h) (2010). The concern is that the person who pays the bill will also call the shots, and that the client's representation will be distorted by the payor's wishes. Thus, a third person can pay for a client's representation only if the client gives informed consent.

Of course, there are many other types of threats involving the competing interests of third persons. Therefore, all state codes have a provision paralleling language in Model Rule 1.7, which bars a lawyer from undertaking or continuing representation where there is a substantial risk that the representation will be materially limited by the interests of a third person. *See* Model Rules of Prof'l Conduct R. 1.7(a)(2) (2010).

One example of a duty to a third person that can create a conflict of interest relates to testifying expert witnesses. A lawyer who serves as a testifying expert witness on behalf of a person does not represent that person, but nevertheless owes the person various duties, such as an obligation to protect the person's confidential information from use or adverse disclosure. (*See* Chapter 3 Part B-3-d.) These duties can create a conflict of interest if the information which must be protected could be useful in the lawyer's representation of another individual. Thus, representation of a client adverse to the party for whom the lawyer is serving as a testifying expert is normally barred by Model Rule 1.7. *See* ABA Formal Op. 97-407 (1997).

Of course, even if a lawyer has a clear conflict of interest relating to a third person, a client can successfully sue for malpractice only if the conflict caused damage. For example, *Herrera v. Hark*, 2007 WL 1319448 (N.J. Super. Ct. App. Div. 2007), a lawyer (Hark) allegedly entered the hospital room of an auto accident victim (Herrera) without authorization, induced Herrera to sign a contingent fee agreement, and did not disclose that the defendant in the forthcoming litigation was the grandfather of Hark's wife. Further, the lawyer allegedly misled the client by telling him that the grandfather could only be held liable for $100,000, the amount of his insurance policy. This was not true because the grandfather had substantial assets. Herrera discharged Hark and then engaged substitute counsel, who secured a $95,000 settlement for the client. In Herrera's subsequent malpractice action against Hark, a New Jersey appellate court affirmed a grant of summary judgment for the defendant. As the court explained:

> Herrera has not shown how he would have obtained a better result than the $95,000 settlement, even if Hark had disclosed his conflict of interest. In short, no showing of damages has been made.

Id. at 3.

B.   SETTLEMENT-RELATED ERRORS

It is not surprising that many malpractice claims are related to settlements. This is true because most disputes are resolved not through adjudication, but by way of compromise, whether before or after a lawsuit is filed.

Some malpractice claims are barred by the client's voluntary resolution of the underlying dispute. However, many settlement-related malpractice claims are viable. The following sections consider whether settlement precludes a client from subsequently recovering damages in a malpractice action.

1.   Failure to Convey an Offer

The failure to convey a settlement offer to a client may amount to actionable malpractice. Thus, in *Stonewell Corp. v. Conestoga Title Insurance Co.*, 678 F. Supp. 2d 203, 213-14 (S.D.N.Y. 2010), a federal court in New York refused to grant summary judgment in favor of the defendant lawyer because there were disputed issues of fact as to whether the defendant neglected to relay a settlement offer to the plaintiff and whether the plaintiff would have accepted the offer.

A settlement offer need not be communicated to a client if previous discussions with the client have made clear than an offer in that range would be unacceptable or if the client has instructed the lawyer not to relay such an offer. *Cf*. Model Rules of Prof'l Conduct R. 1.4 cmt. 2 (2010).

2. "Second Thoughts" About Amounts

A client who has "second thoughts" about the amount of money received or paid in a settlement normally cannot sue a lawyer merely because the amount was too low or too high. *See Muhammad v. Strassburger, McKenna, Messer, Shilobod and Gutnick,* 526 Pa. 541, 587 A.2d 1346 (Pa. 1991). In part, the reason for this rule is that persons must be bound by the agreements they make in order to encourage responsible decision-making. Allowing malpractice claims in cases of "settler's regret," would create chaos in the justice system by discouraging the settlement of disputes. "Lawyers would be reluctant to settle a case for fear some enterprising attorney representing a disgruntled client will find a way to sue them for something that 'could have been done, but was not.'" 587 A.2d at 1349.

3. Actionable Malpractice Related to a Settlement

Notwithstanding the general rule that second thoughts about the adequacy of a settlement are not actionable, a malpractice plaintiff can sometimes state a viable claim related to a voluntary resolution of an earlier dispute. Three such instances are where a lawyer has fraudulently induced, coerced, or negligently caused an inadequate settlement. These situations are discussed in the following sections.

a. Fraudulently Inducing a Settlement

The fact that a client agreed to a settlement does not prevent a client from alleging that a lawyer fraudulently induced the client to settle. "If the lawyer knowingly commits malpractice, but does not disclose the error and convinces the client to settle so as to avoid the discovery of such error, then the client's agreement was fraudulently obtained." *Muhammad v. Strassburger, McKenna, Messer, Shilobod and Gutnick*, 526 Pa. 541, 587 A.2d 1346, 1351 (Pa. 1991). In that type of situation, a malpractice action will lie.

b. Coercing a Settlement

In *Hoffman v. Gotcher & Belote*, 2010 WL 3087468 (N.D. Ill. 2010), the plaintiffs sued their lawyer after settling their personal injury action arising from a trucking accident. In part, the plaintiffs alleged that the lawyer had recommended a settlement that was far lower than would have been recommended by a lawyer who was willing to file a lawsuit. More specifically, the plaintiffs testified "that they felt pressured into settling their claims by Belote [their lawyer] and that they were afraid, if they did not agree to the settlement Belote was recommending, the approaching statute of limitations might expire without suit being filed and they would lose their causes of action arising from the trucking accident." *Id.* at *3. Addressing the facts of the case, a federal court noted that "Illinois courts recognize that a lawyer may be held liable for negligence in the handling of a case that ultimately was settled by the client whether based on deficiencies in preparation that prejudiced the case or a negligent evaluation of the case that caused an inadequate settlement." *Id.* at *3. The court held that there was a question of fact as to whether the plaintiffs had been intimidated or misled in relation to the settlement, and that therefore summary judgment for either party was not appropriate.

c. Negligently Forcing the Client to Settle

A malpractice claim is not barred by a client's agreement to a settlement if the client was forced to settle because of the defendant lawyer's negligence. Thus, in *Bloomberg v. Kronenberg*, 2006 WL 3337467 (N.D. Ohio 2006), a federal court in Ohio held that a client who had entered into a property settlement incidental to a divorce could sue her lawyer for having failed to contact the client's appraiser prior to trial or otherwise introduce evidence prepared by the appraiser to prove that contested properties were worth more than the client's husband contended. As the court explained:

> [T]he Plaintiff's assertion *** is not that the Defendant's strategic decision to recommend settlement constituted error. The Plaintiff's complaint does not focus on strategic choices of any kind. Rather, the Plaintiff alleges that the Defendant completely failed to represent the Plaintiff's interests through his inadequate preparation in the underlying divorce proceedings.

Id. at *3.

In *General Nutrition Corp. v. Gardere Wynne Sewell, LLP*, 2008 WL 4411951 (W.D. Pa. 2008), a law firm advised a client that it would be subject to limited liability for terminating a contract because the contract involved a *sale of goods* governed by the Uniform Commercial Code. However, at trial, the court ruled that the UCC was inapplicable because the contract was for a *sale of services*. Faced with the prospect of multimillion dollar liability, the client settled the underlying dispute. A federal court in Pennsylvania held that the settlement did not bar a malpractice action against the firm for allegedly providing bad advice. The settlement had been based on the advice of replacement counsel and the client "arguably had a duty to mitigate its damages by entering into a reasonable compromise and settlement of the claim." *Id.* at *3.

Similarly, in *Prospect Rehabilitation Services, Inc. v. Squitieri*, 392 N.J. Super. 157, 920 A.2d 135, 141 (N.J. Super. Ct. App. Div. 2007), the plaintiff alleged, in relevant part, that the defendant lawyer had failed to assert certain Medicare denial claims as part of the plaintiff's litigation against nursing homes. A New Jersey appellate court ruled that a malpractice claim was not barred by the fact that the plaintiff, after obtaining substitute counsel, settled with the nursing homes. Effectively accepting the plaintiff's argument that the defendant lawyer's negligence had forced it to accept an inadequate settlement, the court found that the plaintiff had never represented to anyone that its settlement with the nursing homes was a fair and satisfactory resolution of its underlying claims.

Likewise, in *Pike v. Mullikin*, 158 N.H. 267, 965 A.2d 987 (2009), a client entered into a property settlement with his wife because he had grounds to believe that the divorce court would not enforce their antenuptial agreement. The Supreme Court of New Hampshire concluded that the client's agreement with his wife did not bar a malpractice action against the lawyers who drafted the antenuptial agreement. The malpractice suit did not attempt to undermine the final resolution of the divorce, nor was the client pursuing his lawyers for purely monetary gain. Rather, the court found, the client merely sought to put himself into the place that he expected to be if the antenuptial agreement had been enforced by a court.

Negligence by the initial lawyer handling a case may not only force a client to settle, it may limit the options of successor counsel. In a recent Pennsylvania legal malpractice suit, a client followed the advice of her successor counsel and settled her underlying medical malpractice case for $1 million, despite having received a $2.5 million verdict. The settlement was recommended because the complaint had pleaded the wrong theory of liability and, on the facts of the case, amending the complaint was not feasible. The initial attorney, who had filed the deficient complaint, was held liable for malpractice, but the successor attorney who recommended the acceptance of the settlement was not. *See* Amaris Elliott-Engel, "Pa. Jury Awards $1.8 Million in Legal Malpractice Suit," www.law.com, Sept. 3, 2010.

CHAPTER TEN

PREVENTING LEGAL MALPRACTICE

A. ACCEPTING AND REJECTING NEW BUSINESS

Many of the problems that give rise to legal malpractice actions can be avoided by the exercise of care right at the beginning of a possible lawyer-client relationship. By screening prospective clients carefully, checking for conflicts of interest, documenting which proffered engagements have been accepted or declined, and clarifying who is being represented, a lawyer can greatly minimize the chances of being sued.

1. Screening Prospective Clients

If a prospective client is *unreasonably* aggrieved by the conduct of a business partner, a former lawyer, a public official, a commercial establishment, or a family member, there is a possibility the lawyer who is being asked to provide representation will be the next person to "fail" the prospective client. Unhappy clients often turn into malpractice plaintiffs. Therefore, the risk of being sued can be significantly reduced by not commencing a professional relationship with a person destined to be disappointed.

For reasons not related to client temperament, some prospective clients are just not the right fit. They need work in the wrong legal area or on a deadline that is too tight. Or they require help at a moment when the lawyer's time is already fully committed to other clients. These are the kinds of cases that, with the benefit of hindsight, lawyers often conclude it would have been better to decline.

2. Checking Conflicts Thoroughly

As Chapter 9 makes clear, the rules related to conflicts of interest require a lawyer to be vigilant in guarding against a wide range of matters that may threaten the representation of a client. The duties imposed by the conflicts rules make it necessary for a lawyer to think about conflicts starting when a prospective client first seeks legal representation.

The initial step in avoiding conflicts of interest is gathering good information for determining whether a request for representation can be accepted. Assembling this information is more difficult than might first appear because conflicts of interest may arise in many ways. The interests of clients, former clients, lawyers, and third persons must all be considered. Moreover, because conflicts may stem not merely from present facts, but from events that took place in the past, it is essential to preserve and consider material information relating to matters that occurred years earlier.

As any lawyer who has practiced law for more than a decade knows, relying on memory to identify conflicts of interest is risky. Even information that was once well known when a lawyer litigated a case or drafted a document will fade or vanish with the passage of time.

The information needed for assessing possible conflicts generally falls into three categories. Those categories relate to the firm, the prospective client, and the subject matter of the proposed representation.

Some of the information relevant to detecting and guarding against conflicts of interest relates to lawyers and other persons working in the law firm. This information will likely include their names and former names, as well as the names of spouses, former spouses, and other closely related family members. Information about the investments, business interests, and former employers of at least some of these persons could well be important. With respect to the firm's lawyers, it is often critical to know whom they represented in the past, as well as whom they declined to represent.

Other facts needed for evaluating potential conflicts of interest relate to the prospective client. In the case of an individual client, this information is likely to include the client's name and former names, along with the names of spouses, former spouses, and closely related family members. The current and prior employers, investments, and business interests of at least the client may also be material. In the case of an entity client, the lawyer evaluating the conflict will need to learn about related predecessor entities, parent or subsidiary entities, key employees, business partners, and major investors.

With respect to the subject matter of the representation, it may be important to determine not just the nature and scope of the task the lawyer is being asked to perform, but also related information that will vary with the type of work. In litigation, it will often be necessary to gather information about the identities of opposing parties, fact witnesses, and expert witnesses. If the client is requesting legal advice about the client's service as a fiduciary, it will be important to know who are beneficiaries of the fiduciary relationship. Checklists should be developed to guide the collection of information typically relevant to the firm's practice areas. The kinds of persons who may be affected by the handling of a probate matter are likely to be somewhat different than those impacted by bankruptcy work or criminal defense. Of course, it is necessary to consider how the subject matter of the proposed representation relates to the subject matter of other representations handled in the past by lawyers in the firm. Therefore, it will be necessary to know what tasks have been undertaken by the firm's lawyers in prior years.

It is easy to see how checking for conflicts, particularly in large law firms, can become an onerous task. However, the burden of identifying conflicts and complying with applicable rules can be minimized by adopting a systematic approach to these kinds of challenges. Many law firms use conflict-checking software to gather information about the firm and its clients and prospective clients on a regular basis. With respect to the firm's personnel, information will typically be gathered when a lawyer or staff member is being considered for a position or begins employment, and thereafter updated on a periodic basis. Likewise, information about potential clients will be gathered each time a person seeks legal services relating to a new matter.

Conflict-checking software is not infallible. The program may not search for common misspellings or alternative spellings of names and terms (*e.g.*, not just "Alice," but also "Alyce"). Except for the most blatant conflicts (*e.g.*, a firm's appearance on the opposite side of litigation), the program will only identify information that needs to be evaluated. A lawyer still must exercise judgment about what the facts mean. In the usual case, software cannot determine whether there is a "substantial risk" that representation of a client will be "materially limited," as those terms are used by disciplinary rules. *Cf.* Model Rules of Prof'l Conduct R. 1.7(a)(2) (2010).

Even firms that use excellent conflict-checking software normally supplement that process by circulating to lawyers in the firm a "new matter" memo. The memo seeks additional information about possible conflicts that may require the firm to decline a new engagement or seek informed consent.

Some firms have a "conflicts committee" that is charged with resolving disputes about whether a conflict of interest exists and, if so, how the conflict should be handled. These kinds of procedures not only tend to ensure consistent firm practices, but enable lawyers within the firm to develop the type of conflict of interest expertise that may be an asset to the firm.

3. Using Non-engagement Letters

If representation of a prospective client is declined, it is important to confirm that fact in writing. Doing so will dispel any expectation on the part of the person seeking legal services that the lawyer will provide representation. This will make it virtually impossible for the person to sue the lawyer for malpractice by alleging there was an attorney-client relationship created by mistake. (*See* Chapter 3 Part A-1-a-(3).)

A non-engagement letter should clearly state that the lawyer will not represent the prospective client. It should also urge the client to promptly obtain other counsel before any claim is barred by the statute of limitations. In the usual case, the letter should not tell the client which statute of limitations applies to the client's matter or when the statute of limitations will expire. Determining the applicable statute of limitations and whether the running of the statute will be tolled by some special factor is often difficult, and it is easy to get this kind of advice wrong. Erroneous assurances about how much time a person has to file a cause of action will not only mislead the client, but make the lawyer declining the representation subject to a malpractice claim. A lawyer must exercise reasonable care to the extent that a lawyer provides legal services to a prospective client. Advice about the statute of limitations falls within the category of potential liability. *See Restatement (Third) of the Law Governing Lawyers* § 15 (2000).

A non-engagement letter should normally be delivered by both regular and certified mail, return receipt requested. This way the lawyer can prove the letter was delivered to the person asking for representation. If that person later sues for malpractice, claiming to have been a client of the lawyer, the delivery receipt for the certified letter will help to convince a jury that any expectation that the person had, that the lawyer would provide legal services, was unreasonable. Some persons decline to accept certified letter. Therefore, sending the letter by regular mail, too, may be helpful to proving that delivery occurred.

4. Obtaining Signed Engagement Agreements

A lawyer's acceptance of a new client should be promptly followed by the drafting of an engagement agreement. The agreement, which may take the form of a contract or a letter, should clarify at least the following: (1) who is being represented, (2) the fee arrangement, (3) the scope of the representation, and (4) any special conditions of the representation. In the case of an entity client, it may be very useful for the agreement to also state who is not being represented, such as individual officers and employees of the entity. This will help to prevent any misunderstanding, and will demonstrate that the lawyer took pains to ensure that no one was misled.

The client should be asked to return a signed copy of the engagement agreement. That document should then be carefully preserved as part of the law firm's files.

In many malpractice cases, there is uncertainty about whether an engagement agreement was ever written or received by the client. This is because no copy of the agreement can be located in the files of the parties to the litigation. Preserving a copy of the engagement agreement, along with evidence that it was received and acknowledged by the client, is just as important as composing that document.

In drafting the part of the engagement agreement which deals with fees, expenses, interest on unpaid balances, and related matters, a lawyer should remember that it is very difficult to validly change a fee agreement during the course of on-going representation. The lawyer bears the burden of showing that the modification was fair and reasonable *to the client*, and that all material facts were disclosed. Existing precedent in many jurisdictions makes this close to impossible, at least if the original agreement did not provide for periodic adjustment of fees. *See generally Restatement (Third) of the Law Governing Lawyers* § 18 cmt. e (2000).

B. TREATING CLIENTS WELL AND PROVIDING EXCELLENT SERVICE

The surest way to avoid malpractice claims is by treating clients well and providing excellent service. Numerous articles by knowledgeable experts offer the following kinds of advice:

- ■ Be honest and accurate in recording billable hours. Adhere to the same standards you would want a lawyer to follow if you were paying the bill.

- ■ Return phone calls promptly.

■   Hire lawyers and staff members who are polite and naturally inclined to be helpful. Trying to retrofit rude or condescending employees with client-pleasing characteristics is a frustrating proposition with little chance of success.

■   Avoid romantic relationships with clients. Follow this injunction regardless of whether the relationship violates the literal terms and legal interpretations of any disciplinary rule addressing the subject of sexual relations. *See* Model Rules of Prof'l Conduct R. 1.8(j) (2010).

■   Even in the Age of Twitter, make sure that every communication with a client uses good grammar and proper punctuation, and that it is professional and polite. This shows respect for the client. It will also look good to a jury if a dispute later develops.

■   Make sure that letters are clear. Avoid triple-layered legalese as much as possible.

■   In e-mail communications, include a signature block that furnishes useful information, such as phone numbers for the lawyer and, perhaps, the lawyer's secretary.

■   Consult clients about the mode (*e.g.*, letter, e-mail, or phone) and frequency of communications, and about who should be kept "in the loop." Make a record of those instructions and follow them as closely as feasible. (Some lawyers use a checklist to gather this information from new clients. The process may entail not only identifying the decision makers for an entity client, but gathering contact information about key staffers.)

■ Applaud, publicly and privately, the representatives of the law firm (lawyers and staffers) who provide excellent client service. This will reinforce good practices and habits.

■ Ask every person who works for the law firm what can be done to improve client services. This may produce useful suggestions relating to such diverse matters as routing phone calls or arranging parking for clients.

■ Clarify to clients any limitations on the scope of the representation.

■ Preserve copies of all important communications by or on behalf of a client. This may be useful to the client in the future.

■ Let clients know that you appreciate the opportunity to work for them.

C. MANAGING RISKS

1. Risk Management Procedures

Each law firm should have in place standard operating procedures which minimize the risk of malpractice. In many instances, this means that the firm should locate or develop forms and checklists that can be used in handling routine matters.

The law firm's procedures should reflect professional "best practices" with respect to such matters of recurring importance as acceptance or rejection of new clients, handling of funds and property, protection of confidential information from unauthorized access, lawyer-client contracts, and conflicts of interest. Many firms have a risk management partner charged with thinking about what practices should be implemented to reduce a firm's exposure to liability.

Every law firm of more than a few lawyers should have an "ethics committee" or "ethics partner" from whom lawyers in the firm can solicit guidance on questions of professional responsibility. Likewise, a firm should ensure that its lawyers stay current with developments in the law of lawyering (such as important decisions relating to conflicts of interest), either by hosting in-house seminars or taking advantage of other professional education opportunities.

Some of the best risk management advice comes from legal malpractice issuers. Insurers furnish this information to their clients and potential clients through newsletters, lectures, and workshops. Some insurers offer guidance on their websites or provide risk management hotlines.

Consultants specialize in law firm risk management. Money spent on this type of expertise can often greatly reduce the costs that a firm incurs in connection with malpractice claims.

2. Anticipating Problems

The risk of malpractice liability can be minimized by anticipating problems. One common problem is proving that various disclosures were made to a client. With respect to any important matter that may become the subject of dispute, disclosures, warnings, and other important advice should be conveyed to the client in writing. This will help to drive home the importance of what the client is being told, and will enable the firm to prove how it addressed related issues.

As the following sections suggest, difficulties often arise for law firms with respect to tax consequences, estate representation, corporate representation, and deadlines.

a. Tax Consequences

Many legal issues have tax consequences, but most lawyers are not tax experts. Therefore, lawyers who do not specialize in tax law need to be especially vigilant in advising clients about tax-related consequences and in not addressing tax issues.

In some cases, it is reasonable and appropriate for a lawyer to limit the scope of representation by agreeing with the client that the lawyer's responsibilities do not include advising the client about tax matters. However, in other cases, such a limitation might be challenged as unreasonable. *See Restatement (Third) of the Law Governing Lawyers* § 19 (2000).

Whether a client will be taxed on a judgment or settlement is often a complex issue with very significant consequences for the client. *See* Erica Dunmyer, "5 Things Every Plaintiff's Attorney Should Know About Tax Law," law.com (Aug. 17, 2010). In dealing with such questions, it is important to consult appropriate sources of guidance and, if necessary, seek expert advice.

b. Estate Representation

A lawyer doing work related to the administration of an estate needs to clarify the identity of the client. Otherwise, the lawyer may encounter an unexpectedly wide range of potential liability.

In *Spencer v. Gavin*, 400 N.J. Super. 220, 946 A.2d 1051, 1065 (2008), the court noted that there are at least four conceptual possibilities in estate-related representation. A lawyer could represent (1) the executor in the performance of his or her duties; (2) the estate itself; (3) the beneficiaries of the estate; or (4) some combination of the first three alternatives. The *Spencer* court observed that, under New Jersey law, when a lawyer is retained to perform specific tasks in connection with an estate, the lawyer's client is ordinarily the executor, rather than the estate. Nevertheless, the court found that, on the facts of the case, the defendant lawyer, who failed to clarify in a retainer agreement whom he represented, owed duties to the estate as a client. 946 A.2d at 1066-67.

c. Corporate Representation

Misunderstandings often arise as to who is a client in corporate representation. If a law firm intends to represent only the entity, and not particular individuals, such as officers or employees, the law firm must make that clear to persons who might mistakenly think otherwise. In many instances, this needs to be done orally at the moment when there is reason to think there is some misunderstanding. However, it is also important that all paperwork relating to the representation confirm that there was no confusion as to whom was being represented. The law firm's filing system and related documents should clearly indicate that the entity was the client. Billing statements should also name the entity as the client. Likewise, correspondence with the client should be addressed to the entity and directed to the attention of an individual. This will help to document that it was the entity, not the individual, who was being represented by the law firm. Further, care must be taken to ensure that the text of correspondence never carelessly creates the mis-impression that the law firm was looking after the personal legal interests of entity representatives.

d. Calendaring Deadlines

It is essential for a lawyer to carefully calendar all important deadlines related to a client's representation, and to review the calendar on a regular basis. Ideally, all deadlines should be included on the calendars of at least two responsible persons to ensure that the error of merely one person, in ignoring the calendar, will not result in a malpractice lawsuit.

Calendars should include "ticklers," which are reminders of upcoming deadlines. The ticklers should allow enough lead time for completion of required tasks.

A lawyer should never assume that he or she knows which statute of limitations is applicable to a client's claim. Instead, the lawyer should check and double check the statute. Moreover, it is necessary to be alert to special circumstances which may call a different statute of limitations into play (such as, perhaps, the fact that a potentially responsible party is a governmental entity).

A lawyer who refers a client to another lawyer may be subject to liability if the lawyer receiving the referral fails to file a lawsuit before the statute of limitations lapses. (*See* Chapter 8 Part D-1.) Therefore, the referring lawyer's calendar should include reminders for the lawyer to check on whether the referred claim has been properly filed.

D. ENDING REPRESENTATION PROPERLY

A lawyer's duties to a client greatly contract when the representation ends. (*See* Chapter 3 Part A-2-e.) Therefore, exposure to liability for failure to protect a client's interests can be avoided by clarifying that representation has concluded. After that point, a client has little reason to expect the lawyer to act on the client's behalf.

Moreover, the end of the representation may also mean that the statute of limitations begins to run on any claim for which the statute was tolled by the continuing representation doctrine. (*See* Chapter 7 C-2-b.) This can be important to a lawyer who is later sued for malpractice.

At the end of the representation of a client, a termination letter should formally close the client's file. In the letter, the lawyer should thank the client for the opportunity to serve, and perhaps offer to be of assistance in the future, if the need arises. The letter should be sent to the client and a copy permanently retained by the firm in case it is necessary to prove when the representation ended.

CHAPTER ELEVEN

LEGAL MALPRACTICE INSURANCE

A. THE IMPORTANCE OF LEGAL MALPRACTICE INSURANCE

Legal malpractice insurance is important for a variety of reasons. From the perspective of potential defendants, insurance can reduce the costs of settling a claim or paying an adverse judgment. Insurance can also reduce the temptation for defendants to represent themselves in a malpractice lawsuit. Malpractice policies typically cover the costs of defense, as well as liability. (*See* Part C-2-d of this Chapter.) As the previous chapters of this book suggest, legal malpractice law is a complex subject. Lawyers with no particular expertise in this difficult area of the law should not dabble with defending a claim, particularly when their judgment may be impaired by the fact that their own honor and fortune are at stake because *they are the defendants*. It is a great advantage in answering malpractice charges to be represented by a lawyer who specializes in this field.

Malpractice insurance also protects clients. Coverage tends to ensure that money will be available to compensate losses resulting from errors that occur in the practice of law. In addition, the cost of obtaining malpractice insurance, and the requirements insurers sometimes impose on policy purchasers, may focus a lawyer or law firm's attention on the types of mistakes that give rise to malpractice claims. Heightened awareness of such risks often results in improved business practices. That reduces the overall amount of malpractice that occurs in the provision of legal services, thereby protecting clients generally.

Of course, insurance has a downside. Apart from its cost, which can sometimes be substantial, the presence of insurance may increase the likelihood that a person will be sued. In some instances, plaintiffs have named lawyers as defendants simply because they had malpractice insurance. During the Saving & Loan Crisis in the late 1980s, hundreds of S&Ls failed. The federal government was required to pay billions of dollars to clean up the wreckage by reimbursing account holders for the value of their lost deposits. Subsequently, in the 1990s, the federal Resolution Trust Corporation (RTC), as successor to the failed S&Ls, sought to recoup those losses by filing legal malpractice actions against the lawyers who had assisted the allegedly irresponsible conduct of S&L officers, directors, and employees which had caused the crisis. However, the RTC only sued those S&L lawyers who had malpractice insurance. It did not bother to sue the lawyers who did not have coverage, in part because collecting damages from those lawyers might have been difficult absent insurance.

Similar decisions are made all the time by lawyers representing malpractice plaintiffs. In each potential case, a professional judgment must be made about whether it is worth embarking on the troublesome path of litigating a professional liability claim. The presence of malpractice insurance providing possible coverage for the plaintiff's losses makes it easier to answer that question in favor of filing the lawsuit.

In many states, roughly half of all lawyers in some practice areas are covered by malpractice insurance. However, even among lawyers who purchase insurance, coverage varies widely in terms of dollar amounts and contract terms.

1. Mandatory Coverage

Sophisticated clients sometimes require their lawyers to maintain a minimum level of malpractice insurance. Various state laws also may mandate that lawyers have malpractice insurance in order to offer legal services through lawyer referral agencies or to enjoy the legal protections from vicarious liability afforded by practicing law as a member of a limited liability entity. (*See* Chapter 8 Part C.) In some states, a lawyer subject to disciplinary sanctions can be required to maintain adequate malpractice insurance as a condition of any further practice of law.

For decades, Oregon has been the only state that requires all lawyers to carry malpractice insurance. *See* Ore. Rev. Stat. § 9.080 (Westlaw 2010). Lawyers not engaged in the private practice of law may request exemption from this requirement.

2. Disclosure Requirements

The American Bar Association has passed a model rule requiring disclosure of whether or not a lawyer has malpractice insurance. *See* Model Court Rule on Insurance Disclosure (August 2004). A chart on the Client Protection section of the ABA website (www.abanet.org) indicates that, thus far, seven states (AK, CA, NH, NM, OH, PA, and SD) require disclosure directly to clients; eighteen states (AZ, CO, DE, HI, ID, IL, KS, MA, MI, MN, NE, NV, NC, ND, RI, VA, WA, and WV) require lawyers to disclose their lack of malpractice insurance on annual registration statements; and five states (AR, CT, FL, KY, and TX) have decided not to adopt the ABA model court rule. States requiring reporting, but not directly to clients, usually make the information publicly searchable on a website. However, some states provide the information only upon request or do not make it publicly available at all. *See* Jeffrey D. Watters, Comment, "Why Clients Should Know If Their Attorney Does Not Carry Malpractice Insurance," 62 *Baylor L. Rev.* 245, 256 (2010).

B. TYPES OF COVERAGE: "OCCURRENCE" AND "CLAIMS MADE" POLICIES

There are two basic types of legal malpractice insurance policies: "occurrence" and "claims made." An "occurrence" policy covers a lawyer for malpractice that occurs during the policy year, regardless of when the claim is made. Thus, coverage under an occurrence policy extends into the future even if there is no claim during the policy year.

In contrast, a "claims made" policy only covers a lawyer for claims asserted during the policy year. At the end of the year, the policy expires. Claims that are made after that date are not covered. A claim falling within the coverage of a "claims made" policy may arise from acts or omissions that occurred during the policy year, or possibly from earlier events. A "claims made" policy may provide coverage for "prior acts" that took place before the inception of the policy, provided that the insured had no prior knowledge of the claim or facts from which a claim should reasonably have been anticipated. (*See* Part C-1-a of this Chapter.) Moreover, the insured's disclosure of a possible claim during the policy period may be sufficient to preserve coverage even if the claim is not formally made until after the policy expires.

Many legal malpractice insurers have abandoned the sale of "occurrence" policies because providing coverage long into the future is a difficult economic proposition. Therefore, virtually all malpractice policies sold today are of the "claims made" variety. The date that a claim is made is usually the date the insured received notice of a lawsuit or a demand letter. For example, in *Ashby v. Davidson*, 930 N.E.2d 53 (Ind. Ct. App. 2010), the insurance policy defined a "claim" as:

Receipt by an Insured of a demand for money or services (including the service of suit or the institution of arbitration proceedings) against the Insured from one other than that Insured.

930 N.E.2d at 56.

It is important to see how insurance disclosure requirements (*see* Part A-2 of this Chapter) mesh with the fact that most contemporary malpractice insurance is of a "claims made" variety. The fact that a lawyer has insurance at the time a client is represented does not mean that the lawyer will have insurance at the time a claim is made, which may be many years later. During the interim, the lawyer may have stopped purchasing insurance, or may have switched to another insurance carrier whose "claims made" policy does not provide coverage for claims arising from prior acts, or for acts prior to a certain retroactive date (*see* Part C-1-a). Thus, it is possible that insurance disclosure requirements may mislead some clients who think malpractice arising in the course of their representation will be covered, when in fact that may not be the case. Disclosure requirements typically do not ask for revelation of the type of coverage a lawyer has or of limitations related to the coverage. *See* Ronald E. Mallen & Jeffrey M. Smith, 5 *Legal Malpractice* § 36.1 (2009 ed.).

C. POLICY PROVISIONS

A legal malpractice insurance policy has four main parts: the declarations page, the insuring agreements, the exclusions, and the conditions.

1. The Declarations Page

The declarations page of a legal malpractice insurance policy identifies the "named insured" and the policy period. It also specifies the policy limits of liability per claim and per year, and the deductibles that apply per claim and per year.

Further, the declarations page identifies additions or deletions to the insurer's standard form contract. Those changes are handled through "endorsements" to the policy, which are attached to, and incorporated as part of, the policy. Endorsements are not a particular aspect of coverage, but are simply added to the insurance contract to affect one of the four basic parts of the policy mentioned above.

The declarations page sometimes incorporates statements made by the applicant in the insurance application. A typical application requires a lawyer to provide information about the law practice, business interests, disciplinary history, knowledge of potential claims, and other important matters. The applicant's representations are treated as conditions of coverage. The material breach of a condition which causes prejudice enables an insurer to decline coverage for a claim. In some jurisdictions, prejudice is presumed. A misrepresentation may also entitle the insurer to rescind the policy.

a. The Prior Acts Retroactive Date

If the policy restricts coverage for prior acts, the effective date of the prior acts coverage is stated as a retroactive date. In that case, claims must relate to acts or omissions occurring after the retroactive date in order to be covered. In the absence of a retroactive date, prior acts coverage is unlimited, provided that the insured did not know at the inception of the policy of an act or omission that was reasonably likely to give rise to a claim.

Of course, the exact phrasing of the exception to retroactive coverage may be important. However, in *C. Ingram Co. v. Philadelphia Indemnity Insurance Co.*, 303 Ga. App. 548, 694 S.E.2d 181 (2010), application of the exclusion did not pose a close question. The policy said that there was no malpractice coverage "if the insured at the effective date knew or could have reasonably foreseen that *** [a] wrongful act or personal injury might be expected to be the basis of a claim." 694 S.E.2d at 183. An appellate court in Georgia ruled that there was no malpractice coverage under the policy because the law firm had been informed by a client before it obtained the policy that the firm's failure to timely file an action to foreclose on a lien would subject the firm to a suit for malpractice.

Hartford Casualty Insurance Co. v. Moore, 2010 WL 3169517 (C.D. Ill. 2010), was a declaratory judgment action commenced by an insurer (Hartford). The malpractice policy at issue provided that the insurer agreed to:

> pay on behalf of the "insured" all sums in excess of the deductible which the "insured" shall become legally obligated to pay as "damages" by reason of any act, error, or omission, including "claims" arising out of "personal injury," committed or alleged to have been committed prior to the end of the "policy period" and subsequent to the "retroactive date."

Id. at 2. The retroactive date specified in the policy's declaration was December 21, 2006. However, the facts clearly established that the alleged malpractice—failure to properly handle three appeals—took place in 2005 and 2006, ending on July 27, 2006. In an effort to circumvent the fact that the malpractice predated the retroactive date, the insureds (the "LMOJ parties") contended that the policy, as issued, was the product of a mutual mistake of fact, and that therefore reformation of the contract was appropriate. More specifically, the insureds argued that they had asked the insurer's agent (Conklin) for a policy that would cover the law firm from liability for any malpractice that occurred since its inception and its partners from liability for any malpractice that occurred since they were licensed to practice law. In rejecting the request for reformation, a federal court in Illinois stated that such a remedy is appropriate only for *mistake of fact*, but not for *mistake of law*. As the court explained:

> "Mutual mistake of fact 'contemplates a mistake of fact at the time the instrument was drawn, not as to the legal effect of the instrument, but as to the facts of the agreement.'" *** [T]his was a mistake of law, not of fact. According to the LMOJ parties, Hartford, through Conklin, affirmatively represented to them that the December 21, 2006 date would meet their needs—Conklin and thus Hartford, then, were mistaken as to the effect of the December 21, 2006 date, and the LMOJ parties relied on and shared that mistake. ***. Conklin did not represent that she would insert a different date and then made an error in writing the policy. Both parties understood that December 21, 2006 was the date to be written into the policy. They merely misunderstood what the legal effect of that date was. This was thus a

mistake of fact, which cannot support reformation of the policy.

Id. at 5. Because reformation was not appropriate, and the acts giving rise to the malpractice claims occurred before the policy's retroactive date, the insurer was entitled to summary judgment that the claims were not covered by the policy.

In *Byrd & Associates, PLLC v. Evanston Insurance Co.*, 2010 WL 1872740 (5th Cir. 2010), a malpractice policy provided the insured (Byrd) with coverage extending back to February 28, 2003. In 2005, a former client (Butler) sued Byrd for malpractice based on his alleged failure to file notice of a claim in 2000 related to her wrongful death action. The Fifth Circuit held that the legal malpractice policy provided no coverage for Butler's claim because it stemmed from acts prior to February 2, 2003. The court found that the case required no determination as to whether Byrd anticipated Butler's claim, because the acts at issue arose before the retroactive date of the policy.

b. Failure to Disclose Possible Claims

In one recent case, an insurer alleged that coverage for a claim by a former client was properly denied because the matter had not been disclosed by a Maryland lawyer's application to renew his insurance. The lawyer had represented the client in a personal injury suit against her employer. According to the insurer, the lawyer knew about his alleged mistakes. Those errors had resulted in a verdict for the client being thrown out by an appellate court because the lawyer failed to properly transmit records from the state workers' compensation commission. The lawyer also allegedly knew, at the time he submitted his insurance renewal application, that the former client had filed a grievance against him. The insurer argued that in view of this evidence, the lawyer had knowledge of facts which could reasonably support a claim at the effective date of the new malpractice policy, and that therefore the undisclosed matter was not a covered claim under the policy. *See* Jeff Jeffrey, "Solo Practitioner, Insurer Lock Horns Over Malpractice Coverage," *Nat'l L.J.*, Aug. 27, 2010.

Similarly, in *Carolina Casualty Insurance Co. v. Ott,* 2010 WL 1849230, *11 (W.D. Wash. 2010), a federal court in Washington held that a lawyer who had fabricated letters to defend himself in a grievance proceeding filed by a client should have understood that a malpractice claim might arise from the same matter, even if he believed the grievance was without merit. Therefore, the lawyer's insurer had no duty to defend or indemnify him in the malpractice action resulting from the undisclosed matter.

2.   The Insuring Agreements

The insuring agreements of a legal malpractice policy define, in general terms, the scope of the insurance coverage by describing the risks covered under the policy.

a.   Coverage for Money Damages

The insuring agreements normally state that the insurer will pay all sums the insured becomes legally obligated to pay as "money damages." This may ultimately mean that claims for injunctive relief, disciplinary actions, and fee disputes (including fee forfeiture; *see* Chapter 4 Part D) are not covered. Those types of controversies either do not concern "money" or do not deal with "damages." (Remember that "damages" are measured by what the plaintiff lost; "forfeiture" to prevent unjust enrichment is calculated by what the defendant improperly gained. *See* Chapter 6 Part C.)

b. Who Is Insured?

The insuring agreements require that, in order to be covered, a claim for money damages must be made against an "insured." The "named insureds" identified on the declarations page are "insureds." So are other classes of persons identified in the policy. These classes often include a law firm's principals (*i.e.*, partners or shareholders), employed lawyers, other employees, and, perhaps, predecessor law firms. Spouses, former principals, and "of counsel" lawyers sometimes qualify as insureds. Persons who are insureds are usually covered for both direct and vicarious liability.

An applicant for insurance needs to read the policy carefully in order to ensure that coverage is provided to persons the applicant wants to protect and not to persons for whom the applicant does not want to purchase coverage. Movement of lawyers between law firms is now a common phenomenon. A law firm may want to purchase a malpractice insurance policy that provides protection only for claims arising from work performed on behalf of that firm and not for work done by the predecessor firms of some of the firm's current lawyers.

There are special coverage issues relating to contract lawyers (also called "temporary lawyers"; *see* Chapter 8 Part D-7). A law firm will want to be covered for vicarious liability claims associated with the work of a contract lawyer. However, depending on the language of the policy, a contract lawyer may not qualify as an "insured" under the policy's definition of "employees." Because contract lawyers frequently work for different law firms over the course of a year, and will normally find it difficult to be certain that they are covered under every firm's policy, they should arrange their own malpractice insurance, either directly or through their placement agencies.

It is useful to examine the language from an actual policy. In *Ashby v. Davidson*, 930 N.E.2d 53 (Ind. Ct. App. 2010), the malpractice insurance policy at issue defined "insured" in the terms quoted below. Notice how the policy dealt with the coverage of lawyers or employees who, during the term of the policy, were hired by the firm, died, or became incapacitated.

B. "INSURED" means:

1. Any named Insured;

2. Any lawyer who is a former partner, member, officer, director, stockholder, associate, or employee of the Policyholder named in the Declarations of this Policy or the Policyholder's Predecessor Firm(s), but solely for acts or omissions while acting within a professional capacity provid-

ing Legal Services on behalf of the Policyholder or its Predecessor Firm(s);

3. Any lawyer who, during the Policy Period, first becomes associated with the Policyholder either as a partner, member, officer, director, stockholder, associate, or employee, but only for a period of not longer than sixty (60) days from the date the association begins and solely for acts or omissions while acting in a professional capacity on behalf of the Policyholder, all on condition that the Policyholder notify the Company within sixty (60) days of the date of the association. Upon receipt of an application, the Company may, at its discretion, provide prior acts coverage for the new lawyer;

4. The heirs, executors, administrators, beneficiaries, assigns, appointed legal representatives, guardians and conservators of an insured who is dead or incapacitated, and the trustee or estate of an insured in bankruptcy, but solely with respect to such liability of the Insured as is otherwise covered by this Policy; and

5. Any non-lawyer who was, is now, or hereinafter becomes an employee, leased employee or independent contractor of the Policyholder or Predecessor Firm(s), but solely for acts or omissions while acting within the scope of such person's duties as an employee, leased employee or independent contractor of the Policyholder.

930 N.E.2d at 56.

c. Legal Services for Others

Insuring agreements normally state that, in order to be covered, a claim must arise out of the rendition of legal services to others. This requirement is sometimes expressed by coupling the use of the term "professional services" with a definition. Thus, in *Smith v. Ohio Bar Liability Insurance Co.*, 2009 WL 4829998 (Ohio Ct. App. 2009), the court explained, with reference to the policy at issue:

> The policy covers claims made for "an act, error, or omission of the Insured *** in rendering or failing to render Professional Services for others in the Insured's capacity as a lawyer[.]" ***. Professional Services are defined as "all services or activities performed by the insured lawyer in a lawyer-client capacity on behalf of one or more clients ***.

Id. at *1. Consequently, with these types of coverage requirements there are two issues. The first is whether the claim involves legal services, and second is whether those services were rendered to others.

If a loss arises from a lawyer's actions while serving as a broker, realtor, or fiduciary, an insurer may argue that the legal services requirement means there is no coverage. Similar issues arise if a claim stems from a lawyer's nonlegal activities such as managing the funds or property of clients. Many cases have struggled with the question of how closely ancillary services must be related to the practice of law for losses arising from those endeavors to come within the terms of a legal malpractice policy. Sometimes courts resolve these coverage questions by focusing on whether the plaintiff retained the insured *principally* for the purpose of obtaining legal services. In that case, incidental nonlegal services may be covered.

Even if a lawyer's conduct involved the provision of legal services, coverage may be denied because those services were not provided *to others*. This type of issue arises in cases where lawyers in the firm control the the injured enterprise or venture. In such a case, the insurer may argue (possibly with success) that the claim is not covered.

d. Duty to Indemnify Versus Duty to Defend and Pay

The insuring agreements describe the insurer's duty to indemnify or duty to defend and pay damages.

Policies providing for indemnification of covered losses typically do not include a duty to defend. In that case, the insurer is not responsible for arranging and managing the defense of the insured. However, under an indemnification policy, the insurer may have the right to approve the insured's selection of counsel. Normally, the insured must first pay the claimant whatever is owed as a result of a judgment or settlement, then seek reimbursement from the insurer.

More commonly, a malpractice policy includes both a duty to defend and a duty to pay amounts for which the insured becomes liable, even if the insured has not yet paid those amounts. In general, an insurer must defend a suit if the complaint states claims which, if proved, would make the insured liable to pay damages for a loss within the coverage. The question is not whether the claim is meritorious, but simply whether there could be a finding of liability within the terms of the policy. Thus, there may be a duty to defend even if there is ultimately no duty to pay amounts for which the insured becomes liable.

Many malpractice policies cover the costs of an appeal. This is true at least if there are colorable grounds for an appeal.

(1) Noncovered Claims and Reservation of Rights

If there is a duty to defend and only some of the asserted causes of action are covered by a malpractice policy, many jurisdictions hold that the insurer must provide a defense of all claims. This duty continues until the only finding, or possible finding, is liability for losses that are not covered. As a federal court in New York explained:

> If *any* of the claims against the insured arguably arise from covered events, the insurer is required to defend the entire action. ***. If the universe of claims against the insured requires proof of conduct that is excluded from coverage, then the insurer has no duty to indemnify or defend its insured.

Steadfast Insurance Co. v. Stroock & Stroock & Lavan LLP, 277 F. Supp. 2d 245, 252 (S.D.N.Y. 2003), *aff'd* 108 Fed. Appx. 663 (2d Cir. 2004).

In some instances, an insurer may be entitled to reimbursement for amounts spent on the defense of noncovered claims. However, the insurer must have timely asserted its reservation of rights. Otherwise, the insurer may be estopped from denying coverage or seeking reimbursement.

(2) Defense Costs and Self-Liquidating Policies

If a malpractice insurance policy imposes a duty to defend, as well as a duty to pay a resulting settlement or judgment, there is a question as to how amounts paid for the defense should be treated. If, under the terms of the policy, the amounts spent on defense reduce the coverage for payment of claims, the policy is "self-liquidating." Thus, if there is $12 million of coverage, but $2.1 million is spent on defense, only $9.9 million is available to pay a judgment or settlement. A self-liquidating policy is referred to as an "Expenses Within Limits" (EWL) policy.

Some malpractice policies have a special "claims expense allowance." This allowance, up to a certain limit, pays for defense costs, including attorney's fees, without reducing the coverage for liability.

3. Exclusions from Coverage

Whereas the insuring agreements generally define what is covered by the policy, the exclusions identify what is expressly not covered. Exclusions typically fall into three categories: (1) losses not intended to be covered by the legal malpractice policy; (2) extraordinary risks; and (3) "moral" or illegal risks.

a. Losses Not Intended to Be Covered

(1) Personal Injury and Property Damage

Malpractice policies often exclude claims arising from personal injury or property damage. An exclusion of coverage for "personal injuries" may mean that not only is there no coverage for obvious forms of personal injury, such as battery, but also no coverage for defamation, because for some purposes libel and slander may be classified as "personal injury" torts.

The exclusion of coverage for "property damage" may mean that a law firm's malpractice policy does not apply when a lawyer negligently backs a car into a client vehicle in the law firm's parking lot. Coverage for conversion of client property might also be deemed to be excluded on the ground that the exercise of dominion and control over the property of another is a form of "property damage."

However, some malpractice policies provide coverage for claims "arising out of personal injury." *See, e.g., Hartford Casualty Insurance Co. v. Moore*, 2010 WL 3169517, *2 (C.D. Ill. 2010).

(2) Business Pursuits

Malpractice policies frequently contain an exclusion for business pursuits. Depending on the precise language and breadth of the exclusionary provision, this may mean that there is no coverage for a malpractice claim arising from a venture in which a lawyer and client are partners or co-owners. The loss of coverage for this type of claim is especially dangerous for lawyers (and unfortunate for clients seeking to reach malpractice insurance proceeds) because entrepreneurial activities with clients often spawn malpractice claims.

In *Smith v. Ohio Bar Liability Insurance Co.*, 2009 WL 4829998 (Ohio Ct. App. 2009), a lawyer (Smith) was a partner in a law firm and the owner of an insurance agency. After a couple (the Ottos) contacted the insurance agency, the agency issued several annuity policies. Smith also drafted wills and trusts for the couple. The Ottos became dissatisfied with the wills and trusts because of the nature of the annuities, which had been sold to the couple in the names of their daughter and grandson. The Ottos believed that they had inadequate control over the annuities and whether they could be cashed in. In a resulting malpractice action against Smith and his law firm, their malpractice insurer undertook defense of the case with reservation of rights. The insurer then sought a declaratory judgment that the policy did not cover the Ottos' claims because the policy contained a business enterprise exclusion. In relevant part, the policy stated that it did not apply:

> "to any Claim arising out of or in connection with the conduct or sale of any business enterprise not named in the Declarations (including the owner-ship, maintenance or care of any property in connection therewith) wholly or partly owned by an Insured or in which any Insured is a partner, or which is directly or indirectly controlled, oper-ated or managed by an Insured either individu-ally or in a fiduciary capacity."

Id. at *2. The Ohio Court of Appeals found that it did not need to "determine whether the Ottos' claims occurred 'in connection with' the Smith Agency's conduct because it 'arises out of' the conduct of the agency *** [inasmuch as] 'arising out of' means generally 'flowing from' or 'having its origin in.'" The Ottos had first contacted Smith through his agency and it was clear that the Ottos were dissatisfied with the wills and trusts only because of the nature of the annuities. Because the business enterprise exclusion applied to the facts of the case, the malpractice insurer had no duty to defend the claim.

In *Carolina Casualty Insurance Co. v. L.M. Ross Law Group*, LLP, 184 Cal. App. 4th 196, 108 Cal. Rptr. 3d 701 (2010), a malpractice claim arose from bad legal advice related to the distribution of a program entitled "Live! From Las Vegas." The malpractice policy at issue excluded from coverage any claim by a business enterprise "in which the Insured owns more than a 10 percent interest, or in which any Insured is an owner, partner, or employee, or which is directly or indirectly controlled, operated, or managed by any Insured ***." In a declaratory judgment action, a California appellate court ruled that there was no coverage for the malpractice claim. The court offered two reasons. First, the defendant law firm's sole equity partner managed the plaintiff client (an entity) at the time that the malpractice claim was reported to the insurer. Second, a majority interest in the plaintiff client was held at all relevant times by a revocable trust of which the partner was both the settlor and trustee.

(3) Fiduciary Activities

A policy may expressly exclude from coverage claims arising from an insured's service in a fiduciary capacity. On this ground, coverage may be denied for injuries arising from a lawyer's conduct as an officer or a director of a corporation.

Alternatively, a policy may treat performance of fiduciary duties as the equivalent of rendering legal services to others (*see* Part C-2-c of this Chapter), and as therefore covered by a malpractice policy. For example, in *Home Insurance Co. v. Law Offices of Jonathan DeYoung, P.C.*, 32 F. Supp. 2d 219 (E.D. Pa. 1998), the malpractice policy at issue provided:

> When the Insured renders or fails to render services as an administrator, conservator, receiver, executor, guardian, trustee, or in any similar fiduciary capacity, the Insured's acts and omissions in such capacity shall be deemed for the purpose of this section to be the performance of professional services for others in the Insured's capacity as a lawyer, provided that this coverage shall not apply to any loss sustained by the Insured as the beneficiary or distributee of any trust or estate.

32 F. Supp. 2d at 230. In *Home Insurance*, the insurer argued that a claim was not covered because it related to the insured's separate business as an investment advisor. A federal court in Pennsylvania held that there was a question of fact as to whether the lawyer was acting in a fiduciary capacity while serving as an investment advisor, which precluded summary judgment as to whether the claim was covered.

b. Extraordinary Risks

(1) Excluded Areas of Law Practice

Some areas of law practice generate a disproportionate number of malpractice claims or especially large judgments and settlements. For example, lawyers sued for malpractice relating to the validity of patents are often faced with potential liability for huge amounts of damages. *See* Leigh Jones, "Patent Malpractice Claims Hit Firms: Higher Damages Make Firms Skittish," *Nat'l L.J.*, Dec. 10, 2007, at 1.

To avoid liability relating to especially risky practice areas, some insurers refuse to write policies for lawyers specializing in certain fields of law. Insurers can also deal with these problems by excluding from coverage various areas of practice that are thought to involve extraordinary risks. This might include, for example, work relating to intellectual property law, entertainment law (because it often involves intellectual property issues), federal and state securities laws, mass tort litigation, or class actions.

c. Moral and Illegal Risks

It is against public policy for lawyers to obtain insurance against liability for some kinds of "wilful" torts. However, insurance may properly insulate a lawyer from *vicarious liability* for "wilful" wrongdoing. *See Restatement (Third) of the Law Governing Lawyers* § 58 cmt. e (2000).

(1) Specific Kinds of Unlawful Conduct

Malpractice insurance policies often exclude from coverage specific kinds of conduct, such as unlawful discrimination, sexual harassment, misappropriation of property, commingling of client funds, conversion, libel, or slander.

(2) Malicious, Intentional, Criminal, or Otherwise Wrongful Acts

Malpractice policies frequently exclude from coverage various types of bad conduct, sometimes termed "malicious," "intentional," "criminal," or "wrongful." However, the use of any of these words can be problematic, for the terms sometimes raise more questions than they answer. Fortunately, many decisions seem to chart a reasonable course in determining the meaning of these elastic words.

For example, in *Mendel v. Home Insurance Co.*, 806 F. Supp. 1206 (E.D. Pa. 1992), a federal court in Pennsylvania held that a malpractice policy's language disclaiming coverage for "deliberately wrongful acts" excluded from coverage a claim for tortious interference since an "*intentional* and unprivileged interference must be established to prove an intentional interference with contractual relations, or with prospective contractual relations." 806 F. Supp. at 1210-11.

In *Steadfast Insurance Co. v. Stroock & Stroock & Lavan LLP*, 277 F. Supp. 2d 245 (S.D.N.Y. 2003), *aff'd* 108 Fed. Appx. 663 (2d Cir. 2004), the language of a legal malpractice policy excluded coverage for:

(1) any malicious, knowingly wrongful, or criminal act, error, omission, or breach of duty *** or (3) the gaining by any Insured *** of any profit, gain or advantage to which such Insured or person was not legally entitled."

277 F. Supp. 2d at 248. A federal court in New York found that the "wrongful" act exclusion barred coverage with respect to two claims for aiding, abetting, and conspiring to breach fiduciary duties, because those causes of action required actual knowledge of wrongdoing. Further, the court found that the "unfair gain" exclusion barred coverage for three claims related to the transfer of stock because the plaintiff alleged that the law firm had received an unlawful advantage due to the fraudulent nature of the transfers. Because the malpractice policy excluded from coverage all five causes of action pleaded against the defendant law firm, the insurer had no duty to defend the case or to indemnify any resulting losses.

In many cases, it is not easy to say whether coverage may validly be denied under a malpractice policy based on the allegedly malicious, intentional, or criminal nature of the defendant's conduct. An answer to that question may require an exhaustive review of relevant prior rulings in the jurisdiction and perhaps elsewhere. Even then the conclusion may rest only on interpolation of scattered precedents.

(3) Fraud and Dishonest Acts

Fraud and dishonest acts are typically excluded from coverage under a legal malpractice policy. In the usual case, this type of exclusion does not result in a loss of coverage for claims involving merely *negligent* misrepresentation. The same is true of claims for constructive fraud, at least if that term denotes liability despite lack of *scienter*.

Even if fraudulent conduct is excluded from coverage, an "innocent" partner who neither participated in, nor knew about the fraud, is usually entitled to coverage under the terms of the policy.

4. Conditions Affecting Coverage

In order for a claim to be covered by a malpractice insurance policy, it is ordinarily essential that the insured provide timely notice of the claim. Moreover, the insured must cooperate with the insurer in the investigation and defense of the case.

a. Prompt Notice of the Claim

Many cases discuss the notice of claim requirements imposed by malpractice policies. For example, in *Paint Shuttle, Inc. v. Continental Casualty Co.*, 733 N.E.2d 513 (Ind. Ct. App. 2000), the Indiana Court of Appeals wrote:

> Both"occurrence" and "claims made" insurance policies require the insured to promptly notify the insurer of possible covered losses. The notice provision of a "claims made" policy is not simply the part of the insured's duty to cooperate, it defines the limits of the insurer's obligation. If the insured does not give notice within the contractually required time period, there is simply no coverage under the policy.

733 N.E.2d at 522. In *Paint Shuttle*, the court found a legal malpractice insurance policy's notice provi-

sions to be clear and unambiguous. The policy stated the insured's duties as follows:

Your Duties

If, during the policy term, or any applicable extended reporting period:

a. you first become aware that a wrongful act has been committed, arising out of your professional services; and

b. you give written notice to us of the: (1) specific wrongful act, (2) the injury or damage which has or may result from the wrongful act, and (3) the circumstances by which you first become aware of such wrongful act,

then any subsequent claim made against you arising out of such wrongful act shall be deemed to have been made during the policy term or extended reporting period ***.

733 N.E.2d at 520. Because the law firm had only provided *oral* notice of a malpractice suit after it was filed, and did not provide *written* notice until after the policy had lapsed, the court concluded that the law firm had failed to provide adequate notice to trigger coverage of the claim. In explaining its decision, the court wrote:

[T]he notice was insufficient because the law firm voluntarily undertook the defense of the malpractice suit without allowing Continental to exercise its rights of investigation and defense of a claim under the malpractice policy. Notice is a term of art within the insurance context and sufficient notice by an insured to an insurer involves more than just promptly notifying an insurance company of a claim. *** [N]otice also encompasses an insurer's right to promptly investigate a claim or to control the defense of a lawsuit with which it might be subjected to liability as an insurer of an insurance policy.

733 N.E.2d at 720-21.

Occasionally, a court will excuse failure to provide notice as required by the terms of the policy. For example, in *Ashby v. Davidson*, 930 N.E.2d 53 (Ind. Ct. App. 2010), a lawyer (Davidson) abandoned his practice without providing notice to his clients, embarked on a multi-state crime spree, and ultimately ended up in prison. Several clients filed malpractice actions against Davidson. The former lawyer's insurer (Bar Plan) intervened and sought a declaratory judgment that there was no coverage for the claims because the lawyer had failed to notify the insurer about the suits and failed to cooperate or assist in the investigation and defense of the claims. The Indiana Court of Appeals reversed a judgment in favor of the insurer, explaining:

> Here, by the terms of the policy, Davidson was the person required to provide written notice to Bar Plan but was running from the law ***. For the same reason, Davidson was unavailable to receive demands from the Clients within the policy period. The Clients themselves provided actual notice of their claims against Davidson to Bar Plan within the policy period. Consequently, Bar Plan received actual written notice of the claims within the policy period. ***

*** [U]nder the facts of this case, notice provided by Davidson to Bar Plan was an impossibility ***. Bar Plan has been able to investigate and defend the Clients' claims against the insured after receiving prompt, actual written notice of the claims. It seems to us that the purpose behind the notice provision at issue here has more to do with the ability of the carrier to investigate and defend against claims in a timely manner than with the ability of a carrier to deny coverage because actual notice was supplied by the wrong individual, *i.e.*, "gotcha." We decide as a matter of law that the actual notice Bar Plan received from the Clients was proper.

930 N.E.2d at 57-58.

(1) Claims Related to Criminal Representation

The exoneration and innocence requirements that are imposed on malpractice claims related to criminal representation (*see* Chapter 7 Part B-2) make it difficult to say when a malpractice claim is sufficiently likely to be filed that it must be disclosed to a malpractice insurer in order to preserve coverage for that claim. This is particularly true because post-conviction relief may be sought by a convicted client in many courts, at both the state and federal levels, with some tribunals ruling that the client's legal representation was constitutionally adequate, and any decision to the contrary is usually subject to being reversed on appeal.

In *Lemke v. Zurich North America*, 26 Misc. 3d 1084, 896 N.Y.S.2d 603 (2009), a New York court ruled that once a federal court had found that a lawyer's conduct was constitutionally deficient, the lawyer was required to disclose a possible malpractice claim to his insurer. On the facts of the case, no such notice was provided. However, New York law grants an injured person a right to give notice to an insurer about a claim. Unfortunately, the malpractice plaintiff had waited more than a year after obtaining post-conviction relief to sue his lawyer and provide notice of the claim to the insurer. The court held that because there was no excuse for this delay, the insurer had no obligation to indemnify the the defendant lawyer or pay any benefits to the malpractice plaintiff.

b. Disclosure of Material Changes

An insured is expressly required by the terms of most malpractice policies to notify the insurer of "material changes" related to information submitted in the insurance application. A material change can result from an influx or exodus of lawyers, or from such things as the opening of new offices, merger with another firm, or conversion of a partnership to a limited liability entity. Failure to disclose material changes in the firm's operations can result in loss of coverage.

D. DISCLOSING MALPRACTICE TO CLIENTS

Related to the issue of whether a lawyer must disclose a potential malpractice claim to an insurer is the issue of whether the claim must be revealed to the client who is the victim of the malpractice. *See generally* Benjamin P. Cooper, "The Lawyer's Duty to Inform His Client of His Own Malpractice," 61 *Baylor L. Rev.* 174 (2009).

Mindful of the well-recognized duty of a lawyer to keep a client reasonably informed about material developments in the representation, the *Restatement* takes the position that:

> If the lawyer's conduct of the matter gives the client a substantial malpractice claim against the lawyer, the lawyer must disclose that to the client.

Restatement (Third) of the Law Governing Lawyers § 20 cmt. c (2000). Under this formulation, the key issue is determining when is a malpractice claim is "substantial." The *Restatement* offers as an example a lawyer who missed the statute of limitations. In that case, there is a duty to inform the client of the right to sue for malpractice and to disclose the resulting conflict of interest that may require the lawyer to withdraw from further representation. *Id.*

In an ethics opinion, a committee in Colorado took the position that a lawyer must disclose an error "if the error is material, meaning that it will likely result in prejudice to a client's right or claim." Colo. Bar Ass'n, Ethics Comm. Formal Op. 113 (2005). However, the opinion—which focused on ethical responsibility, rather than malpractice liability—further opined that:

> "Unless there are steps that can be taken now to avoid the possibility of future harm, there is probably no immediate duty to disclose the mere

possibility of lawyer error or omission." Lawyers should be given the opportunity to remedy any error before disclosing the error to the client.

Id. This might be true, for example, if the lawyer missed a nonjurisdictional deadline, a potentially fruitful area of discovery, or a theory of liability or defense. *Id.*

Focusing on whether there is anything that a client needs to do at the moment, rather than in the future, to mitigate the effects of malpractice, and on whether it is reasonable to allow a lawyer an opportunity to cure the malpractice, is a sensible way of approaching the question of whether disclosure is required. However, an even better question may be to ask whether a disinterested lawyer would conclude that the client should be told. If so, disclosure is required. Presumably, any error serious enough to require a lawyer to advise his malpractice insurer of a possible claim is sufficiently "substantial" to require disclosure to the client.

In the legal malpractice field, nondisclosure of malpractice is unlikely to lead to liability independent of the underlying malpractice. This is true because in order to be actionable, the nondisclosure must cause damage. That is likely to be the case with respect to nondisclosure of malpractice only if the underlying errors caused harm and were actionable.

In *Leonard v. Dorsey & Whitney LLP*, 553 F.3d 609 (8th Cir. 2009), the Eighth Circuit predicted that:

the Minnesota Supreme Court would not hold a lawyer liable for failure to disclose a possible malpractice claim unless the potential claim creates a conflict of interest that would disqualify the lawyer from representing the client. *** Thus, the lawyer must know that there is a non-frivolous malpractice claim against him such that "there is a substantial risk that the lawyer's representation of the client would be materially and adversely affected by" his own interest in avoiding malpractice liability. ***.

553 F.3d at 629.

Nevertheless, it is important to see why nondisclosure of malpractice can be seriously disadvantageous to a lawyer. There are least three reasons. The first relates to the statute of limitations, the second to trial tactics, and the third to client relations.

As to the statute of limitations governing a malpractice action, there is a possibility that nondisclosure will be treated as fraudulent concealment of the kind that tolls the running of the statute of limitations. (*See* Chapter 7 Part C-3-c.) More likely, nondisclosure will extend the filing period for a malpractice action because the plaintiff did not discover the malpractice, and could not reasonably have done so, absent disclosure by the lawyer. (*See* Chapter 7 Part C-3-a.) These tolling issues may be important in cases where the lawyer withdraws from further representation of the client or where the running of the statute of limitations is otherwise not barred by a "continuous representation" rule. (*See* Chapter 7 Part C-3-7.)

Second, nondisclosure of malpractice to a client gives the client's malpractice lawyer potent ammunition for arguing a case to the jury. During counsel's opening and closing arguments, and during the cross-examination, the defendant lawyer will be hammered repeatedly as to why important facts were never disclosed to the client. The plaintiff's expert is sure to say there was a duty to disclose this type of material information. If the arguments and testimony are effective, they will tar the defendant with the brush of dishonesty and insensitivity to the client's interests. The defendant may be painted as not merely careless or incompetent, but lacking in candor and concern for the client.

Finally, clients sometimes forgive lawyer's mistakes. Many authorities urge professionals to acknowledge and apologize for their errors. Some research has shown that when doctors disclose and apologize for their mistakes, they are less likely to be sued for malpractice. Whatever chance there is for client understanding is probably lost if important matters are concealed from the client, but later discovered.

INDEX